Preface

In recent years, the evolution of the financial service industry has blurred traditional distinctions between broker-dealers and investment advisers and made it difficult to design appropriate regulatory schemes for their professional services. To better understand the industry's dynamics and its effects on individual investors, the U.S. Securities and Exchange Commission (SEC) commissioned RAND to conduct a study of broker-dealers and investment advisers from two perspectives: first, examine investment advisers' and broker-dealers' practices in marketing and providing financial products and services to individual investors; and second, evaluate investors' understanding of the differences between investment advisers' and broker-dealers' financial products and services, duties, and obligations.

The research on which this document reports was conducted within the LRN-RAND Center for Corporate Ethics, Law, and Governance within the RAND Institute for Civil Justice.

The LRN-RAND Center for Corporate Ethics, Law, and Governance

The LRN-RAND Center for Corporate Ethics, Law, and Governance is committed to improving public understanding of corporate ethics, law, and governance and to identifying specific ways in which businesses can operate ethically, legally, and profitably at the same time. The center's work is supported by voluntary contributions from private-sector organizations and individuals with interests in research on these topics.

The center is part of the RAND Institute for Civil Justice (ICJ), which is dedicated to improving decisionmaking on civil legal issues by supplying policymakers with the results of objective, empirically based, analytic research. ICJ facilitates change in the civil justice system by analyzing trends and outcomes, identifying and evaluating policy options, and bringing together representatives of different interests to debate alternative solutions to policy problems. ICJ builds on a long tradition of RAND research characterized by an interdisciplinary, empirical approach to public-policy issues and rigorous standards of quality, objectivity, and independence.

ICJ research is supported by pooled grants from corporations, trade and professional associations, and individuals; by government grants and contracts; and by private foundations. ICJ disseminates its work widely to the legal, business, and research communities and to the general public. In accordance with RAND policy, all ICJ research products are subject to peer review before publication. ICJ publications do not necessarily reflect the opinions or policies of the research sponsors or of the ICJ Board of Overseers.

Robert Reville, Director
RAND Institute for Civil Justice
1776 Main Street, P.O. Box 2138
Santa Monica, CA 90407-2138
310-393-0411 x6786
Fax: 310-451-6979
Email: Robert_Reville@rand.org

Michael Greenberg, Research Director
LRN-RAND Center for Corporate Ethics,
Law, and Governance
4570 Fifth Avenue, Suite 600
Pittsburgh, PA 15213-2665
412-682-2300 x4648
Fax: 412-682-2800
Email: Michael_Greenberg@rand.org

Contents

Figures

Tables

Executive Summary

The financial service industry is at a crossroads regarding its regulatory and legal status. As the industry has become more complex, it has become increasingly difficult for regulators to design regulations that govern the different financial services available in this market. In theory, financial professionals are relatively distinct: A *broker* is defined as someone who conducts transactions in securities on behalf of others; a *dealer* is defined as someone who buys and sells securities for his or her own accounts; and an *investment adviser* is defined as someone who provides advice to others regarding securities. Broker-dealers and investment advisers are subject to different federal regulations: The Securities Exchange Act of 1934 (48 Stat. 881) regulates brokers and dealers, and the Investment Advisers Act of 1940 (54 Stat. 847) regulates investment advisers.

In light of these differences in definitions and regulations, the dividing line between broker-dealers and investment advisers has always been an important one. However, trends in the financial service market since the early 1990s have blurred the boundaries between them. Firms are constantly evolving and bundling diverse products and services in response to market demands and the regulatory environment. Although the SEC has attempted to clarify the boundaries between broker-dealers and investment advisers—first in a 1999 proposed rule that was then modified and became the 2005 rule, "Certain Broker-Dealers Deemed Not to Be Investment Advisers" (SEC, 2005)—the regulation was challenged and eventually overturned.

During the rule-making process, the SEC received more than 1,700 letters from financial professionals, investors, and consumer groups expressing concerns about what investors understand about the differences between brokerage and advisory accounts, the legal obligations of each type of account, and the effect of titles and marketing on investor expectations. As a result, the SEC recognized that any future regulatory reform would have to be based on a clearer understanding of the industry's complexities, including the changing business practices of broker-dealers and investment advisers and how investors perceive these practices. In response, the SEC commissioned RAND to conduct this study.

Study Purpose and Approach

The main purpose of this study was to provide the SEC with a factual description of the current state of the investment advisory and brokerage industries for its evaluation of the legal and regulatory environment concerning investment professionals. This study did not evaluate the legal or regulatory environment itself; nor does this resulting report make policy recommendations. Specifically, the study addressed two primary questions:

- What are the current business practices of broker-dealers and investment advisers?
- Do investors understand the differences between and relationships among broker-dealers and investment advisers?

To describe industry practices, we collected and analyzed information from a number of sources: previous studies of the subject, primarily in economics and business publications and in popular sources, such as trade journals and financial media; data derived from regulatory filings submitted by investment advisers and broker-dealers from 2001 to 2006; business documents used by a sample of firms; and two sets of personal interviews: one set with 26 interested parties with different perspectives on the industry and one set with financial service firms.

To assess investor understanding, we collected and analyzed data from an extensive household survey and from focus groups consisting of experienced and inexperienced investors. The survey, which was completed by 654 U.S. households, asked about perceptions of the differences between investment advisers and broker-dealers, experience with financial service providers, and the level of satisfaction with the services received. Six focus groups with 10 to 12 participants each allowed for interactive discussion of the same topics and offered the opportunity to probe for the assumptions and reasoning that lay behind certain responses.

Overall, we found that the industry is very heterogeneous, with firms taking many different forms and offering a multitude of services and products. Partly because of this diversity of business models and services, investors typically fail to distinguish broker-dealers and investment advisers along the lines that federal regulations define. Despite their confusion about titles and duties, investors express high levels of satisfaction with the services they receive from their own financial service providers.

Current Business Practices of Investment Advisers and Broker-Dealers

We provide a descriptive analysis of the business practices of thousands of investment advisers and broker-dealers based on data they report in regulatory filings. We focus attention on firms that report that they offer both brokerage and advisory services or are affiliated with firms that offer the complementary service. We attempt to clarify the differences between such firms and those that specialize solely in brokerage or advisory services. Our analysis confirms what many stakeholders expressed in their interviews: The industry is composed of heterogeneous firms that provide a range of services and are engaged in a variety of relationships with one another, and, therefore, it is not surprising that investors fail to distinguish financial service providers along the regulatory lines.

Number of Firms and Firm Size
A relatively small number of large firms provide a full range of services, are often affiliated with other financial service providers, and conduct an overwhelming proportion of the investment advisory and brokerage businesses. On the other end of the spectrum are a great number of relatively small firms that provide a limited range of either investment advisory or brokerage services, but they frequently report affiliations with firms providing complementary services.

Figure S.1 displays year-end industry snapshots of the number of brokerage and investment advisory firms from 2001 through 2006, as described in data we obtained from the SEC Division of Investment Management and from the Financial Industry Regulatory Authority (FINRA). During this time period, the following changes took place:

- The number of investment advisers in the Investment Adviser Registration Depository (IARD) database grew substantially, from 7,614 in 2001 to 10,484 in 2006, whereas the number of broker-dealers declined from 5,526 to 5,068.
- The number of broker-dealers in the Financial and Operational Combined Uniform Single (FOCUS) Report database declined from 5,526 to 5,068.
- The number of dual registrants (firms in both databases) in these data remained relatively constant (between 500 and 550 each year).
- The share of broker-dealers that were dually registered increased slightly, from 9.5 percent to 10.6 percent, while the share of investment advisers that were dually registered fell from 6.9 percent to 5.1 percent.

Although some investment advisory firms are very large, most are rather small. Among investment advisory firms with individuals as clients at the end of 2006, more than half reported having no more than ten employees. Only about one-fourth of these firms reported having more than 50 employees, and less than 8 percent reported having more than 100 employees. However, 69 investment advisory firms with individual clients reported that they

Figure S.1
Broker-Dealers, Investment Advisers, and Dually Registered Firms (2001–2006)

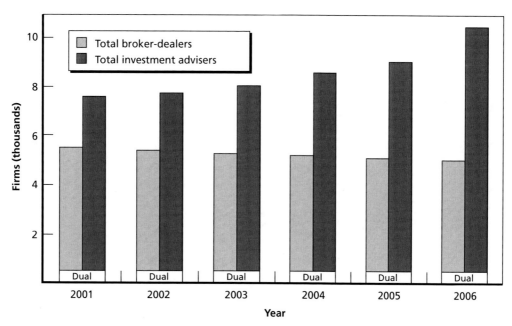

SOURCES: Broker-dealer data are from FOCUS reports. Investment adviser data are from IARD .
NOTE: *Dual* indicates firms listed in both databases.
RAND *TR556-S.1*

employed more than 1,000 individuals each. Almost 40 percent of investment advisory firms reported that some of their employees were registered representatives of a brokerage firm.

We also analyzed data on more than 5,000 broker-dealers registered at the end of 2006, but these data do not contain reports on employment and clientele. Much more information is available on firm finances. A defining attribute of a broker-dealer is whether it clears or carries customer accounts. Those firms that do must file a FOCUS report, Part II, while the others need file only the abbreviated Part IIA report. The Part II filers constitute only about 10 percent of registered broker-dealers but tend to be much larger than Part IIA filers.

Among broker-dealers, distributions of assets and ownership equity are heavily skewed, with one group of firms being vastly larger than the rest. The mean of total assets reported in the fourth quarter of 2006 is more than $1 billion, but the median is less than $500,000. The difference between mean of ownership equity ($32 million) and the median ($340,000) is also quite striking. Much of this variation is associated with filing status. The means of reported assets and ownership equity among Part II filers are $10 billion and $250 million, respectively, whereas the corresponding means among Part IIA filers are about $25 million and $7 million.

Financial Services

Most firms reported being engaged strictly as either an investment adviser or as a broker-dealer without any affiliations with those that provide the complementary service. Many others, however, were directly engaged in only one type of activity but were affiliated with a firm engaged in the other type. The remainder, a minority of firms, were directly engaged in both brokerage and advisory activities.

As the economic scope of a firm grows, it tends to engage in a much fuller range of services and consequently is affiliated with other financial service firms or conducts a significant amount of business in both the investment advisory and brokerage fields. Smaller firms, which are much more numerous, tend to provide a more limited and focused range of either investment advisory or brokerage services, although they frequently report some sort of affiliation with firms providing the complementary service.

Almost 95 percent of investment advisory firms with individual clients provide portfolio management for individuals or small businesses, with about 14 percent of those firms managing a wrap-fee program. Overall, about 6 percent of investment advisory firms with individual clients sponsor a wrap-fee program. After portfolio management, the most frequently provided advisory service is financial planning, reported by about half of the firms. Almost 20 percent engage in pension consulting. More than 25 percent of investment advisory firms with individual clients reported being engaged in business activities other than advisory services, including broker-dealer (7 percent), registered representative of a broker-dealer (12 percent), and insurance agent or broker (12 percent). Our assessment of these data, in combination with other evidence, indicates the presence of substantial reporting error in the regulatory filings.

Among broker-dealers in the Central Registration Depository (CRD) database at the end of 2006, the most frequently reported business activities were mutual fund retailer (52 percent), retailing of corporate-equity securities over the counter (50 percent), and private placement of securities (50 percent). Part II filers were more likely than Part IIA filers to report engagement in all but 7 of the 28 different business activities described in the data. More than 20 percent of the broker-dealers reported being engaged in the investment advisory service business. Overall, about 7 percent of total quarterly revenues of broker-dealers were reported for a fee category that included *but was not limited to* investment advisory service fees. Even among firms that reported being engaged in investment advisory services, this share is just 8 percent. However, further inspection of the data indicates that investment advisory service fees may have accounted for a large share of revenues at smaller firms.

Dual Activity and Affiliations

The number of firms dually registered in the FOCUS and IARD databases remained relatively constant at 500 to 550 from 2001 through 2006. However, the number of dually registered firms grew as a proportion of all broker-dealers, and these dually registered firms grew substantially in terms of mean reported revenues, expenses, and, generally, net incomes over the entire period. With respect to assets under management by these dually registered firms, the total amount in discretionary accounts increased slightly from 2001 to 2006, while the amount in nondiscretionary accounts increased by about 75 percent.

Firms that directly provide either investment advisory or brokerage activities but not both may be affiliated with firms that provide other financial services. Overall, almost one out of every four investment advisers with individual clients has a related person who is also an investment adviser, and this other adviser could, of course, engage in other business activities. Moreover, more than one out of every five advisers reported that a related person was a broker-dealer, municipal-securities dealer, or government-securities broker or dealer. About 17 percent reported that a related person was an insurance company or agency, and 11 percent reported that a related person was an investment company.[1]

Among broker-dealers, more than 20 percent of registered firms in the fourth period of 2006 reported current or expected engagement in investment advisory services. Only about half of these firms are included in the contemporaneous IARD database. Many, but certainly not all, of the other half were confirmed to be state-registered investment advisers. We also obtained data on broker-dealers' affiliations, but these data are much less detailed than the data on investment advisers. About 40 percent of broker-dealers either directly or indirectly control, are controlled by, or are under common control with a firm engaged in the securities or investment advisory business. About 8 percent of broker-dealers are directly or indirectly controlled by a bank holding company or other banking institution.

Firms reporting such affiliations play a disproportionately large role in the market. For example, investment advisory firms that report no direct engagement in brokerage activities but that a related person is a broker-dealer constitute less than 15 percent of all reporting firms but managed more than one-fourth of all accounts and almost two-thirds of all assets reported at the end of 2006. Among broker-dealers, 69 percent of Part II filers reported affiliations with securities or investment advisory businesses, as opposed to 38 percent of Part IIA firms, which tend to be much smaller.

These affiliations further blur the boundaries among types of financial services. In many cases, we found it difficult disentangle the services and business relationships of firms that were dually registered or affiliated with other firms. Some corporations may have multiple subsidiaries or business units, each registered separately as an investment adviser or broker-dealer, but these data do not identify these relationships. By comparing details across databases, we noted many inconsistencies and inaccuracies in the information reported. For example, many invest-

---

[1] In regulatory filings, *person* can indicate a person or other legal entity, such as an affiliate business.

ment advisory firms that were not sole proprietorships reported being engaged as registered representatives of broker-dealers. Other investment advisers reported being engaged as broker-dealers, but we could find no evidence that they were dually registered. In most of these cases, the firms appear to be affiliated in some way with a broker-dealer with a distinct CRD number, including one investment advisory firm that reported having more than 1,000 employees who were registered representatives of a broker-dealers.

In a few case studies, we attempted to classify firms based on reported activities and affiliations and found that we had to piece together the evidence based on multiple sources of information, such as regulatory filings, business documents, Web sites, and firm interviews. What became clear was that the registered firms may be involved in multifaceted relationships spanning a variety of business activities. Given such complexity, it is not surprising that the typical retail investor finds it difficult to understand the nature of the business from which he or she receives investment advisory or brokerage services.

Disclosures

Both investment advisers and broker-dealers are required to provide certain disclosures to clients and potential clients. In interviews with interested parties, many claimed that the disclosures themselves are problematic. First, they are not written in a way that is easily understandable to the average investor, and the information they provide is inadequate. Second, the financial service provider does not do enough to help investors understand disclosures—that is, they present the required disclosures without taking time to explain them. Third, many said that investors do not take the necessary time and effort to fully read and understand disclosures.

Participants in firm interviews described the lengths to which these firms go to make full disclosure, including efforts to produce booklets written in plain English rather than legal language. Several of these participants acknowledge that, regardless of how carefully they craft documentation, investors rarely read these disclosures.

We examined many types of disclosures: descriptions of the differences between investment advisers and broker-dealers, conflicts of interest, compensation structure, code of ethics and fiduciary oath, future performance, and so forth. We referred to multiple sources—published studies, business documents and Web sites, and interviews with both financial service professionals and investors.

In the business documents submitted by investment advisers, the most frequently identified disclosures concerned the code of ethics and fiduciary oath. In the documents submitted by broker-dealers, the most frequently identified disclosures concerned issues of compensation—e.g., how clients compensate the firm, how other firms compensate the firm, and how employees are compensated. In contrast, the most frequently found disclosure on the Web sites of both investment advisers and broker-dealers was related to future performance.

Investor Understanding

To assess the level of investor understanding about a range of issues, we administered a large-scale, national household survey and conducted six intensive focus-group discussions with both experienced and inexperienced investors. Both methods were designed to identify investor understanding of the distinctions between investment advisers and broker-dealers and the relationships among them. Our analysis confirmed findings from previous studies and from our interviews with stakeholders: Investors had difficulty distinguishing among industry professionals and perceiving the web of relationships among service providers.

About two-thirds of all survey respondents were classified as "experienced" investors (that is, they held investments outside of retirement accounts, had formal training in finance or investing, or held investments only with retirement accounts but answered positively to questions gauging their financial understanding). Of the 349 respondents who reported using a financial service provider, 73 percent seek professional assistance for advising, management, or planning, and 75 percent seek professional assistance for conducting stock-market or mutual fund transactions.

We presented respondents with a list of services and obligations and asked them to indicate which items applied to investment advisers, brokers, financial advisors or consultants, or financial planners. Their responses indicate that they view financial advisors and financial consultants as being more similar to investment advisers than to brokers in terms of services and duties. However, regardless of the type of service (advisory or brokerage) received from the individual professional, the most commonly cited titles are generic titles, such as *advisor, financial advisor,* or *financial consultant.* Focus-group participants shed further light on this confusion when they commented that the interchangeable titles and "we do it all" advertisements made it difficult to discern broker-dealers from investment advisers.

Comments from focus-group participants expand on the survey responses. Like survey respondents, focus-group participants indicated that they would be willing to seek services from an investment adviser or a broker, but for different reasons. The compensation structures, disclosure requirements, and legal duties make investment advisers appealing. However, account minimums, industry certification, and costs make brokers appealing. Even though we made attempts to explain fiduciary duty and suitability in plain language, focus-group participants struggled to understand the differences in standards of care. Furthermore, focus-group participants expressed doubt that the standards differ in practice.

However, despite their confusion about titles and duties even among experienced investors, most survey respondents and focus-group participants are happy with their own financial service provider. It is clear from their responses that that personal service given by the financial service provider is a very important dimension of the business relationship. For survey respondents, the most common types of positive comments attributed to financial service providers are personal, service-related attributes, such as attentiveness and accessibility. These attributes were mentioned more than dimensions such as expertise or performance. For focus-group respondents, attentiveness and accessibility were also mentioned as important dimensions, but the most commonly mentioned attribute they sought was trustworthiness. We do not have evidence on how levels of satisfaction vary with the actual financial returns arising from this relationship. In fact, focus-group participants with investments acknowledged uncertainty about the fees they pay for their investments, and survey responses also indicate confusion about the fees.

Acknowledgments

We could not have conducted this study without the contributions of many people who agreed to share their expertise and opinions with us. We thank the individuals from dozens of organizations and firms who shared business documents and participated in interviews. We also thank the survey respondents and focus-group participants who participated in the study. We are also grateful to FINRA in providing data as well as contributing their time and expertise.

We thank Terrance T. Odean of the University of California, Berkeley, for his expert advice. Georges Vernez of RAND, Constantijn Panis of Deloitte Financial Advisory Services, and Jerry W. Markham of Florida International University provided detailed comments in their formal reviews of an earlier draft of this report. The final report is much improved as a result.

Throughout the duration of the study, we have also benefited from the assistance of a number of RAND researchers: Michael Thompson, Emre Erkut, Melissa Bradley, Jennifer Pevar, and Erica Czaja.

Lastly, we thank Laura Zakaras for her valuable assistance in writing the report. Brian Grady and Christopher Dirks provided excellent administrative assistance.

Abbreviations

ALP	American Life Panel
CD	certificate of deposit
CRD	Central Registration Depository
FINRA	Financial Industry Regulatory Authority
FOCUS	Financial and Operational Combined Uniform Single
FPA	Financial Planning Association
HNW	high net worth
IARD	Investment Adviser Registration Depository
MMA	money-market account
NASD	National Association of Securities Dealers
NOPR	notice of proposed rule making
NYSE	New York Stock Exchange
RDD	random-digit-dial
SEC	U.S. Securities and Exchange Commission
SRC	Survey Research Center
SRO	self-regulating organization

CHAPTER ONE

Introduction

A 2005 rule by the U.S. Securities and Exchange Commission (SEC), "Certain Broker-Dealers Deemed Not to Be Investment Advisers" (SEC, 2005) sought to clarify which of a broker-dealer's investment advisory activities are subject to regulation by the Investment Advisers Act of 1940 (SEC, 2005; 54 Stat. 847). The 1940 act regulates activities of investment advisers, whereas the Securities Exchange Act of 1934 (48 Stat. 881) regulates the activities of broker-dealers, who are also subject to oversight by self-regulating organizations (SROs). The 1940 act (§202[a][11]) defines an *investment adviser* as

> any person who, for compensation, engages in the business of advising others, either directly or through publications or writings, as to the value of securities or as to the advisability of investing in, purchasing, or selling securities, or who, for compensation and as part of a regular business, issues or promulgates analyses or reports concerning securities.

To avoid duplicate regulation of brokerage activities, the 1940 act (§202[a][11][C]) makes an exception for "any broker or dealer whose performance of [advisory] services is solely incidental to the conduct of his business as a broker or dealer and who receives no special compensation therefor."

The 1940 act does not define two important concepts: (1) advisory services that are "solely incidental" to the business of a broker or dealer or (2) "special compensation" for advisory services. The 2005 rule clarifies these definitions (SEC, 2005). Under the 2005 rule, a broker-dealer is excepted from the 1940 act if it charges an asset-based or fixed fee (rather than commissions, markups, or markdowns) for its services, as long as the broker-dealer (1) does not charge a separate fee for advisory services; (2) does not provide advice as part of a financial plan or in connection with financial planning services; (3) does not exercise investment discretion over any customer accounts; and (4) includes the following statement in any advertisements for the account and for contracts, agreements, applications, and other forms governing the account:

> Your account is a brokerage account and not an advisory account. Our interests may not always be the same as yours. Please ask us questions to make sure you understand your rights and our obligations to you, including the extent of our obligations to disclose conflicts of interest and to act in your best interest. We are paid both by you and, sometimes, by people who compensate us based on what you buy. Therefore, our profits, and our salespersons' compensation, may vary by product and over time.

Background

During the tenure of chair Arthur Levitt, the SEC commissioned the 1995 *Report of the Committee on Compensation Practices* (Tully and Levitt, 1995) in response to a concern about conflicts of interest in the retail brokerage industry. The report identified *best practices* as those that attempted to more closely align the interests of the investor, the registered representative, and the firm. Fee-based accounts were highlighted as a best practice because they reduce the likelihood of abusive selling practices, such as churning, high-pressure tactics, and recommending unsuitable transactions. Fee-based accounts allow for registered representatives to be compensated based on the amount of assets in an account regardless of transaction activity.

The release of the Tully-Levitt report coincided with an increase in competition in the retail brokerage industry as well as falling transaction-based commissions, the traditional source of income for registered representatives. As a result, more brokerage firms began to offer fee-based programs. Since such fee-based accounts were similar to advisory programs offered by investment advisers, there was some concern that brokerage firms that offered such accounts would be providing advice that was more than "solely incidental" to the transaction and trigger application of the Investment Advisers Act.

The SEC studied these new fee-based brokerage programs and concluded that they were traditional brokerage offerings that had been repriced, not new advisory programs. In 1999, the SEC proposed a rule (§202[a][11]-1 of the Investment Advisers Act), that, among other things, exempted broker-dealers offering fee-based brokerage accounts from being subject to the terms of the Investment Advisers Act. The SEC argued that, if the 1940 act applied to broker-dealers providing such fee-based programs, it would discourage the offering of such programs that would be beneficial to brokerage customers (SEC, 2005).

Many of those who commented on the 1999 proposed rule argued that such an exclusion would blur the lines between broker-dealers and investment advisers and confuse investors about their rights and obligations under each type of financial relationship. In response to these and other comments, the SEC modified the rule and reproposed it in 2005. The reproposed rule expanded the disclosure requirements of broker-dealers offering investment advice by ensuring that any advertisement or literature identify the account as a brokerage account, as discussed previously.

The 2005 rule has since been vacated, but the rule-making process raised important questions about investor perceptions of differences between brokerage and advisory accounts (including the legal obligations of each type of account) and the effect that titles and marketing that investment professionals use have on investors' expectations.

To address these questions, the SEC commissioned RAND to study the current business practices of broker-dealers and investment advisers, as well as investor understanding regarding distinctions between broker-dealers and investment advisers.

Purpose of the Study

The main purpose of our study was to provide to the SEC a factual background for its evaluation of the legal and regulatory environment concerning investment advisers and broker-dealers. The study itself did not evaluate the legal and regulatory structure, nor does this resulting report provide recommendations on policies or regulations.

To gain better insight into the current business practices of investment professionals, as well as what investors understand about the differences between broker-dealers and investment advisers, our research addresses two main questions:

- What are the current business practices of broker-dealers and investment advisers?
- Do investors understand the differences between and relationships among broker-dealers and investment advisers?

This report offers a description of current industry practices in marketing and providing financial products and services to individual investors by investment advisers and broker-dealers. We describe how each of these investment professionals interacts with individual investors today. The report also evaluates investor understanding of information received from investment advisers and broker-dealers about financial products and services. The unit of analysis throughout the report is the financial service provider, such as the firm or its individual professionals, rather than the products or services that they offer.

Approach

We used several methods to study current practices in the financial industry and analyze whether investors understand differences between types of financial service professionals:

- **Literature review.** We examined the relevant literature on the subject, which exists primarily in the fields of economics and business. The relevant economic studies focus on finance, industrial organization, contracts, and law and economics; business studies focus on management and marketing within the financial industry.
- **Quantitative analysis of industry data.** We conducted a large-scale, empirical inquiry of the investment adviser and broker-dealer industries, using data derived from regulatory filings submitted by investment advisers and broker-dealers. Our analysis focuses on a snapshot of firms at the end of 2006 but also includes some findings on changes in the preceding five years. In our analyses, the definition of a firm is determined by a unique registration in these regulatory filings. For investment advisers, we use data from the Investment Adviser Registration Depository (IARD). The 2006 data include 10,484 firms. For broker-dealers, we use two data sets. Data from the Central Registration Depository (CRD) include 5,224 firms. Data from the Financial and Operational Combined Uniform Single (FOCUS) Report describe 5,068 firms.
- **Business-document collection.** We collected and examined business documents used by a sample of selected investment advisers and broker-dealers. Using a probability-sampling scheme, these firms were selected from the registration data described above. Collected documents include marketing and sales documents advertising the firm itself, its range of services, or individual products; regulatory documents, such as disclosure statements and disclaimers required by federal and state regulators and SROs; account-based documents (e.g., application forms, account agreements, transaction confirmations, account statements); and interfirm agreements and contracts between investment advisers or broker-dealers and other possible financial institutions, such as mutual fund managers.

- **Interviews.** We conducted two sets of interviews—one set of interviews with interested parties and one set with financial service firms. The interested-party interviews provided us with a general view of how those parties perceived the financial service industry to work with individual investors. We interviewed knowledgeable people with a variety of perspectives on the financial service industry to gain a better understanding of how broker-dealers and investment advisers work with individual investors. Topics included opinions on trends affecting the investment adviser and broker-dealer markets, the current regulatory scheme, important issues that the current industry faces, and investor choice and sophistication.

  We also interviewed investment professionals in the financial service industry. The firm interviews allowed us to investigate how the financial service industry interacts, in practice, with investors. Participants were asked specific questions about their firms and those firms' business practices. We also asked about level of investor knowledge and industry trends and sought comments on the current regulatory structure.

- **National household survey.** To assess investor understanding of distinctions between investment advisers and broker-dealers, we conducted a large-scale survey on household investment behavior and preferences, experience with financial service providers, and understanding of the different types of financial service providers. The survey was administered to members of the RAND American Life Panel (ALP), a longitudinal survey of U.S. households, via the Internet. The survey was administered for six weeks, from September 26, 2007, through November 6, 2007. During this time, 654 households completed the survey. The household survey included questions on investment experience, beliefs about differences between investment advisers and broker-dealers, and experience with financial service providers.

- **Focus groups.** To gain additional evidence on investor beliefs about and experience with financial service providers, we conducted six focus groups with investors in Alexandria, Virginia, and Fort Wayne, Indiana. Each location included two groups of experienced investors and one group of inexperienced investors. Discussion topics included participants' investment background, general impressions of the financial service industry, financial decisionmaking and experience with financial service professionals, perceived differences between investment advisers and broker-dealers, and expectations of business relationships based on both broker-dealers' and investment advisers' advertisements.

Organization of This Report

The next chapter discusses the policy context for this study. It describes the evolution of the current regulatory and legal environment for broker-dealers and investment advisers. It also presents assessments of the industry and its regulatory structure, as expressed by interested parties. Chapter Three reviews published studies and media reports on various dimensions of the financial service industry, such as its structure, services, revenues, forms of compensation, and disclosure practices. Chapters Four through Six present our key empirical results: Chapter Four presents our empirical analysis of data derived from regulatory filings by broker-dealers and investment advisers; Chapter Five provides our analysis of the business documents and personal interviews with representatives of select firms; Chapter Six presents the results of surveys and focus groups on investor perceptions of distinctions between broker-dealers and investment advisers. We used diverse data sources and methods for the various components of the empirical analysis. Each chapter begins with a summary of our methodology and directs the reader to appendixes for further details about our data sources and data-collection and analytic techniques. Chapter Seven offers concluding observations about current business practices of broker-dealers and investment advisers and investor understanding of those practices.

CHAPTER TWO

Regulatory and Legal Background

To set the stage for subsequent analysis, it is important to have a basic understanding of key aspects of the legal and regulatory landscape within which broker-dealers and investment advisers navigate. This chapter describes the main features of that terrain. In the first part of the chapter, we offer the central highlights of the regulatory environment, first for broker-dealers, then for investment advisers. We focus on key policy issues related to fee structures, the rendering of advice, and the 2005 rule change that are most relevant to this research project.[1] We conclude with a summary of the results of interviews with "interested parties"—stakeholders with a variety of perspectives on the industry, from trade groups to consumer-interest groups and regulators—who express concern about today's regulatory environment and help illuminate the key policy issues facing the industry.

Regulation of Broker-Dealers

The Securities Exchange Act of 1934 (48 Stat. 881; herein, the 1934 act) and its implementing rules comprise the most central regulatory apparatus for broker-dealers. The act defines a *broker* as a "person engaged in the business of effecting transactions in securities for the account of others" (§3[a][4]), while a *dealer* is a "person engaged in the business of buying and selling securities for his own account" (§3[a][5]).

Brokers and dealers generally cannot do business unless they are registered with the SEC (48 Stat. 881, §15[a]).[2] The SEC has ability to revoke or suspend broker or dealer registration or censure the broker or dealer if the broker or dealer has violated federal law or engaged in other misconduct.

Although the SEC has the authority to set rules regarding broker-dealers, the commission has delegated much of this authority to SROs—in particular, the Financial Industry Regulatory Authority (FINRA).[3] In addition, a broker-dealer must also become a member of FINRA and must abide by applicable rules established by state law.[4]

---

[1] This is by no means a complete exegesis of the copious regulatory distinctions within these fields, which would require volumes. For more extended analysis of the legal and regulatory environment, see Plaze (2006).

[2] There are some exceptions, such as broker-dealers who deal with municipal and government securities only or broker-dealers who do business entirely within one state.

[3] FINRA was created in 2007 through the consolidation of the National Association of Securities Dealers (NASD) and the member regulation, enforcement, and arbitration functions of the New York Stock Exchange (NYSE).

[4] If a broker-dealer conducts business on only one national securities exchange (and meets certain other requirements), it is not required to become a member of FINRA if it is a member of that exchange.

Both the SEC and FINRA have several rules that govern the conduct of broker-dealers. The "regulatory-conduct" duties for broker-dealers are significant.[5] We begin with discussion of registration requirements for broker-dealers. We then list some of the more important regulatory requirements in the sections that follow.[6] We conclude the section on regulation of broker-dealers with discussion of the extension of fiduciary duties to broker-dealers handling discretionary (or "discretionary-like") accounts.

Registration Requirements

Applications for FINRA membership involve several filed forms and documents. Membership applications must include Form BD, the Uniform Application for Broker-Dealer Registration, which requires information on the broker-dealer; its business practices; persons, firm, and organizations that are controlled, controlling, or under common control; and criminal, civil, and other actions (for more information on Form BD, see Appendix A). Included in the application materials that registrants must also submit are a detailed business plan that describes all material aspects of the business, such as monthly projections of income and expenses for the first 12 months, an organizational chart, and a list of the types of securities to be offered and the types of customers to be solicited. Other required information includes names and fingerprints for all "associated persons" and any regulatory, civil, or criminal actions against the firm or any associated persons. Furthermore, each associated person must register with FINRA.

For active members, Form BD must be updated "not later than 30 days after learning of the facts or circumstances giving rise to the amendment" (FINRA, 2007b). SEC rules require that all registered broker-dealers file an annual audit report that includes a statement of financial condition, a statement of income, a statement of cash flow, a statement of changes in stockholders', partners', or sole proprietor's equity, and a statement of changes in liabilities subordinated to claims of general creditors. SEC rules also require that broker-dealers file the FOCUS report monthly or quarterly.[7] The main sections of the FOCUS report include a statement of financial condition describing assets, liabilities, and ownership equity; computation of net capital; statement of income or loss; and computation for determination of reserve requirements (for more details on the FOCUS report, see Appendix A).

All professionals—including partners, officers, directors, branch managers, department supervisors, and salespersons—associated with a registered broker-dealer must register with FINRA. As part of the registration process, individuals are required to submit information on prior employment and any disciplinary history as well as pass mandatory examinations

---

[5] Note that these conduct regulations do not necessarily give investors direct, actionable legal rights against a broker-dealer. In particular, when a broker-dealer violates the suitability requirement, it does not necessarily follow that the client (as opposed to FINRA) has the authority to take legal action. Traditionally, legal actions for suitability violations have followed a case-by-case assessment (*Colonial Realty Corp. v Bache and Co.*, 358 F.2d 178, 2nd Cir., 1966). But in many jurisdictions, courts have come down more firmly on the side of an absolute prohibition on private rights of action (*Jablon v Dean Witter and Co.*, 614 F.2d 677, 9th Cir., 1980). On the other hand, courts have found that violation of the suitability requirement (even if not directly actionable itself) may bear on other legal rights that an investor possesses, such as implied rights of action under securities-fraud laws (such as SEC Rule 10b-5, 48 Stat. 881, §10[b]), contractual rights, or fiduciary obligations (*Clark v Lamula*, 583 F.2d 594, 2nd Cir., 1978).

[6] FINRA rules include both NASD rules and certain NYSE rules. In this report, we follow FINRA's convention of specifying whether rules are NASD rules or NYSE rules.

[7] Whether a broker-dealer is required to file monthly or quarterly depends on whether he or she clears transactions and holds customer accounts.

administered by FINRA. Topics on the qualification exams include the markets, the securities industry, and securities regulation. Principals of broker-dealers, such as officers, partners, or managers, must pass additional examinations.

Suitability

Under NASD rule 2310, the broker-dealer making a recommendation to a retail customer must have grounds for believing that the recommendation is suitable for that customer with respect to his or her portfolio, financial situation, and needs.

Before executing a transaction recommended to a customer, the broker-dealer is required to make "reasonable efforts" to discover

> i. the customer's financial status; ii. the customer's tax status; iii. the customer's investment objectives; and iv. such other information used or considered to be reasonable by such member or registered representative in making recommendations to the customer. (NASD rule 2310)

Broker-dealers may also have additional suitability requirements, depending on the products that they offer. For example, a new rule that is scheduled to become effective in May 2008 establishes suitability standards for transactions related to variable annuities (NASD rule 2821).

Reasonable Basis

Before recommending a specific security, a broker-dealer must ensure that an investment is suitable for some investors (as opposed to being made suitable for a specific customer). A broker-dealer cannot recommend a security unless there is an "adequate and reasonable basis" for such a recommendation (*Hanly v Securities and Exchange Com.*, 415 F.2d 589, 2nd Cir., 1969).

Prohibition of Excessive Markups

NASD rule IM-2440-1 describes the markup policy. Since 1943, FINRA has used the "5 percent policy," which states that a markup of 5 percent for a security is a reasonable one. But the 5 percent policy is a guide, not a rule. In evaluating whether a markup is excessive, FINRA considers a number of factors, including the following:

- type of security involved[8]
- availability of the security in the market
- price of the security
- amount of money involved in a transaction
- disclosure
- pattern of markups
- nature of the member's business.

Prohibition of Excessive Trading Activities

NASD rule IM-2310-2 prohibits excessive trading, or "churning." In general, churning involves three elements:

---

[8] For example, the 5 percent policy may be too generous for certain instruments, such as government bonds.

- The broker-dealer must have control of the account (e.g., a "discretionary" account).
- Once the account is turned over more than four times its total value annually (this is called *excessive trading*), a presumptively suspect case arises.
- The intent of trading is to generate commissions.

Supervision of Registered Representatives

FINRA imposes strict regulations on broker-dealers to supervise the activities of their employees (NASD rule 3010).

Best Execution

There are also requirements that broker-dealers who receive orders from customers must execute them promptly and with reasonable diligence and must seek the most favorable terms for customers available under the circumstances (NASD rule 2320).

Record-Keeping Requirements

Registered broker-dealers are also required to make and keep a number of records relating to their business. Such records include account-record information, records of transactions, statements of financial accounts, memoranda of orders, transaction confirmations, records of associated persons of the firm (including disciplinary history), and a list of beneficial owners of securities held in street name (17 C.F.R. §240.17a-3).

Broker-Dealers and Fiduciary Duties

An important factor in the legal obligations of financial service providers (and the rights of their clients) is the extent to which such financial professionals owe *fiduciary duties* to their clients. Unlike a contractual duty (which allows a party relatively broad discretion to pursue its own self-interest, subject to a loose good-faith constraint), fiduciary duties require a heightened duty to act on another's behalf, in good faith, with honesty, with trust, with care, and with candor. Nearly 80 years ago, U.S. Supreme Court Justice Benjamin N. Cardozo famously described the distinct nature of the fiduciary duty:

> Many forms of conduct permissible in a workaday world for those acting at arm's length are forbidden to those bound by fiduciary ties. A trustee is held to something stricter than the morals of the market place. Not honesty alone, but the punctilio of an honor the most sensitive is then the standard of behavior. (*Meinhard v Salmon*, 249 N.Y. 458, 1928, p. 458)

Unlike the case of investment advisers (addressed below), broker-dealers are not categorically bound—by statute, regulation, or precedent—to a per se rule imposing fiduciary obligations toward clients. Instead, the existence of fiduciary obligations within a broker-client relationship has historically been significantly more contingent, turning ultimately on the factual nature of the relationship (usually as interpreted by courts and arbitrators).

Perhaps the most critical distinction along these lines is that between *nondiscretionary* accounts (for which the broker-dealer simply carries out specific market or limit orders on behalf of its client) and *discretionary* accounts (for which the client has given consent for the broker-dealer to purchase and sell securities on his or her behalf without consent for each transaction—often with restrictions on the categorical domain of such securities). By both title and description, discretionary accounts give a broker-dealer significantly more freedom to exercise judgment for the client. Instead of merely executing the client's transactional instructions, a broker for a discretionary account will tend to make trades on his or her own accord, on an ongoing basis, on the client's behalf. It is not surprising, then, that such freedom comes at additional potential risk that the broker may abuse that discretion or otherwise run afoul of the client's best interests. Accordingly, brokers who handle discretionary accounts are generally thought to owe fiduciary obligations to their clients. Not only do such duties transcend the basic regulatory constraints placed on the broker, but they also give rise to individual enforcement rights by the client.[9]

In contrast, brokers handling nondiscretionary accounts are generally thought to owe a much more limited and shallow pool of duties to the customer, principally concerning many of the rules that apply to all registrants, including prompt order execution, knowing one's security, knowing one's customer, disclosing conflicts of interest, and refraining from engaging in securities fraud.[10] Significantly, this set of duties is generally perceived not to rise to the level of a fiduciary relationship (see, e.g., *Independent Order of Foresters v Donald, Lufkin and Jenrette*, 157 F.3d 933, 2nd Cir., 1998, pp. 940–941).

At least two additional factors further cloud this landscape. First, some brokerage accounts may possess some characteristics of both discretionary and nondiscretionary accounts. For example, a broker handling a putatively nondiscretionary account may simply begin to make decisions on behalf of his or her client, effectively exercising de facto control over not only executions of client orders but also over the contents of those orders themselves. Even when the client is continuously apprised of such orders, courts have, on occasion, found that the broker's course of performance in exercising control created a fiduciary obligation (see *Hecht v Harris, Upham and Co.*, 430 F.2d 1202, 9th Cir., 1970). Over the years, courts have developed a number of tests to diagnose whether fiduciary-like control exists, usually turning on multifactor tests that are sometimes difficult to predict in practice.[11]

---

[9] One oft-cited federal-court opinion has ruled that brokers handling discretionary accounts owe a broad spectrum of fiduciary duties, including the duties to

(1) manage the account in a manner directly comporting with the needs and objectives of the customer as stated in the authorization papers or as apparent from the customer's investment and trading history, . . . (2) keep informed regarding the changes in the market which affect his customer's interest and act responsively to protect those interests[,] (3) keep his customer informed as to each completed transaction; and ([4]) explain forthrightly the practical impact and potential risks of the course of dealing in which the broker is engaged. . . . (*Leib v Merrill Lynch, Pierce, Fenner and Smith, Inc.*, 461 F. Supp. 951, E.D. Mich., 1978, p. 951).

[10] Brokers handling nondiscretionary accounts have been held to owe more limited duties:

(1) the duty to recommend a stock only after studying it sufficiently to become informed as to its nature, price and financial prognosis; (2) the duty to carry out the customer's orders promptly in a manner best suited to serve the customer's interests; (3) the duty to inform the customer of the risks involved in purchasing or selling a particular security; (4) the duty to refrain from self-dealing or refusing to disclose any personal interest the broker may have in a particular recommended security; (5) the duty not to misrepresent any fact material to the transaction; and (6) the duty to transact business only after receiving prior authorization from the customer. (*Leib v Merrill Lynch, Pierce, Fenner and Smith, Inc.*, 461 F. Supp. 951, E.D. Mich., 1978, p. 953)

[11] These tests include such factors as

(1) the broker's past activities as investment advisor; (2) the extent to which the customer followed the broker's advice; (3) the extent to which the broker trades without the customer's prior approval; (4) the frequency of communication between the broker and customer; (5) the investment sophistication of the customer; and (6) the degree of trust and confidence reposed in the broker. (Goforth, 1989, pp. 428–429)

Second, for nearly two decades, the jurisprudential tests for divining the existence and extent of fiduciary obligations among brokers have remained in a form of doctrinal stasis, with little or no evolutionary development of legal precedents. The reason for this hiatus is that virtually all disputes in this period involving brokers' allegedly breached duties to their clients have been adjudicated through arbitration, a process that does not generate published, written opinions. Challenges to the validity of such binding arbitration requirements, moreover, are both rare and rarely successful, leaving much of the current set of disputes beyond the public view. It is difficult to tell with much certainty, then, whether courts hearing such cases today would adopt a fiduciary-duty jurisprudence for brokers that is stronger, weaker, or roughly the same as the one that developed during the 1970s and early 1980s (see, e.g., Markham and Hazen, 2006, §12:33).

Regulation of Investment Advisers

The federal Investment Advisers Act of 1940 (54 Stat. 847, herein the 1940 act) regulates the collection of financial professions that typically includes financial planners, money managers, and investment consultants. The act (§202[a][11]) defines an *investment adviser* as any person who, for compensation, is engaged in a business of providing advice to others or issuing reports or analyses regarding securities. This test is conjunctive (and thus both parts must be satisfied for a party to be deemed an investment adviser under the act). However, the SEC—which is authorized under statute to administer the act—has interpreted its ambit relatively broadly.

Falling under the 1940 act's prescriptions entails three sets of general obligations: heightened fiduciary duties, reporting and record-keeping obligations, and other requirements. We discuss registration requirements as well as these obligations below.

Registration Requirements

Under the 1940 act, any investment adviser who does not fall under a specific exception must register with the SEC.[12] Those whose assets under management amount to less than $25 million are specifically precluded from federal registration and are subject to state requirements (if they exist), while those managing more than $25 million are required to file under federal law, and state registration requirements are preempted.[13] (It is important to note, however, that, while federal law may preempt state registration requirements, it generally does not supersede other state mandates, such as licensing or renewal fees and state blue-sky antifraud laws.)

When applicable, SEC registration takes place at the firm level, and employees and others under control of the firm are deemed to be registered by the advisory firm's registration. The precise vehicle for registration is Form ADV, which must be filed at least once a year (and, in some cases, more frequently). The form contains two parts. Part I contains general informa-

---

[12] Exceptions include advisers who do all of their business within a state and not pertaining to securities sold on a national exchange, private advisers with fewer than 15 clients, hedge-fund advisers, commodity-trading advisers, and investment advisory firms that are themselves charitable organizations. Some of these exceptions are not as clear as they first appear. For example, in assessing the number of clients maintained by the adviser, the SEC has had difficulty determining whether to treat corporate clients as a single client or to pierce through to the actual number of shareholders. See Pekarek (2007) and Markham (2006, pp. 101–105).

[13] In special cases, such as with Wyoming, which has no state requirements, investment advisers are required to register under federal law.

tion about the nature and size of the adviser's business and disciplinary history within the firm (pertaining to either the company or individual employees). Information on Part II includes disclosures of conflicts, such as the practice of using of an affiliate firm to execute client trades. (See Appendix A for more about Form ADV.)

Fiduciary Duties

In addition to registration requirements, and unlike broker-dealers, federally registered investment advisers owe fiduciary obligations to their clients as a *categorical* matter. As noted already, such obligations require the adviser to act solely with the client's investment goals and interests in mind, free from any direct or indirect conflicts of interest that would tempt the adviser to make recommendations that would also benefit him or her. Although the specific standards for fiduciary obligations are not laid out clearly in the statute, they are unambiguously a centerpiece of the 1940 act's differential treatment of investment advisers, and their categorical application has since been upheld in numerous specific circumstances (see, e.g., *Lowe v SEC*, 472 U.S. 181, 1985, p. 210). Some of these requirements are similar to those that apply to nonfiduciary broker-dealers, including a suitability requirement, a requirement that the adviser have a reasonable basis for his or her recommendations, and a best-execution requirement. However, the universal duties imposed on investment advisers differ in number, degree, and mechanism of enforcement. As noted, the kernel of the fiduciary obligations that investment advisers owe to clients is to refrain from any undisclosed conflicts of interest, a requirement that constrains only some broker-dealers. In addition, even for those requirements that appear similar to those for broker-dealers, violation may be viewed as much more significant.[14]

The fiduciary duties imposed on investment advisers require any adviser either to refrain from acting with a conflict of interest or to fully disclose the conflict and receive specific consent from the client to so act. Examples of such conflicts include various practices in which an adviser may have pecuniary interest (through, e.g., fees or profits generated in another commercial relationship, finder's fees, outside commissions or bonuses) in recommending a transaction to a client. Moreover, these duties have been held to apply both to current and to prospective clients, and thus even deceptive advertising falls under the act's proscriptions.

Record-Keeping Requirements

The SEC also requires investment advisers to keep and maintain a significant number of records pertaining to client accounts, interactions, and business operations for no less than five years. The types of records required to be maintained include both typical records reflecting specific client interactions as well as records that the SEC deems to be pertinent to discharging fiduciary obligations. These include (among other things) records of an investment advisory firm's transactions and its employees' personal transactions, copies of advertisements, copies of client communications, and evidence substantiating performance-based advertising. Although these records are not required to be filed with the SEC, the commission has significant inspection rights and can demand access to an adviser's records as frequently as every other year (and more frequently if the commission has cause to believe that an ongoing violation is occurring).

---

[14] The commission takes the position that violation of suitability requirements is tantamount to committing securities fraud.

Other Requirements

Finally, the SEC and the 1940 act require investment advisers to refrain from particular sorts of business practices that have been deemed inconsistent with the adviser's role as a fiduciary. For example, the commission has placed significant restrictions on the advertising practices of investment advisers when soliciting new clients. Moreover, the 1940 act restricts the use of various types of fee structures—and, in particular, performance fees beyond a simple asset-management fee—to relatively sophisticated or high–net-worth (HNW) clients. In addition, advisory contracts are required to prohibit the adviser from assigning client accounts without consent.

The Dividing Line Between Investment Advisers and Broker-Dealers

Because of the distinct regulatory structures of registration, disclosure, and legal duties placed on investment advisers and broker-dealers, the dividing line between these two categories has always been an important (though also an elusive) one. Under the 1940 act, registered brokers and dealers are excluded from the terms of the 1940 act so long as the following are true:

- Any advice that the broker-dealer gives to clients is "solely incidental" to its business as a broker-dealer.
- The broker-dealer does not receive any "special compensation" for rendering such advice.

The proscription on special compensation has traditionally meant that broker-dealers receive compensation from their brokerage clients in the form of commissions, markups, and markdowns on specific trades. In essence, then, investment advisers' business practice of charging a general fee, rather than broker-dealers' practice of charging transaction-specific fees, has evolved into one of the hallmark distinctions between investment advisers and broker-dealers. Although a broker-dealer could, in theory, charge a management fee and avoid being deemed an investment adviser by giving solely incidental investment advice, the judicial interpretation of *solely incidental* is fraught with ambiguity, and thus the mechanism by which broker-dealers and investment advisers charge clients for services has become a significant issue from a regulatory perspective. Consequently, over the past two decades, broker-dealers have begun to drift subtly into a domain of activities that (at least under the regulatory regime) have historically been the province of investment advisers.

Simultaneously, investment advisers have also begun to enhance the scope of advisory activities they offer in a way that has not been part of the traditional norm. Some investment advisers, for example, may offer services that employ computerized trading programs and may take an active, discretionary management role over customer accounts. From the retail investor's prospective, these activities may not be obviously distinct from those in which brokers typically engage.

Adding further ambiguity to the mix is the emergence, also during the past 20 years, of a category of financial service provider known as *financial planners*. This field is itself highly professionalized, with a certification program that involves rigorous training and testing. Moreover, the financial planner is sometimes identified as an entity independent of either the broker-dealer or the investment adviser, offering *generalized advice* about a *general* financial plan for a client and not handling client accounts or executing transactions (see SEC, 1988, at ¶89,011).

However, it is widely acknowledged that financial planners typically offer a range of services, which need not correspond with this description (see SEC, 1988, at ¶89,011).

In the 1990s, a number of other types of brokerage accounts, including "discount" brokerage accounts and "fee-based" accounts, further blurred the distinction between broker-dealers and investment advisers. The popularity of discount brokerage programs grew in the 1990s because they were attractive to brokerage customers who wanted to trade securities at a lower commission rate and who did not want assistance from a registered representative. Full-service broker-dealers began to introduce discount brokerage accounts to compete with discount broker-dealers. However, they continued to offer full-service brokerage accounts that still included assistance from registered representatives, for a higher commission rate than that charged for discount brokerage accounts. There was concern that offering both discount and full-service brokerage accounts would require full-service accounts to come under the proscription of the 1940 act. This concern arose because, with a two-tiered commission structure, the difference in commission rates between full-service and discount brokerage accounts could be viewed as special compensation in return for investment advice.

During this same period, fee-based brokerage programs were gaining popularity as well, in part as reaction to the 1995 Tully-Levitt report (Tully and Levitt, 1995). In 1994, at the request of then–SEC chair Arthur Levitt, a committee was formed to identify conflicts of interest in the retail brokerage industry and to identify best practices to reduce these conflicts. Formation of the Committee on Compensation Practices was, in part, motivated by concerns that commission-based compensation may encourage registered representatives to churn accounts or make unsuitable recommendations. The chair of the committee was Daniel Tully, and the resulting report (Tully and Levitt, 1995) came to be known as the Tully report. In terms of compensation policies, the Tully report defined *best practices* as those "designed to align the interest of all three parties in the relationship—the client, the registered representative, and the brokerage firm" (Tully and Levitt, 1995, p. 1). Among the best practices that the committee found was "paying a portion of [registered-representative] compensation based on client assets in an account, regardless of transaction activity, so the [registered representatives] received some compensation even if they advise a client to 'do nothing'" (Tully and Levitt, 1995, p. 1). In further discussion of compensation based on client assets, the report specifically mentions fee-based accounts as potentially being "particularly appropriate for investors who prefer a consistent and explicit monthly or annual charge for services received, and whose level of trading activity is moderate" (Tully and Levitt, 1995, p. 10).

Fee-based brokerage accounts typically provide customers with a bundle of brokerage services for either a flat fee or a fee based on assets in the account. As with discount brokerage accounts, there was concern that the introduction of fee-based accounts would trigger the 1940 act, due to violation of the special-compensation exemption.

The burgeoning size, scale, and intertwined scope of activities among various financial service providers likely enhanced a general sense of uncertainty about the regulatory categorization of such providers. This sense of uncertainty, in turn, contributed to additional rule-making activity by the SEC. The most pertinent for this study concerns the proposed rule regarding the creation of a safe harbor for the certain exceptions to the 1940 act. We give an overview of that activity below.[15]

---

[15] In addition, we should note that the SEC also briefly adopted a rule that required hedge funds to register under the 1940 act. That rule was subsequently struck down in 2006 (*Goldstein v SEC*, 371 U.S. App. D.C. 358, 2006). It is not directly

Policy Response to Blurring of the Line

In 1999, the SEC issued a notice of proposed rule making (NOPR) that exempted broker-dealers offering fee-based accounts from being deemed to be investment advisers under the 1940 act. Although the proposed rule change would not alter the determination that asset-based or flat fees constituted special compensation, the receipt thereof would not trigger the 1940 act's requirements so long as three requirements were met:

1. The broker-dealer did not exercise investment discretion over the brokerage accounts.
2. Any advice provided by the broker-dealers with respect to the accounts was incidental to the brokerage services provided to those accounts.
3. Prominent disclosure was made to the client regarding the fact that the account was a brokerage account and not an advisory account.

The 1999 NOPR further allowed full-service broker-dealers to offer discount brokerage accounts "without having to treat full-price, full-service brokerage customers as advisory clients" (SEC, 2005, p. 10). The 1999 NOPR was issued in concert with a no-action position taken by the SEC, effectively assuring brokers even before the rule was finalized that they would be fully protected in abiding by the NOPR. In January 2005, the SEC reproposed the rule with some key changes: The revised version of the proposed rule expanded the disclosure-statement requirements and further clarified the circumstances under which investment advice from a broker-dealer is solely incidental to its business as a broker or a dealer. In particular, a broker-dealer must register as an investment adviser if it charges a separate fee or offers separate contracts for advisory services (such as sponsors of wrap-fee programs), holds itself out as a financial planner, or if it offers discretionary accounts. In April 2005, the commission finalized its proposal as "Certain Broker-Dealers Deemed Not to Be Investment Advisers" (SEC, 2005).

A short time later, the Financial Planning Association (FPA) challenged the new rule in court. In March 2007, the U.S. Court of Appeals for the District of Columbia Circuit invalidated it on a split 2-1 decision (*Fin. Planning Ass'n v SEC*, 375 U.S. App. D.C. 389, 2007). A core aspect of the FPA challenge was that, by excluding from the definition of *investment adviser* any broker-dealers who offer fee-based accounts, the rule exceeded what the SEC, as an administrative agency, was empowered to do. Furthermore, it claimed, even if within the SEC's power, the rule constituted an unreasonable interpretation of the empowering statutes. These two challenges correspond to what is known as the *Chevron test* for challenging rule-making in administrative agencies (and is named after the case *Chevron, USA, Inc. v NRDC, Inc.*, 467 U.S. 837, 1984).

In the March 30 opinion, the FPA prevailed on the first part of a *Chevron* challenge—i.e., that the statutory acts at issue, in particular §202(a)(11) of the Investment Advisers Act, was very specific on the issue of who could be exempted from the definition of *investment adviser* and thus limited the SEC's power. On this basis, the rule was vacated. In addition, the court vacated the rule in full because it did not have a severability clause, which would have allowed the court to deem only the offending portion of the rule to be invalid.

---

pertinent to our study, but it does have some effect on the interpretation of our larger data set in Chapter Four. We shall revisit this topic there.

The court's opinion revolved exclusively (or nearly so) around statutory interpretation, using a set of interpretational canons—such as plain-meaning interpretation, dictionary definitions, contextual interpretation, observations of grammatical differences among the subsections, and the like—to conclude that §202(a)(11)(C) made up the sole and exclusive exemption for broker-dealers and that §202(a)(11)(F), which gives the SEC broad discretionary powers over future exemptions, could not be used to broaden that tailored and precise exemption for broker-dealers in §202(a)(11)(C).

In May 2007, the SEC announced that it would not seek appeal of the *Fin. Planning Ass'n v SEC* ruling and instead asked the court for a 120-day stay of the ruling so that firms and investors would have adequate time to review their options, because clients with fee-based brokerage accounts would have to decide what to do with their assets in these accounts. The SEC also announced its intention to review the regulation of broker-dealers and investment advisers.

Prior to the vacating of the rule, the SEC adopted a temporary rule and proposed a new rule 202(a)(11)-1. Temporary rule 206(3)-3T allows that broker-dealers that are also registered as investment advisers may engage in principal trading on nondiscretionary advisory accounts under several conditions. Principal trades are transactions in which a broker fills customer orders with the firm's own inventory rather than with shares it obtains on the open market. Dually registered firms are required to provide disclosures on the conflicts of interest that may arise in principal transactions, obtain the customer's consent before engaging in any principal transactions, identify principal trades on confirmation statements, and provide the customers' annual reports showing principal-trading activity in the account. The temporary rule, which expires in 2009, allows for dually registered firms to offer fee-based brokerage clients an alternative account that offers similar services.

Proposed rule 202(a)(11)-1 reinstates guidance from the now-vacated rule on the clarification that

> (i) a broker-dealer provides investment advice that is not "solely incidental to" the conduct of its business as a broker-dealer if it exercises investment discretion (other than on a temporary or limited basis) with respect to an account or charges a separate fee, or separately contracts, for advisory services, (ii) a broker-dealer does not receive "special compensation" solely because it charges different rates for its full-service brokerage services and discount brokerage services, and (iii) a registered broker-dealer is an investment adviser solely with respect to accounts for which it provides services that subject it to the Advisers Act. (SEC, 2007b, p. 55,127)

Stakeholder Concerns with Proposed Changes

We have just reviewed how the law distinguishes between investment advisers and broker-dealers and alluded to the fact that the functional distinction has started to break down. To dig further into the erosion of differences between investment advisers and broker-dealers, we undertook a series of interviews with stakeholders or interested parties. During the rule-making process, the SEC received more than 1,700 comment letters from investment advisers, broker-dealers, SROs, and investor- or consumer-interest groups. There were concerns that business practices of investment advisers and broker-dealers were becoming more similar to one another, especially with the introduction of fee-based brokerage programs. There were also concerns as to what investors understand regarding similarities and differences of brokerage and advisory accounts, the legal obligations of each type of account, and the effect of titles and marketing used by investment professionals on the expectations of investors. To further understand these issues, the RAND research team conducted interviews with interested parties, including those who submitted comment letters.

We conducted 26 interviews with representatives from interested parties. The interviews included members of seven financial service industry association groups representing investment advisers, broker-dealers, and financial planners; five consumer-protection, -education, or -research groups; nine interviews with regulators (both federal and state regulators); and five academic experts. About half of the associations or organizations interviewed included two to three participants. The remainder were individual interviews. Participants were asked a series of questions aimed at gaining a better understanding of the important issues facing the financial service industry today, specifically related to the structure of regulations of broker-dealers and investment advisers.

The interviews were conducted in December 2006 and April and May 2007. In consultation with the SEC, interview participants were drawn from two pools—those who had provided public comment and those who had not. We began with prominent parties who submitted public comments to the SEC on the proposed rule during the Federal Register's open comment period. Those who commented on the rule were then categorized based on the industry they were representing (e.g., broker-dealers, investment advisers, consumer protection), if any. Each comment letter was reviewed by members of the research team and then weighted on a 1 to 5 scale, based on level of endorsement or opposition to the proposed rule. Potential participants were selected from each of the various industry categories to reflect a range of views of the proposed rule. By reviewing industry and academic publications and Web sites for additional potential experts, we also solicited participants who had not submitted public comments. Invitation letters were sent via FedEx to 32 parties that were invited to participate in the interview. Research-team members followed up with phone calls or email and then scheduled an interview date.

We followed the same interview protocol for all interested-party interviews. Since interviews follow the format of a conversation rather than answers to a survey, we cannot exactly quantify responses to topics presented. For example, in his or her response, a participant may not actually address the question asked. Additionally, respondents volunteered information not directly related to a particular question. When presenting the findings below, we identify prominent themes that emerged from these interviews. When possible, we assign a relative value, such as *majority* to indicate that more than 50 percent of respondents expressed that view or *most* to represent closer to 75 percent agreement. The term *many* indicates less than 50 percent agreement, whereas *some* represents 10 to 20 percent agreement.

Limited Investor Understanding

Most of those interviewed agreed that whether a financial service professional is a broker-dealer or an investment adviser is indistinguishable to investors. Many interviewees reported believing that investors think that broker-dealers and investment advisers offer the same products and services. According to these interviewees, most investors do not know the differences between a broker-dealer and an investment adviser; nor do they know that their regulatory burdens may be different. The primary view was that most investors believe that the financial intermediary is acting in the investor's best interest.

Trends Blurring the Distinction Between Broker-Dealers and Investment Advisers

We asked participants for their views on past and future trends that shaped and will shape the industry and marketplace. Many interviewees said that they felt that two factors have encouraged brokerage houses to move away from transaction-based commissions and toward more asset-based fees: the decline in transaction fees and the results from the Tully report. As a result, they claim that broker-dealers expanded their form of compensation to include fee-based accounts. Many participants reported that they thought that offering such products and services meant that broker-dealers and investment advisers became less distinguishable from one another. They claimed that bundling of advice and sales by broker-dealers also added to investor confusion. Participants mentioned that the line between investment adviser and broker-dealers has become further blurred, as much of the recent marketing by broker-dealers focuses on the ongoing relationship between the broker and the investor and as brokers have adopted such titles as "financial advisor" and "financial manager."

As for future trends, some participants noted that the baby-boom generation has been pouring money into the financial markets over the past 25 years. These participants expressed concern that, within the near future, large numbers of these people will be retiring, shifting a large amount of wealth out of corporate retirement plans and into the hands of individual investors. This issue is of primary concern to the regulators. These investors will face new challenges regarding managing their finances over the remainder of their lives, and most will need professional help doing so. Participants said that access to good financial information will be critical for those investors to make wise financial decisions.

Questionable Value of Disclosures

We asked interviewees for their opinions on the disclosures that investment advisers and broker-dealers are required to provide to clients and potential clients. One participant expressed the belief that clients do not have trouble understanding disclosures and, in particular, do not have difficulty distinguishing brokerage and advisory accounts once they have seen the disclosures. However, the majority of interviewees expressed the opposite viewpoint—that disclosures do not help protect or inform the investor, primarily because few investors actually read the disclosures. Many participants said that they think that the disclosures themselves are the root of the problem. The way that they are written is not easily understandable to the average investor, and the information in disclosures is not sufficient. Some participants mentioned their opinion that investment advisers' disclosures are more complete than broker-dealers' disclosures, but participants generally felt that both investment advisers' and broker-dealers' disclosures should provide more information and in plainer language. Some interviewees reported their opinion that the financial service provider does not do enough to help investors understand disclosures: Financial service providers present the required disclosures but do not take time to explain them. Many participants also mentioned that many investors do not take the necessary time and effort to fully read and understand disclosures.

Many participants interviewed acknowledged that the timing of presentation of the disclosures is also important—broker-dealers tend to give disclosures at the point of sale, whereas investment advisers are required to provide Form ADV Part II in advance or at the time of contract if rescission is permitted within a specifically allotted time. These interviewees said that they think that disclosures at the point of sale are often too late to make a difference.

Assessment of the Current Regulatory Structure

The majority of those interviewed felt that the current regulatory scheme treats broker-dealers and investment advisers differently when, in practice, their role is essentially the same, especially from the viewpoint of the individual investor. Most of these respondents felt that the recently vacated rule that exempts broker-dealers from the 1940 act based on the form of compensation (asset-based fees) misses the mark. They argue that it is the services provided, rather than the form of compensation, that should trigger the type of regulation that applies. Most interviewees said that, if the services provided are the same, then the same rules should apply, because an investor's expectation will be the same.

Some participants were cautious of encouraging additional regulation and worried that it would become an even greater obstacle to commerce. Others felt that the existing regulatory structure could still function but with some needed adjustments. Some of these suggested changes included clearly defining the term *solely incidental*, addressing the issue of how to handle principal trades, and having a uniform disclosure statement across broker-dealers and investment advisers.

Need for Greater Financial Literacy

Many participants argued that the primary concern of regulation should be the investor and creating an investor-friendly industry. They believe that investors need to have confidence in the industry and know that financial service providers are being regulated vigorously and disciplined properly if need be.

Most of those interviewed felt that financial literacy was very low across all income levels. They expressed that investors must take more personal responsibility in their investments but that there is a role for the industry as well. Many participants expressed a clear need for financial education, and several indicated that the financial service industry must step up to provide or fund more financial-literacy and -education programs. Some participants mentioned that financial literacy becomes even more important as the amount of money that moves into the hands of individual investors in the form of self-directed retirement accounts grows each year.

Conclusion

In many ways, the financial service industry finds itself at a crossroads regarding its regulatory and legal status. The legal distinctions that define investment advisers and broker-dealers date back to the 1930s and 1940s. As the beginning of this chapter describes, in the past few decades, the functional difference between investment advisers and broker-dealers has arguably become more blurred, thereby calling into question the wisdom of traditional definitions and regulatory and legal distinctions between the two types of service providers.

The interested-party interviews suggest that individual investors do not distinguish between investment advisers and broker-dealers. Marketplace changes that have resulted in investment advisers and broker-dealers offering similar services have added to investor confusion. This has led many to question the value of two regulatory schemes when, in practice, investment advisers and broker-dealers serve similar roles, especially in investors' eyes. Those interviews also suggest that disclosures, which are meant to inform investors of their rights and of the responsibilities of the financial service provider, are of little value because few investors read them.

Future regulatory and legal reform may clarify, dissolve, or smooth these blurred boundaries. Regardless, a comprehensive, empirical analysis of these markets will assist policymakers as they evaluate the regulatory and legal environment. The analyses presented in the following chapters are designed to provide such a foundation.

CHAPTER THREE

View of the Industry from Published Sources

To further examine the business practices of investment advisers and broker-dealers, we reviewed the academic literature in economics and business, with a focus on finance, industrial organization, contracts, law and economics, and management and marketing in the financial industry. We also surveyed trade journals, financial media, and national news media.[1] Because practices in the financial sector have been changing rapidly, we focused on studies published in the past five years. Our aim in undertaking this review is to address our two basic research questions: What are the current business practices of investment advisers and broker-dealers (at least as reflected in the literature), and what do investors know about them? As we will explain in this chapter, the academic and trade literature present some important, but incomplete, insights regarding these two questions.

The academic literature is strong in some areas and weak in others. There are many studies, for example, on the topic of investment advisers' compensation, typically built around some conception of principal-agent theory. On other topics, such as the specific composition of fee structures, however, there is discernibly less academic research. And in some areas, the research is meager to nonexistent, most notably on revenue streams and compliance practices of firms. We suspect that these patterns are largely a reflection of the dearth of readily available, structured, and representative data on these issues.

In areas in which the academic literature is thin, we have used other sources to help fill in our understanding of current practices in the industry. In some sections, we synthesize information gleaned from a large number of sources, such as trade journals, financial media, and other similar publications. While popular literature certainly reflects the actual situation in certain cross-sections of the financial service industry at given points of time, these sources may not provide a perfectly reliable account of typical, current practices in the entire sector. For that reason, we complement these sources with a review of business documents and interviews with investment advisers and broker-dealers, which we present in Chapter Five.

We begin our overview of the industry by describing firms: the structure of the industry, services they provide, fee structures associated with those services, and sources of revenue. We then describe marketing and sales practices of financial service firms, including disclosure and compliance practices; investment professionals, their compensation, and training; and, finally, investor perceptions and expectations.

---

[1] In our search for relevant sources, we used major research databases in business, economics, and social sciences. Specific channels included EconLit, the American Economic Association's electronic bibliography of economic literature; ABI/INFORM®, covering refereed journals in business and trade publications; LexisNexis®, covering a host of trade and financial media; Social Science Research Network, covering social-science working papers in the publication pipeline; and ProQuest National Newspapers 5, covering large, national newspapers with authoritative financial content.

Characteristics of Firms

Structure of the Financial Service Industry

Industry reports describe that, for both the investment advisory and brokerage industries, a relatively small numbers of firms tend to dominate their respective markets. Our analysis in Chapter Four of data on investment advisers and broker-dealers yields a similar finding.

Investment advisers. A relatively small number of investment advisory firms dominate the industry, in terms of total assets under management. From 2001 to 2007, roughly 5 percent of firms reported discretionary assets under management of more than $10 billion. These firms account for more than 80 percent of assets under management across the industry. However, small firms are the majority among SEC-registered investment advisory firms. From 2001 to 2007, 60 to 70 percent of firms had ten employees or fewer (National Regulatory Services and Investment Counsel Association of America, 2001; Investment Counsel Association of America and National Regulatory Services, 2002, 2003, 2004; Investment Adviser Association and National Regulatory Services, 2005, 2006; National Regulatory Services and Investment Adviser Association, 2007).

Broker-dealers. As with the investment adviser industry, relatively few brokerage firms dominate the market. Broker-dealers do not report assets under management, but an indicator of retail-market activity is revenue. According to data compiled and analyzed by Mills (2005), the top ten brokerage firms accounted for 45 percent of commission revenues as of 2004. Over the majority of the past two decades, with the exception of the late 1990s, this share fluctuated between 38 and 45 percent. The share of the ten largest players bottomed in 1999 at 32 percent. Of fee-based brokerage, one firm dominated the market in 2005 in terms of assets in fee-based brokerage accounts (Tiburon Strategic Advisors, 2005).[2]

Other Firms

Our analysis of the financial service industry focuses on services offered by broker-dealers and investment advisers. However, the financial service industry includes other types of firms that provide services that broker-dealers and investment advisers typically provide, and this injects even more complexity and confusion into the retail-investor market for financial services. See Appendix A for a brief summary of the literature describing mutual fund direct purchase and financial services by banks and accountants.

Fee Structures Associated with Services

We report here on findings from existing sources on fee structures for brokerage and advisory services. Our empirical analysis, document collection, and firm interviews in Chapters Five and Six will shed further light on fee structures within the industry. Furthermore, our research also gives insight on the effects of the recent regulatory developments.

Brokerage services. Before the recent regulatory developments (see Chapter Two), many large brokerage firms had been relying less on commissions and offering fee-based accounts as an option to customers (Smith, 2003). Fees that are based on account size generally range from 1 to 3 percent of assets, whereby larger accounts are subjected to lower fees, and wealthier cli-

---

[2]   However, with the recent regulatory developments, the market for fee-based brokerage service is evolving, as we observe from our firm interviews and as reported in Chapter Five.

ents are often in a position to negotiate the fee rate. In general, brokerage firms find fee-based products and services appealing because they generate revenue regardless of how actively the customer conducts transactions (Horowitz, 2004). Furthermore, as competition from discount brokers has driven down the profits from commissions, fee-based products and services have become even more attractive (Black, 2005). Overall, broker-dealers' commission revenues have deteriorated steadily since 1980 as a result of declining commission rates (Mills, 2005). In a survey of 83 broker-dealers, Eckblad and Black (2006) found that fee revenues grew by 36 percent in 2005, comprising 19 percent of total broker-dealer revenues for the year. The highest reported share of fee revenues was 53 percent (Eckblad and Black, 2006).

Advisory services. National Regulatory Services and the Investment Adviser Association (2007) found that more than 95 percent of SEC-registered investment advisers charge asset-based fees according to 2007 SEC registration data. In addition, one-third charge hourly fees, 41 percent offer fixed-fee arrangements, and 32 percent charge performance-based fees. Only 9 percent of investment advisers reported that they charge commissions for advisory services.

Revenue Streams of Financial Service Firms

In addition to fee structures associated with services, many financial service providers have other sources of revenue. Below, we describe revenue from interfirm arrangements in which both investment advisers and broker-dealers may engage, as well as the phenomenon from finance known as *dual trading*, which tends to apply to broker-dealers most centrally.

Interfirm arrangements. Many financial service providers collect sales commissions from insurance firms, banks, and mutual fund companies (Smith, 2003). Sales arrangements between broker-dealers and mutual fund companies are known as revenue-sharing deals (Lauricella, 2004). Fund companies pay the broker-dealers a certain percentage of the sales that brokers bring in, on top of the commissions that investors pay the broker. For example, one broker-dealer justifies such revenue sharing on the basis of marketing support. This broker-dealer receives from fund companies up to 0.25 percent of the value of shares purchased, plus up to 0.10 percent on fund shares held in its accounts. Another broker-dealer charges fund families up to 0.12 percent and 0.09 percent of funds sold for equity and bond funds respectively.

Brokerage firms have recently begun to disclose details about interfirm agreements to clients (Lauricella, 2004; Segal, 2004). Until recently, revenue sharing was not part of standard written agreements that fund companies had with dealers. Instead, such schemes may have been mentioned in other distribution documents, in an addendum to the main agreement, or structured as an oral understanding, or were sometimes detailed in less formal, side letters (Segal, 2004).

Managed accounts have been growing in popularity in recent years. Managed-account programs, such as unified managed accounts, separately managed accounts, or wrap accounts, may involve interfirm arrangements. Typically, the broker for such an account offers to bundle all of the client's various investments and services, including advice, execution, custody, and clearing pursuant to a single contract. The broker steers the client to a portfolio manager of the client's choice (PLI, 2007, pp. 528–529). The investor pays the broker a fee, which typically varies, across the industry, from 0.4 to 3.0 percent of assets under management. The portfolio manager may be an independent investment adviser or may be employed by the brokerage firm (Kim, 2006, 2007). In our review of the literature, we did not find any details on how the fee is shared between the broker and the investment adviser, although we did come across one article that cited a source urging the managed-account industry to disclose how these fees are shared (Jamieson, 2004).

Another common business relationship for small brokerage or small investment advisory firms is a structure in which independent brokers or investment advisers become a partner with a large-scale brokerage platform. In such a setup, the independent player can rely on the platform firm for execution, research, training, administrative support, custody, and any software (Clark, 2003). The independent broker or investment adviser pays an asset-based fee to the large brokerage firm whose platform it uses for trading and account management. These fee rates typically vary from 0.05 to 0.17 percent, depending on the competitive positioning and bargaining power of the parties involved ("On the Cutting Edge," 2006). There may also be other fees, such as setup and monthly fees (Oberlin and Powers, 2003).

Multiple roles of broker-dealers and dual trading. Broker-dealers are often put in a position of carrying out different (and sometimes blurred) roles in effecting transactions. In some cases, the broker-dealer merely executes an order on behalf of a customer in the trading market. In other instances, the broker-dealer acts as a principal in the transaction, selling the security to or purchasing it from the client, or submits client orders to a market maker that is a corporate affiliate of the broker-dealer. In yet other instances, the broker-dealer attempts to match up buy-side and sell-side clients, collecting commissions from both sides (and—in some circumstances involving internalized orders—claiming a larger portion of the spread). In practice, moreover, these alternative roles can often be conflated. An emerging area of research in financial economics analyzing the effects of these multiple roles has come to be known as the *dual-trading* literature. (This term is frequently used in a general way that does not bear directly on similar legal or regulatory terms, such as *dual registration*, in which a financial service firm is registered with the SEC both as a broker-dealer and as an investment adviser.) By whatever name one attaches to it, however, the conflicts of interest that sometimes attend the hazy boundaries between broker, dealer, and market maker have generated considerable interest among finance scholars, on both theoretical and empirical grounds. We consider some of them below.[3]

A sizable portion of the academic literature on dual trading concentrates on potential advantages of the practice. Indeed, if acting as a dual trader increases profits significantly, one should expect to see more entry into the market by brokers who are anxious to capture those profits. This entry, in turn, could drive commissions down and increase the depth of the market. And, if the market has greater depth, spreads may well decrease, thereby reducing the profits that broker-dealers can make even from undetected or legally permissible conflicts of interest.

The finance literature has explored such conflicts from both theoretical and empirical perspectives. Garbade and Silber (1982) analyzed optimal compensation and "best-execution" rules in a theoretical model. They found that there were a number of compensation or incentive schemes that gave rise to best-execution rules but that the most helpful intervention is one that encourages public dissemination of accurate securities prices. Thus, one inference from their study is that perhaps the most important measure of regulatory effectiveness is the bid-ask

---

[3]   Although the studies referenced in this section do not relate to the identical set of practices and institutions, nor do they use the same methodologies, their common focus on conflicts among brokers who act for a client and for some pecuniary side interest makes it most natural to address them collectively. Moreover, these studies tend to be grouped together by financial economists who study securities-trading practices.

spread, or the amount by which the asking price exceeds the bid, which is itself a measure of market depth and the presence of private information or agency costs.

A number of other theoretical papers largely corroborate that theme. Chakravarty and Sarkar (2002), for example, developed a theoretical model that suggests that retail investors would prefer, under many circumstances, the banning of dual trading. However, if there is sufficiently free entry and entry costs are relatively low in the dual-trading market (i.e., lots of parties willing and able to be dual traders), then the market will remain viable (but still less desirable for retail investors). Even within this framework, however, a reduction in bid-ask spreads may signal a reduction in informed traders generally, which would make retail investors better off.

Fishman and Longstaff (1992) found empirical evidence that dual trading helps uninformed customers and hurts informed ones. Moreover, they found that prohibitions on front running decrease bid-ask spreads in the market and force commissions up. Prohibitions on dual trading, however, have ambiguous effects on bid-ask spreads.

Smith and Whaley (1994) analyzed the top-step rule introduced in the Chicago Mercantile Exchange in 1987, which effectively reduced the practice of dual trading within futures markets. They found an unambiguous increase in spreads, indicating that the regulation increased costs to the customer.[4]

There also is a small but interesting associated literature on payments made by market makers for order flow. This practice corresponds to making side payments to a broker in exchange for the broker's willingness to channel his or her customers' orders to a specific market maker. The aggregation of order-flow payments can be extremely profitable to brokers. Much like the other literature on dual trading, the social desirability of order-flow payments appears to hinge on the degree of competitiveness of the market. As Ferrell (2001, 2002) noted, the significant competition among discount and fee-based brokerage houses in the late 1990s and 2000s likely caused order-flow payments to be passed on largely to customers.

Marketing of Financial Service Firms

There is scant research on the marketing of financial service firms, and the literature does not tend to distinguish between marketing of brokerage firms and marketing of investment advisory firms. Much of the research indicates that advertisements for financial service providers tend to appeal to emotion rather than provide information that a potential customer would need to make a well-informed decision.

Lawson, Borgman, and Brotherton (2007) conducted a content analysis of financial service print advertisements in 12 magazines, including general-audience magazines, magazines targeted to men, and magazines targeted to women. They found that the most common marketing messages in advertisements in men's and women's magazines involved convenience, safety, economy, family, and effectiveness. The most common marketing messages in advertisements in general-audience magazines involved wisdom, expertise, effectiveness, and productivity of the financial service provider.

Black (2005) briefly touched on advertising practices of brokerage firms. She contrasted the advertising practices of the late 1990s with those of early 2000s. Advertisements in the earlier period encouraged investors to believe that almost everybody could build enormous

---

[4] It should be noted that the Chicago Mercantile Exchange conducted its own study and concluded that the introduction of the top-step rule had no appreciable impact on market depth or liquidity.

wealth by trading. In contrast, the commercials of the later period promoted the image of the relationship with the broker as a long-term one.

Likewise, in the mutual fund industry, researchers have found that most mutual fund advertisements do not include such information as transaction costs that an investor needs to make a well-informed decision (see Huhmann and Bhattacharyya, 2005, for an overview of mutual fund–advertisement studies as well as their own research).

Disclosure Practices

In our research, we did not come across any academic studies on disclosure practices. We rely here on information that we gleaned from the popular press. The majority of articles on disclosure practices of financial service providers focus on disclosures that pertain to broker-age services. As discussed in Chapter Two, investment advisers are required to provide Form ADV, Part II to clients. While brokers have disclosure requirements as well, they do not have a standard disclosure form, such as Form ADV. Furthermore, the regulations regarding their disclosures have changed with the recent rule-making process. Therefore, it is not surprising to find more discussion of brokerage disclosure than of advisory disclosure. Articles that pertain to advisory services are mainly concerned with hedge-fund disclosures, which were outside the scope of this study.

Although there have been allegations of brokerage firms failing to properly disclose fees and conflicts of interest (for examples, see Damato, 2005; Kristof, 2004; or Lauricella, 2004), several recent articles (summarized next) indicate that brokerage firms are working to improve disclosure practices.

Pessin (2006b) reported that several large brokerage firms were in the process of streamlining disclosure documents in an effort to "inform, not confuse" investors. Such efforts included (1) collating information previously spread out over many documents into a single one, (2) cutting down on legal jargon to make disclosures more understandable, (3) using tables of contents and instructions, (4) giving the client only those disclosures pertaining to the specific type of account opened, and (5) implementing technology that allows professionals see what is being mailed to their clients. According to the article, making disclosures more accessible could also reduce a firm's liability in the event that customers claim not to have understood the disclosures.

As a further example of recent changes in brokerage disclosure practices, Opdyke (2005) reported that a global financial group with 2 million U.S. customers was about to roll out a new, 21-page document pointing out key differences between brokerage and advisory accounts, advisers and brokers, and discretionary and nondiscretionary accounts. Details on the compensation mechanisms of the firm and its employees across account and product types would also be disclosed.

Lauricella (2004) discussed the trend in the brokerage industry toward providing investors with information on revenue sharing between mutual fund companies and broker-dealers.

Armstrong and Hechinger (2004) drew attention to disclosure practices associated with the brokerage of bond purchases. Unlike the stock market, prior transaction prices in the bond market are not accessible to investors, making it hard for them to know the amount of markup they are paying the broker in addition to the going price for the bond. The article reports on the newly embraced bond-disclosure policy of a major dually registered group. This group is beginning to disclose how much it charges for each bond trade and adding to its Web site access to NASD's Trade Reporting and Compliance Engine (delayed corporate-bond prices) and fair-value pricing estimates from a third-party data vendor.

Internal-Monitoring and Compliance Practices

We found very few sources of information about compliance practices. Research on this topic is virtually absent, probably because so little data are publicly available.

Broker-dealers. Carlson and Fernandez (2006) analyzed data from a Securities Industry Association survey of member firms on compliance. They analyzed survey responses from 56 member firms accounting for 40 percent of industry employment and 28 percent of industry revenues.[5] They estimated that the industry spent $25.5 billion on compliance activities in 2005. Staffing-related costs comprised almost 94 percent of compliance spending. Compliance spending equaled 13 percent of the firms' net revenue. This ratio was highest for mid-sized firms and lowest for small firms. As small firms tend to outsource many compliance-related activities, they do not have to keep full-time compliance staff, which reduces their total compliance costs. Large firms, on the other hand, benefit from economies of scale in terms of personnel costs and infrastructure spending for monitoring.

Pessin (2005) reported that new and increased compliance requirements were altering branch managers' work routines. Branch managers reported that compliance concerns were increasingly dominating their workloads. As a response, some firms were transferring compliance tasks to in-house compliance professionals located at branches or at the main office.

Investment Advisers. ACA Compliance Group, the Investment Adviser Association, *IM Insight*, and Old Mutual Asset Management (2007) recently conducted a survey of compliance personnel at SEC-registered investment advisory firms. They received responses from 457 firms. Most firms have very small compliance staffs: Roughly a third of firms have one employee engaged full time in compliance activities, and 28 percent of firms do not have any full-time compliance employees. Moreover, the vast majority (78 percent) of chief compliance officers perform noncompliance duties in addition to their compliance duties. However, many firms reported that they promote a "culture of compliance" and cite evidence including annual compliance training (65 percent of firms) or ongoing compliance testing (57 percent of firms).

Compensation Structures of Investment Professionals

In the area of broker compensation, we found many articles in the popular press detailing the various forms of compensation structures. However, we found no academic articles. On the other hand, we found several academic articles on investment adviser compensation structures and no popular-press articles. The academic articles analyze the conflicts of interest inherent in principal-agent relationships, such as those between the investment adviser and the client.

Broker Compensation. Across broker-dealer firms, compensation to individuals accounts for roughly 40 percent of a firm's cost structure (Mills, 2005). The literature reports a wide variety of compensation structures for brokers.

A common source of compensation is payout, the amount that a broker receives from total revenue that he or she generated for the firm. The payout percentage depends on the type of relationship between the firm and the broker, the level of production, the products involved,

---

[5] Note that the survey response rate is 13.5 percent.

and the broker's rank in the firm. Firms can have ten or more different payout levels. In general, payouts are structured to increase incrementally as production increases (Oberlin and Powers, 2003). However, Schaeffer (2001) noted that payout can also involve a fixed percentage.

Clark (2003) found that, as the relationship between the broker and the firm becomes more independent and remote, the payout increases: Large brokerage firms pay out 35 to 50 percent, independent broker-dealers 80 to 95 percent, and clearing firms 100 percent. Tibergien and Clark (2002) found that integrated firms pay out 25 to 40 percent and independent broker-dealers 60 to 90 percent, with the average independent broker-dealer's payout being 82 percent. Furthermore, as professionals gain experience, they progress to arrangements with higher payouts.

Horowitz (2004) explained one brokerage firm's payout structure as follows: monthly, 20 percent of the first $9,000 and 50 percent of anything above $9,000. There are other incentives, such as incentives that promote fee-based accounts: The firm charged its brokers $15 for a stock or option trade made outside a fee-based program and put 1 to 2 percent of the production of brokers who derived at least 50 percent of their annual production from fees into an investment plan that vests after five years.

Even within a firm, compensation structures may vary depending on location. Cowan (2002) reports that, in the branches of a major brokerage firm, broker pay was 100 percent based on production. For the call center–based brokers of the same firm, pay was structured as a base salary and a bonus, which is a function of service skills, production, and net asset inflow.

Investment adviser compensation. In the area of investment adviser compensation, we found several academic articles. The economic and finance theory articles analyze the conflicts of interest inherent in the relationship between the investment adviser and the client. In these sorts of relationships, the investment adviser is the agent and the client is the principal. The client hires the investment adviser to act on his or her behalf, but the investment adviser's interests may not always coincide with those of the client. The client may not be able to perfectly monitor the principal. From the client's point of view, then, the important question is what kind of compensation structure best aligns the parties' interests. These articles generally report that a bonus-compensation structure, in which the adviser is paid a bonus (either a fixed sum or a percentage) if the portfolio return exceeds a predetermined benchmark, is the optimal contract from the client's point of view.

For example, Liu (2005) analyzed a situation in which the conflict of interest between the client and adviser arose because the client could not evaluate the effort or quality of the adviser's work as well as the adviser could. Liu found that the optimal contract was not an asset-based fee. In fact, an asset-based fee may induce the adviser to take excessive risks. When returns are not very volatile, a bonus-compensation structure is the optimal contract. Likewise, Das and Sundaram (2002) found that clients were generally better served by a bonus-compensation structure than by fulcrum fees. However, unlike Liu, they found that a bonus contract leads to the adoption of riskier portfolios than fulcrum fees do. Finally, Palomino and Prat (2003) found that, when the conflict of interest between client and adviser arises due to potential differences in their willingness to undertake risk, the optimal contract was a bonus contract.

Empirical academic articles that analyze the effect of compensation structure tend to use fund data, as those data are more readily available than data from other types of adviser-investor relationships. These analyses further support the theory articles' hypotheses on optimality of bonus-compensation structures. For example, Elton, Gruber, and Blake (2003) found that mutual funds with a bonus-compensation structure perform better than did funds without. Similarly, Coles, Suay, and Woodbury (2000) found that closed-end fund premiums are larger when the adviser's compensation structure has a bonus component to it.

Investor Perceptions and Expectations of Financial Service Providers

Motivated in part by the SEC's investment adviser and broker-dealer rule-making process, a few studies have examined investors' understanding of the differences among types of financial service providers and particularly between investment advisers and broker-dealers.

In 2005, the SEC commissioned a study by Siegel and Gale and Gelb Consulting Group. The study team conducted four focus groups of investors in Tennessee and Maryland. Focus-group participants generally did not know the differences among brokers, financial advisors, financial consultants, investment advisers, and financial planners (Siegel and Gale, LLC, and Gelb Consulting Group, Inc., 2005).

The Zero Alpha Group and the Consumer Federation of America commissioned a survey by Opinion Research Corporation of 1,044 investors regarding regulation of brokers and investment advisers. When asked, "Based on your knowledge of stockbrokers, such as Merrill Lynch, Morgan Stanley, and Edward D. Jones, which ONE of the following statements do you believe BEST describes the services they provide to their customers?" 28 percent of respondents reported that financial advice is the primary service, and 26 percent reported that conducting stock-market transactions is the primary service (ZAG, 2004). When asked the following question, 86 percent of respondents answered affirmatively:

> Stockbrokers receive financial incentives from INVESTMENT product sponsors to recommend particular investments to their customers. If, for example, a stockbroker receives cash payments, vacation trips or other forms of compensation from a mutual fund company AS AN INDUCEMENT TO sell a particular mutual fund to his or her clients, should the stockbroker BE REQUIRED TO DISCLOSE THAT FACT TO A CUSTOMER BUYING THE MUTUAL FUND? (Opinion Research Corporation, 2004, slide 13)

Almost all (91 percent) of respondents reported that they thought that, if stockbrokers and financial planners offer the same type of investment advisory services, the same investor-protection rules should apply to both. Lastly, 65 percent of respondents reported that they would be much or somewhat less likely to use a stockbroker for investment advice if brokers were subject to weaker investor-protection rules than a financial planner would be (Opinion Research Corporation, 2004).

In a 2006 survey of 1,000 investors, TD AMERITRADE found that, even with the new disclosure rules from the 2005 rule (§202[a][11]-1), investors were still generally unclear about the distinction between brokers and investment advisers. When asked, "Are you aware that stockbrokers and investment advisors offer fee-based financial advice but provide different levels of investor protection?" 43 percent of respondents reported that they were unaware of this, and 47 percent of respondents reported that they were not aware that brokers do not have to disclose all conflicts of interest. More than 60 percent of respondents believed that brokers have a fiduciary duty, and 90 percent of respondents believed that investment advisers have a fiduciary duty. The majority of respondents would not seek services from a broker if they knew that brokerage services provided fewer investor protections, that brokers did not have a fiduciary duty, or that brokers were not required to disclose all conflicts of interest. After being presented with the disclosure statement specified by the 2005 rule, 79 percent of respondents reported that they would be less likely to seek financial advice from a brokerage firm. Moreover, 64 percent reported that they did not expect to get an unbiased response if they were to ask a broker about the differences between brokerage and advisory accounts (TD AMERI-TRADE Holding Corporation, 2006).

There are also a few studies that focus on dimensions of service that help determine investors' satisfaction with their brokers. Fusilier and Schaub (2003) set out to examine brokerage clients' perceptions and points of satisfaction. They conducted two surveys of investors: one in 1998 (bull market) of 760 respondents and another in 2002 (bear market) of 388 respondents. Survey items included questions about perceptions of broker practices and satisfaction. Fusilier and Schaub found that satisfaction was influenced by the investor's perception of the broker's honesty, expertise, knowledge, and service. Furthermore, they found that investor perceptions and levels of satisfaction did not change significantly from the bull to the bear markets.

Yang and Fang (2004) performed a content analysis of 740 customer reviews of online brokerage services and identified quality dimensions that were closely related to satisfaction: responsiveness (e.g., prompt service, order execution, order confirmation), service reliability (e.g., accurate quotes, order fulfillment, calculation of commissions), competence (e.g., research capacity), and security (e.g., privacy).

To investigate features that matter to online traders, Chao, Mockler, and Dologite (2002) surveyed 139 investors with assets ranging from $1,000 to $1.3 million. The most highly ranked features were cheaper trading costs, trading security, customer service, and technical support. The dimensions that mattered the least were reputation of the firm, ease of use of the Web site, reliability of trades, and ease of account opening and access. Such service dimensions as execution speed, real-time quotes, and access to IPOs came out as only moderately important.

Conclusion

Overall, our review of the literature offers some insights about both our research questions concerning the business practices of investment advisers and broker-dealers and investor understanding of distinctions between the two. Our review suggests that the financial service industry is perpetually evolving. We summarize the key findings as follows:

- Both the investment adviser and broker-dealer industries have relatively few firms that dominate their respective markets.
- Almost all investment advisers charge asset-based fees for their services, while very few charge commissions for advisory services. While broker-dealers typically charge commissions for brokerage services, there was tremendous growth in fee-based brokerage services before the 2005 rule (§202[a][11]-1) was vacated.
- While we did not find articles related to investment advisers' disclosure practices, we did find a number of articles on broker-dealer disclosure practices. Many of the articles reported a trend toward increasing and improving disclosures to clients.

- Self-reports from brokerage firms and investment advisory firms indicate that these firms spend significant money and effort on internal monitoring and compliance.
- Existing studies suggest that investors do not have a clear understanding about the distinction between broker-dealers and investment advisers and their different levels of fiduciary responsibility.

Our review of the existing literature indicates that important, unanswered questions remain concerning business practices and investor perceptions of financial service providers. In the following chapters, we present the results of our own empirical work by analyzing administrative data on broker-dealers and investment advisers (Chapter Four), by examining the business documents of select firms and interviewing firm professionals (Chapter Five), and by analyzing survey and focus-group responses on investor perceptions of the financial service industry (Chapter Six).

Insights from Industry Data

We report in this chapter on a large-scale analysis of data derived from regulatory filings made by investment advisers and broker-dealers. We use these data to describe relevant aspects of the current state and recent evolution of the investment adviser and broker-dealer industries, focusing attention on the services that these provide and the relationships among them. This analysis reflects the best available empirical evidence on systematic patterns of activities, affiliations, and business growth among the many thousands of firms that the data describe.

All of the administrative data for this study came from regulatory filings submitted by registered investment advisers and registered broker-dealers. We rely on three sources of data, which we obtained either from the SEC Division of Investment Management or from FINRA:

- IARD data based on Form ADV filings by investment advisers
- CRD data based on Form BD filings by broker-dealers
- FOCUS report filings, parts II and IIA, by broker-dealers.

Taken together, the data have impressive scope, describing the attributes of more than 10,000 investment advisers and 5,000 broker-dealers in the fourth quarter of 2006. Moreover, some of this information is available quarterly back to the fourth quarter of 2001 for investment advisers and 1999 for broker-dealers. As a result of the different regulatory regimes, however, the content of the data sets varies greatly between these two types of firms. A firm's regulatory filing requirements in one domain (e.g., investment advisory firms handling more than $25 million in assets) may be quite different from those in another (e.g., brokerage firms that do not handle client accounts). This limitation tends to preclude direct "apples-to-apples" comparisons of firms in the various constituent groups. Nevertheless, it does give us a reasonably informative picture of the state of each industry, along with some limited opportunities to conduct a comparison.

For more detail on key characteristics of these filings, the architecture of the data sets, and detailed descriptions of data sources, see Appendix A. Appendix A also includes details about our efforts to identify dually registered firms, as well as firms that may appear to investors to engage in dual activities, using these three data sources along with searchable databases maintained by the SEC and by FINRA.

Throughout this chapter, we take the firm as the unit of analysis, but the data we received determine the definition of a *firm*. That is, each registered investment adviser is a separate firm, and each registered broker-dealer is a separate firm. Some firms are dually registered as both an investment adviser and a broker-dealer. Of course, some corporations may have multiple subsidiaries or business units, each registered separately as an investment adviser or broker-dealer, but these data do not identify these relationships. To complicate matters further, there are other types of relationships that are not completely identified by our data. For example, some solely registered investment advisory firms have employees who are registered representatives of broker-dealers. Quite frequently, one such employee is the sole proprietor or founder of a small investment advisory firm.

This chapter attempts to identify the relationships among firms that emerge from the administrative data. (We then used these data on the population of individual registrants to select firms for further data collection and analysis in Chapter Five.) The portrait that arises from these data reveals an industry that is extremely heterogeneous in terms of firm size, services offered, activities of affiliated firms, and nearly every other dimension we describe. This variation is true of investment advisers and broker-dealers, as well as across these industries. A fraction of the firms in our data—about 5 percent of investment advisers and 10 percent of broker-dealers—appear to be dually registered; that is, these firms are listed in both the database of investment advisers and the database of broker-dealers. Our data also indicate that many firms registered solely as one type are affiliated with firms engaged in the other type of business. We use these indicators of dual and affiliated activity to classify firms within each industry. This classification scheme captures important aspects of the heterogeneity across firms.

Our analysis is organized as follows. First, we present a brief overview of firms included in our data from 2001 through 2006. Next, we turn to separate discussions of investment advisers and broker-dealers. In each case, we first present summary statistics describing firms at the end of 2006, and then we compare firms based on our indicators of dual and affiliate activity. Our conclusions highlight the key comparisons between investment advisers and broker-dealers that we can make with the available data.

Overview of Firms in the Data: 2001–2006

We begin the analysis by tracking the number of firms at year end from 2001 through 2006. As displayed in Figure 4.1, the number of investment advisers in our IARD data grew substantially over this period, from 7,614 to 10,484, whereas the number of broker-dealers submitting a FOCUS report declined from 5,526 to 5,068. We also used these IARD and FOCUS data to identify dually registered firms based on a match of the unique identifier—the CRD number—in the fourth-quarter filing of each year from 2001 though 2006. We see in the figure that the number of dually registered firms consistently hovered between 500 and 550, with little discernable temporal trend. Taken together, these results indicate that the share of broker-dealers that were dually registered (i.e., listed in both databases) increased slightly from 9.5 percent to 10.6 percent, while the share of investment advisers that were dually registered fell from 6.9 percent to 5.1 percent.

Two important caveats (discussed at greater length in Appendix A) deserve explicit mention here with regard to the number of investment advisers in our IARD data. First, many investment advisers complete Form ADV for state registration but are not included in our IARD data on SEC-registered advisers. Soon after the first electronic filings were submitted to IARD, National Regulatory Services and the Investment Counsel Association of America issued their 2001 *Evolution Revolution* report, in which they estimated that upward of two-

Figure 4.1
Broker-Dealers, Investment Advisers, and Dually Registered Firms (2001–2006)

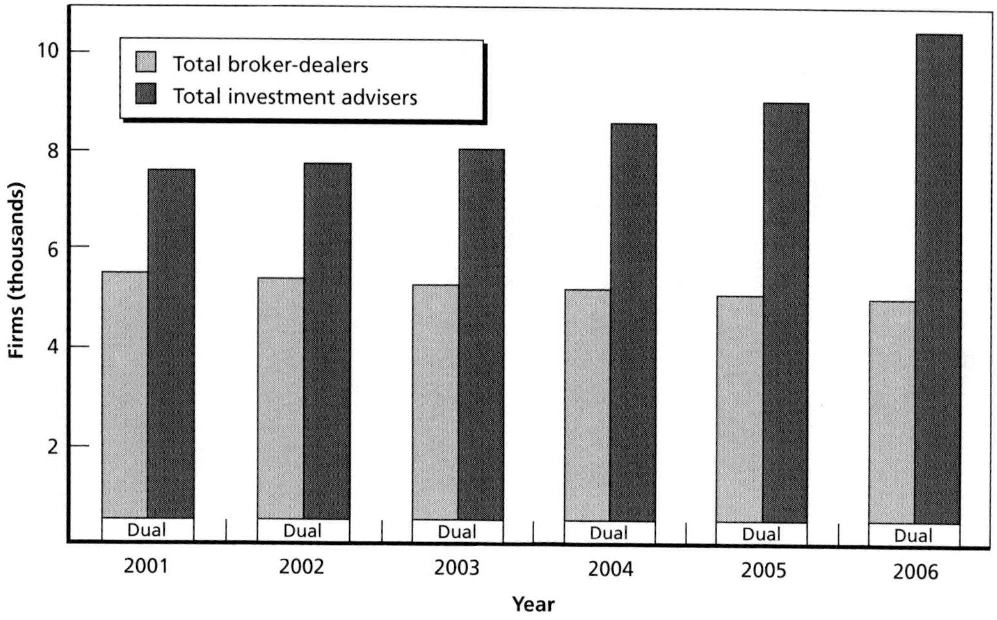

SOURCES: Broker-dealer data are from FOCUS reports. Investment adviser data are from IARD .
NOTE: *Dual* indicates firms listed in both databases.
RAND *TR556-4.1*

thirds of registered investment advisers were state registered (National Regulatory Services and Investment Counsel Association of America, 2001). Unfortunately, we did not have access to direct cross-sectional or trend data on state registration as opposed to SEC registration. We attempted, however, to identify registered broker-dealers that were also state-registered investment advisers at the end of 2006, and these findings are discussed in the section on broker-dealers.

Second, our findings on trends in the number of investment advisers are affected by changes in the registration requirements of hedge funds. As described in the 2006 *Evolution Revolution* report (Investment Adviser Association and National Regulatory Services, 2006, p. 4), a sizable fraction of the growth in investment advisory firms during 2006 were "new registrations pursuant to SEC rule changes requiring that certain previously unregistered hedge-fund managers register as investment advisers by February 1, 2006." And indeed, the data we received for the first quarter of 2006 include a total of 10,274 advisers, indicating that most of the increase in registrants from 2005 to 2006 (see Figure 4.1) did occur in the first quarter. During 2006, however, a court decision invalidated the SEC rule requiring registration of hedge funds (*Goldstein v SEC*, 371 U.S. App. D.C. 358, 2006). According to the 2007 *Evolution Revolution* report (National Regulatory Services and Investment Adviser Association, 2007), more than 700 hedge funds deregistered subsequent to this ruling. If we restrict attention to the period 2001 through 2005, the number of investment advisers in our IARD data grew at an average annualized rate of 4.5 percent. The rate is 6.7 percent if we extend the period through the end of 2006.

Investment Advisers

Attributes of Investment Advisory Firms: Fourth Quarter of 2006

The IARD data describe a heterogeneous collection of 10,484 investment advisory firms listed in the database in the fourth quarter of 2006. About 99 percent of these firms are SEC registered, with the remainder indicating that that they are no longer eligible to remain registered with the SEC. As a point of comparison, we note that the annual *Evolution Revolution* publications describe all SEC-registered firms (see National Regulatory Services and Investment Counsel Association of America, 2001; Investment Counsel Association of America and National Regulatory Services, 2002, 2003, 2004; Investment Adviser Association and National Regulatory Services, 2005, 2006; National Regulatory Services and Investment Adviser Association, 2007). In contrast, we focus on the reports given by all firms in our IARD database that indicate that they have individuals as clients. About 70 percent of the advisory firms report that they have individuals as clients, leaving us with 7,395 investment advisory firms. Descriptive statistics for the full set of firms and the set of firms with individual clients are reported in Table C.1 in Appendix C.

Among advisers with individual clients, more than 80 percent have clients that represent a range of asset holdings, from high to relatively low net worth. Almost 17 percent work strictly with HNW individuals, leaving less than 3 percent who reportedly work only with individuals who are not classified as having an HNW.

Employees. Although some investment advisory firms are very large, most are rather small. As reported in the first column of Table 4.1, more than half of the investment advisory firms with individual clients reported that they employ no more than ten individuals. Only about one-fourth of the firms reported having more than 50 employees, and less than 8 percent

Table 4.1
Advisers with Reported Number of Employees, by Employee Type (7,395 Investment Advisory Firms That Have Individual Clients)

Employees of This Type at the Firm	Employees (%)		
	All Types[a]	Perform Investment Advisory Functions	Registered Representatives of a Broker-Dealer
0	0.0	1.3	61.9
1 to 10	54.4	70.5	23.9
11 to 50	19.4	13.7	4.9
51 to 100	18.3	10.3	5.5
101 to 250	5.3	2.9	2.3
251 to 500	0.9	0.6	0.6
501 to 1,000	0.7	0.3	0.3
>1,000	0.9	0.4	0.6
Any number	100.0	100.0	100.0

SOURCE: IARD data for fourth quarter of 2006.
[a] Column does not total 100 percent due to rounding.

reported having more than 100 employees. However, 69 investment advisory firms with individual clients reported that they employ more than 1,000 individuals each.

The data also describe the number of employees performing "investment advisory functions (including research)" and the number of employees who are "registered representatives of a broker-dealer" (see SEC, 2006). As Table 4.1 shows, there is a good deal of variation across firms in the number of employees who are registered representatives. Although more than 60 percent of firms reported having no such employees, many reported a relatively large number of such employees. For instance, almost 10 percent of firms reported having at least 50 employees who are registered representatives of a broker-dealer, and almost 4 percent reported having at least 100 such employees. Note that a small percentage of investment advisory firms report that they have no employees performing advisory functions.

Assets under management. Other indicators of the heterogeneity in firm size arise from the data on assets under management, in which we found that a small fraction of firms manage a large fraction of the assets. Reports of assets under management are given if the advisory firm first reports that it provides "continuous and regular supervisory or management services to securities portfolios" (SEC, 2006). Table 4.2 describes the reports given by 7,177 advisory firms with individual clients and a positive number of accounts.

More than two-thirds of the accounts are discretionary accounts, totaling more than $15 trillion in assets. These firms manage an average of just fewer than 1,000 discretionary accounts, with an average of total assets in these accounts exceeding $2 billion. However, firms typically manage far fewer accounts and assets than the average. For example, the median number of discretionary accounts is just 128, and the median of total assets in these accounts is about $75 million. In fact, more than 90 percent of firms have fewer accounts and fewer assets than the average. One firm manages about 4 percent of all reported assets in discretionary accounts.

Not only are nondiscretionary accounts fewer in number, but more than 25 percent of firms have no such accounts, 50 percent have no more than one, and 75 percent have no more

Table 4.2
Assets Under Management (7,177 Advisory Firms That Reported Having Individual Clients and Providing Continuous and Regular Supervisory or Management Services to Securities Portfolios)

Account	Mean	Standard Deviation	Minimum	Median	Maximum
Discretionary					
Number	991	10,741	0	128	600,141
Dollars (thousands)	2,143,795	17,200,000	0	75,555	613,000,000
Nondiscretionary					
Number	457	9,826	0	1	466,527
Dollars (thousands)	230,906	2,410,753	0	361	115,000,000
Total					
Number	1,448	16,917	1	190	699,386
Dollars (thousands)	2,374,701	18,200,000	10	106,764	651,000,000

SOURCE: IARD data for fourth quarter of 2006.

than 35. A total of almost $2 trillion in assets are reported to be managed in these accounts, and one firm reported managing about 7 percent of these assets.

Summing together discretionary and nondiscretionary accounts, the 7,177 firms reported managing a total of more than $17 trillion, with a mean across firms of 1,448 accounts and nearly $2.4 billion in assets. Thus, mean account size is $1.6 million.

Of course, a very different picture arises from analysis of medians rather than means. The median number of accounts at a firm is just 190, and the median total of assets under management at a firm is just less than $107 million. The median account size cannot be calculated from the available data. One firm reported a total of $651 billion in assets under management. In contrast, 90 percent of advisers reported managing less than $1.7 billion each.

Compensation. Not surprisingly, the primary form of compensation is based on a percentage of assets under management. More than 97 percent receive such compensation, and the share is even higher among the 98 percent of firms that report providing "continuous and regular supervisory or management services to securities" (language from SEC, 2006). The second-leading form of compensation is "fixed fees (other than subscription)" (language from SEC, 2006), which are reported by 50 percent of advisers with individual clients, followed by hourly fees (44 percent). Only 13 percent of these advisers reported receiving commissions.

In fact, more of these advisers (20 percent) reported receiving performance-based fees than reported receiving commissions. Many of these reports are sure to pertain to hedge funds. For instance, of the 1,505 advisers reporting performance-based fees, almost 60 percent are classified as possible hedge funds according to a methodology based on that adopted in the *Evolution Revolution* reports.[1] A total of 1,177 advisers with individual clients (16 percent) are classified as possible hedge funds.

Business activities. The advisers also reported on business activities in which they or related persons are engaged. They first reported on the advisory services they provide. Almost 95 percent provide "portfolio management for individuals and/or small business" (language from SEC, 2006), with about 14 percent of those firms managing a wrap-fee program. Overall, about 6 percent of advisers with individual clients sponsor a wrap-fee program. After portfolio management, the most frequently provided advisory service is financial planning, reported by about half of the firms. About 18 percent engage in pension consulting.

More than 25 percent of investment advisers reported that they are engaged in activities other than advisory services, including brokerage services, among others. These reports may provide indicators of dual activity. As reported in Table C.1 in Appendix C, the most frequently reported activity is insurance broker or agent (16 percent). In addition, about 7 percent of the investment advisers with individual clients reported being engaged as a broker-dealer. Another 12 percent reported that they are registered representatives of a broker-dealer, with the overwhelming majority of these reports given by firms that are not sole proprietorships. According to Investment Adviser Association and National Regulatory Services (2006), this response pattern indicates confusion about the question (see also Appendix A).

However, almost 75 percent of firms did not report any of the listed "other business activities." Of these 5,424 firms, 4,160 also reported that they neither are "actively engaged in any other business not listed in Item 6.A. (other than giving investment advice)" nor "sell

---

[1]   We classify a firm as a possible hedge fund if it reported that its clients include "other pooled investment vehicles (e.g., hedge funds)" and the adviser or a related person is "a general partner in an investment-related limited partnership or manager of an investment-related limited liability company" (SEC, 2006).

products or provide services other than investment advice to advisory *clients*" (language from SEC, 2006).

Affiliated activities. Firms that do not directly engage in other business activities may instead be affiliated with firms that engage in these activities. Overall, almost one out of every four investment advisers with individual clients has a related person who is also an investment adviser. This other adviser could, of course, engage in other business activities. Moreover, more than one out of every five advisers reported that a related person is a broker-dealer, municipal-securities dealer, or government-securities broker or dealer. About 17 percent reported that a related person is an insurance company or agency, and 11 percent reported that a related person is an investment company. A smaller share of advisers reported having related persons that are banks or thrifts (9 percent); pension consultants (5 percent); or futures-commission merchant, commodity-pool operator, or commodity-trading adviser (5 percent).

The advisers also reported on other aspects of relationships with broker-dealers, with the overwhelming majority reporting some such relationship, either directly or via a related person. Whereas only 5 percent reported that the adviser or a related person engages in "agency cross transactions" (language from SEC, 2006), more than 60 percent reported that the adviser or a related person has discretionary authority to determine the broker or dealer to be used for a purchase or sale of securities for a client's account. Almost 80 percent reported that they or a related person recommends brokers or dealers to clients, and almost 60 percent receive research or other products or services other than execution from a broker-dealer or a third party in connection with client securities transactions.

Comparison of Investment Advisory Firms by Dual and Affiliated Activity Classification

In this section, we provide more detailed evidence of the relationships among investment advisers and broker-dealers. In particular, we consider advisory firms with individual clients, and we track various firm attributes from 2001 to 2006. Moreover, we further compare these attributes between firms that reported involvement in brokerage activities and those that did not.

There are different ways to identify whether an advisory firm reports involvement in brokerage activities (see Appendix A). One way to do so, for example, is simply to flag any firm that commonly appears in both the IARD data and the data on broker-dealers. But other approaches exist as well. For example, some investment advisory firms indicate on their IARD forms (i.e., Form ADV) that they are also broker-dealers, but not all of these firms are registered in a database of broker-dealers, so we cannot confirm their claims. Still other firms reported being a registered representative of a broker-dealer, but we found no evidence of this status in our other databases.[2]

Given the heterogeneity of methods for identifying firms that are active both as investment advisers and as broker-dealers, we created five classes of firms that indicate what different sources of data reveal about their activities. We specifically classified each of the investment advisory firms into one of five mutually exclusive and exhaustive types:

---

[2] We suspect that many of these inconsistencies emanate from confusion among individual filers about whether they should be reporting information about themselves or about their firm. Indeed, our data show that a great many of these firms have founders or principals who are employed as registered representatives of a broker-dealer.

1. *Dually registered:* A matching, unique, firm identifier (the CRD number) exists in both the IARD database and a database of broker-dealers (either CRD data or FOCUS reports) for the corresponding business quarter.
2. *Reportedly engaged as a broker-dealer:* IARD data indicate that the firm has reported itself to be engaged in business as a broker-dealer, but no matching CRD number is found (i.e., not of type 1, dually registered).
3. *Registered representative:* IARD data indicate that the firm is a registered representative of a broker-dealer, and the firm is not of type 1 or 2 (not dually registered and not reportedly engaged as a broker-dealer).
4. *Affiliated activity:* IARD data indicate that a related person is a broker-dealer, municipal-securities dealer, or government-securities broker or dealer, and the firm is not of type 1, 2, or 3 (not dually registered, not reportedly engaged as a broker-dealer, and not a registered representative).
5. *Neither dual nor affiliated activity:* The firm is not of type 1, 2, 3, or 4.

The great majority of firms in the IARD data are of the fifth type—neither dual nor affiliated activity. Moreover, as reported in Table 4.3, it is these firms that account for most of the previously mentioned growth in the number of firms in our IARD data from 2001 through 2006.[3] However, the firms in the other classifications dominate the market in the sense that they manage the overwhelming majority of assets and account for most of the growth in assets under management since 2001.

We turn our attention now to a comparison of firms across these types. We restrict the analysis to those firms reporting that they have individual clients. Most of the discussion

Table 4.3
Advisers of Each Type, by Year

Fourth Quarter of Year	Dually Registered (FOCUS)	Reportedly Engaged as Broker-Dealer	Registered Representative	Affiliated Activity	Neither Dual nor Affiliated Activity
2001	527	124	826	1,803	4,334
2002	538	131	841	1,810	4,455
2003	548	112	858	1,850	4,724
2004	525	105	868	1,872	5,253
2005	518	101	819	1,904	5,742
2006	536	94	855	2,009	6,990

SOURCE: Activities and affiliations reported in IARD. Dually registered firms were determined by a match between IARD and FOCUS data.

---

[3] The numbers in this table include all firms in the IARD data and therefore correspond to those in Figure 4.1. However, we restrict attention in the remainder of this section to the firms that reported having individual clients. The trends for this subset of firms are similar to those reported in Table 4.3. Note also that dually registered firms are classified here based on matches with the FOCUS-report data, which are available back to 2001. For our analysis of the fourth quarter of 2006, we used the slightly more inclusive set of matches that we obtained with the CRD data, which are available only in this final quarter but that include additional data that allow us to identify broker-dealers who are dually registered with one or more states but not the SEC (see Appendix A).

focuses on the firms in the IARD data in the fourth quarter of 2006. Detailed descriptive statistics are reported in Table C.2 in Appendix C.

Employees. As of the fourth quarter of 2006, dually registered firms tended to employ a much larger workforce than did the other investment advisers. Firms in the affiliated-activity group tended to be the next largest in this regard. For example, as reported in Table 4.4, 40 percent of dually registered firms reported having more than 100 employees, and 11 percent reported having more than 1,000. More than one-quarter of the affiliated-activity firms reported having more than 100 employees, but only 1 percent of these firms reported having more than 1,000 employees. In contrast, most of the firms of the other three types employed ten or fewer individuals. Only a small fraction of these other firms reported having more than 100 employees.

As one would expect, the reported frequency with which employees work as registered representatives of a broker-dealer varies greatly across these types of firms. As reported in Table 4.5, dually registered firms were the most likely to report large numbers of this type of employee, followed again by the affiliated-activity firms. Firms classified as neither dual nor affiliated were the least likely to report many, if any, employees who are registered representatives of a broker-dealer. About 37 percent of dually registered firms had at least 100 employees described this way, whereas 87 percent of firms in the neither-dual-nor-affiliated classification have no such employees. Only three of the 478 dually registered advisers reported having no such employees.

The entries in the table also indicate that 44 firms reported having more than 1,000 employees who are registered representatives of a broker-dealer. Not surprisingly, most of these firms—38, to be exact—were large, dually registered firms. Five of the six remaining firms fall in the affiliated-activity group, suggesting that these large numbers of employees are registered representatives of a broker-dealer that is a "related person." The remaining firm is classified as reportedly engaged as a broker-dealer, based on its Form ADV filing, but available information suggests that it too should be in the affiliated-activity classification. According to this large

Table 4.4
Advisers with Reported Number of Employees, by Adviser Type (7,395 Investment Advisory Firms That Have Individual Clients)

Employees	Dually Registered (478 firms) (%)	Reportedly Engaged as Broker-Dealer (75 firms) (%)	Registered Representative (798 firms) (%)	Affiliated Activity (1,051 firms) (%)	Neither Dual nor Affiliated (4,993 firms) (%)
1 to 10	15.9	52.0	65.2	23.0	63.0
11 to 50	11.7	14.7	21.4	16.5	20.5
51 to 100	31.0	25.3	11.9	34.4	14.5
101 to 250	18.8	4.0	1.4	19.4	1.7
251 to 500	5.2	0.0	0.0	3.8	0.1
501 to 1,000	6.1	1.3	0.1	1.7	0.1
>1,000	11.3	1.3	0.0	1.1	0.0

SOURCE: Employees, activities, and affiliations are from IARD data for the fourth quarter of 2006. Dually registered firms are determined by a match in IARD and CRD data.

Table 4.5
Advisers with Reported Number of Employees Who Are Registered Representatives of a Broker-Dealer, by Adviser Type (7,395 Investment Advisory Firms That Have Individual Clients)

Employees Who Are Registered Representatives of Broker-Dealers	Dually Registered (478 firms) (%)	Reportedly Engaged as Broker-Dealer (75 firms) (%)	Registered Representative (798 firms) (%)	Affiliated Activity (1,051 firms) (%)	Neither Dual nor Affiliated (4,993 firms) (%)
0	0.6	5.3	2.4	21.8	86.6
1 to 10	23.4	66.7	80.8	39.2	11.0
11 to 50	12.8	12.0	10.8	12.2	1.5
51 to 100	26.4	13.3	5.4	17.7	0.8
101 to 250	17.6	1.3	0.6	7.2	0.1
251 to 500	6.5	0.0	0.0	1.1	0.0
501 to 1,000	4.8	0.0	0.0	0.2	0.0
>1,000	7.9	1.3	0.0	0.6	0.0

SOURCE: Employees, activities, and affiliations are from IARD data for the fourth quarter of 2006. Dually registered firms are determined by a match in IARD and CRD data.

firm's Web site, it provides advisory services for a holding company, whereas a company with a similar name offers securities. That securities firm has a distinct CRD number in the CRD database; therefore, the advisory firm is not dually registered, according to our classification.[4]

As mentioned earlier, many firms also appear to be misclassified as registered representatives because of Form ADV reporting problems. The Investment Adviser Association and National Regulatory Services (2006) reported that only sole proprietorships should fall into this category, but fewer than 10 percent of these firms are sole proprietorships. Our Web searches, described in Appendix A, indicate that a great majority of the remaining firms have founders or principals who are employed as registered representatives of a broker-dealer, often a large firm with a distinct CRD number but with the same reported business address.

Assets under management. The IARD data on assets under management provide another indication of the disproportionate role of the firms that are dually registered as broker-dealers and the firms that are affiliated with registered broker-dealers. These findings, summarized in Table 4.6, are perfectly compatible with findings on the relative size of the workforce among these firms. Overall, dually registered firms constitute just more than 6 percent of all reporting firms but managed almost half of all accounts and more than 9 percent of all assets reported by the investment advisory firms with individual clients. Affiliated-activity firms constitute less than 15 percent of all reporting firms but reportedly managed more than one-fourth of all accounts and almost two-thirds of all assets. In contrast, the firms that are neither dually registered nor affiliated constitute more than two-thirds of all reporting firms but reportedly managed only about one-fifth of all accounts and one-fifth of all assets.

---

[4]   In fact, we conducted searches for each of the firms that was reportedly engaged as a broker-dealer but was not contained in our databases of broker-dealers. As discussed in Appendix A, a small number of these firms were classified in FINRA's searchable database as inactive. A much larger number appear to be affiliated with broker-dealers, such as the large firm just discussed.

Table 4.6
Assets Under Management, by Adviser Type (7,177 Investment Advisory Firms That Have Individual Clients and Continuous and Regular Supervisory or Management Services to Securities Portfolios)

Assets Under Management	Dually Registered (455 firms) (per firm, $ millions)	Reportedly Engaged as Broker-Dealer (70 firms) (per firm, $ millions)	Registered Representative (785 firms) (per firm, $ millions)	Affiliated Activity (1,008 firms) (per firm, $ millions)	Neither Dual nor Affiliated (4,859 firms) (per firm, $ millions)
Discretionary accounts					
Mean	2,340	1,370	911	10,341	635
Median	79	49	41	385	74
Nondiscretionary accounts					
Mean	1,155	57	113	550	100
Median	35	0	10	0	0
Total					
Mean	3,495	1,427	1,024	10,891	735
Median	205	76	67	543	97

SOURCE: Employees, activities, and affiliations are from IARD data for the fourth quarter of 2006. Dual registrations are determined by a match in IARD and CRD data.

To characterize assets under management by these various types of firms, we report the means and medians of the distributions in Table 4.6. We see that the affiliated-activity firms tend to be the largest, managing more than $10 billion on average, with a median value of more than $500 million. The mean and median of total assets under management at dually registered firms are about $3.5 billion and $200 million, respectively. With about one-third of their reported assets under management in nondiscretionary accounts, the dually registered firms report a much larger share of assets in nondiscretionary accounts than do firms in any of the other classifications.

The mean of total assets under management by firms that are neither dually registered nor affiliated, $735 million, is by far the lowest among all five classifications. However, the distribution of assets across firms is less skewed than in the other cases. The median of total assets, $97 million, actually exceeds that of two groups, and the median of assets in discretionary accounts almost equals that of dually registered firms—$74 million versus $79 million. The median of assets in discretionary accounts at affiliated-activity firms is far greater than either of these—$385 million.

The amount and distribution of reported assets under management has changed markedly since 2001. As shown in Table 4.7, total assets under management reported by firms with individual clients fell slightly from the fourth quarter of 2001 to the fourth quarter of 2003 and then increased by more than 50 percent over the next three years. Almost one-third of this reported increase took place between 2005 and 2006, during which time it appears that the registration of hedge funds accounts for a sizable share of the jump in the number of firms.

Note that all the overall growth in assets at firms with individual clients is attributable to assets in discretionary accounts. However, this finding does not apply equally to all types of firms. Figures 4.2 and 4.3 depict the overall growth in assets under management in

Table 4.7
Assets Under Management, 2001–2006: Investment Advisers That Have Individual Clients and Continuous and Regular Supervisory or Management Services to Securities Portfolio

Fourth Quarter of Year	Firms	All Accounts (assets, $ trillions)	Discretionary Accounts (assets, $ trillions)	Nondiscretionary Accounts (assets, $ trillions)
2001	5,442	11.85	10.05	1.81
2002	5,589	11.74	9.96	1.78
2003	5,754	11.29	9.66	1.64
2004	6,102	12.95	11.61	1.34
2005	6,483	15.16	13.65	1.52
2006	7,177	17.04	15.39	1.66

SOURCE: Assets under management reported in IARD.

Figure 4.2
Total Assets Under Management in Discretionary Accounts, by Year and Firm Type

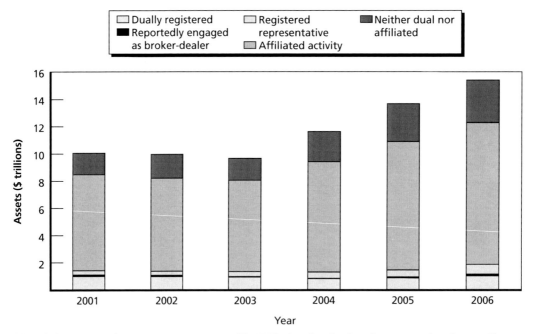

SOURCES: Assets under management reported in IARD data for the fourth quarter of each year. Firm type based on IARD and CRD data.
RAND TR556-4.2

discretionary accounts and the overall decline in those in nondiscretionary accounts, as well as the changing compositions of firm types at which these assets are managed. For example, dually registered firms actually reported a 17 percent decline in assets in discretionary accounts from 2001 through 2004, an 11 percent increase from 2004 to 2005, and another 16 percent increase from 2005 to 2006. In contrast, assets in nondiscretionary accounts at dually registered firms increased every year from 2001 through 2006, for a total increase of 75 percent over the period.

Figure 4.3
Total Assets Under Management in Nondiscretionary Accounts, by Year and Firm Type

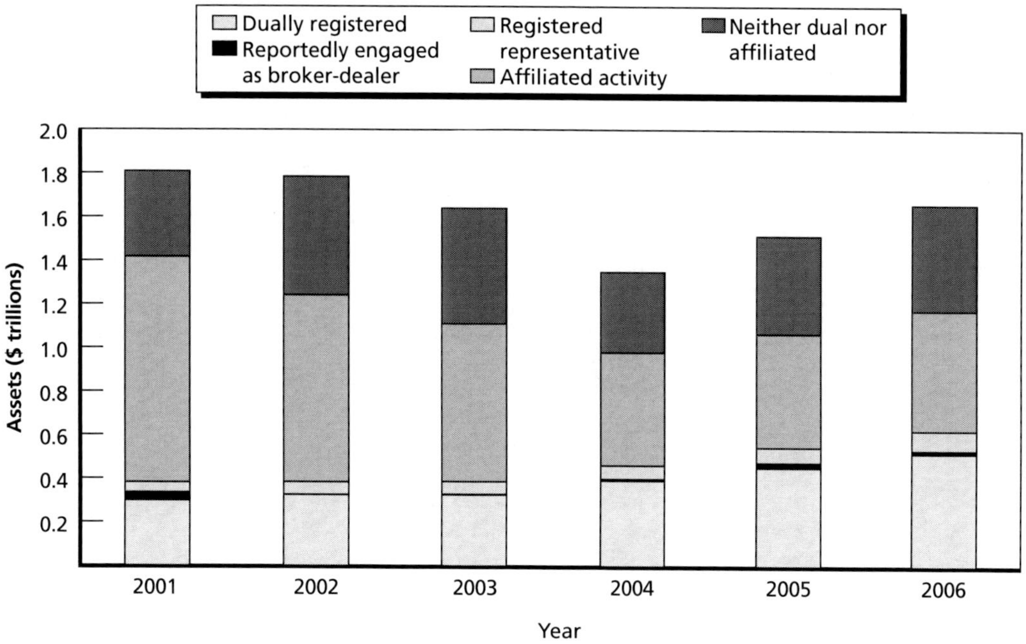

SOURCES: Assets under management reported in IARD data for the fourth quarter of 2006. Firm type based on IARD and CRD data.
RAND *TR556-4.3*

Clearly, most of the growth in assets managed in discretionary accounts occurred at firms in the affiliated-activity group. The number of firms in this category grew by about 7 percent. The total amount of assets in discretionary accounts that these firms managed grew by almost half, constituting two-thirds of all assets in discretionary accounts at the end of 2006. Over the same period, firms classified as neither dual nor affiliated grew quickly. The number of firms in this group rose by almost half, and total assets in discretionary accounts that they managed nearly doubled, constituting one-fifth of all assets in discretionary accounts by the end of 2006.

Compensation. Almost all firms of each type reported receiving compensation based on a percentage of assets under management. Other forms of compensation vary widely from one group to another. For example, about half of the dually registered firms and firms classified as registered representatives reported receiving commissions, as do about one-third of firms reportedly engaged as broker-dealers. In contrast, less than 10 percent of the affiliated-activity firms and less than 5 percent of those firms that are neither dual nor affiliated receive commissions. (See Table 4.8.)

Firms in these last two groups, especially the affiliated-activity group, frequently reported receiving performance-based fees, as did those firms reportedly engaged as broker-dealers. In a related result shown in Table C.2 in Appendix C, we found that about one-third of affiliated-activity firms are classified as possible hedge funds using our methodology adapted from the *Evolution Revolution* reports. Almost 15 percent of firms that are neither dual nor affiliated are classified as possible hedge funds.

Table 4.8
Reported Forms of Compensation, by Adviser Type

Form of Compensation	Dually Registered (478 firms) (%)	Reportedly Engaged as Broker-Dealer (75 firms) (%)	Registered Representative (798 firms) (%)	Affiliated Activity (1,051 firms) (%)	Neither Dual nor Affiliated (4,993 firms) (%)
Assets under management	97.3	96.0	97.7	97.5	97.1
Hourly	45.8	41.3	66.5	29.0	42.8
Subscription	1.0	2.7	1.8	2.4	1.6
Fixed	55.6	42.7	59.9	47.5	48.3
Commissions	50.4	36.0	47.7	9.9	4.0
Performance based	12.3	25.3	8.4	38.5	19.1
Other	14.0	5.3	9.1	13.6	7.5

SOURCE: Forms of compensation, activities, and affiliations are from IARD data for the fourth quarter of 2006. Dual registration was determined by match in IARD and CRD data.

Business activities. Almost all firms of each type reported providing portfolio management for individuals or small businesses, but the types vary considerably in the other advisory activities they reported. As shown in Table 4.9, more than 40 percent of dually registered firms sponsored a wrap-fee program, whereas the largest share of any other group is just more than 10 percent—both the affiliated-activity firms and those reportedly engaged as broker-dealers. Less than 2 percent of firms that are neither dual nor affiliated reported sponsoring a wrap-fee program. The results for actually managing a wrap-fee program are very different. The largest share is found in the affiliated-activity group (30 percent), followed by dually registered firms (27 percent). The shares for the remaining three groups range from 8 to 12 percent.

Firms in the affiliated-activity category were the least likely to report providing financial planning (33 percent) and the most likely to report providing portfolio management for investment companies (32 percent). In contrast, firms classified as registered representatives were the most likely to report providing financial planning (79 percent) and least likely to report providing portfolio management for investment companies (5 percent). The percentages for dually registered firms varied similarly (62 versus 7 percent).

Our classification scheme captured other variations in business services other than advisory activities. We note here that all but eight of the firms that are classified as dually registered actually reported that they were engaged in business as a broker-dealer. About 8 percent of dually registered firms reported being engaged as a registered representative of a broker-dealer, and half reported being engaged as an insurance broker or agent. More than half of the firms classified as reportedly engaged as a broker-dealer also reported being engaged as a registered representative of a broker-dealer, and two-fifths reported engagement as an insurance broker or agent (see Table 4.10). Almost three-quarters of the firms in the registered representative group also reported being engaged as an insurance broker or agent. The remaining two groups—affiliated-activity firms and neither-dual-nor-affiliated-activity firms—rarely reported any of the other business activities listed on Form ADV.

Table 4.9
Reported Advisory Activities, by Adviser Type

Advisory Activity	Dually Registered (478 firms) (%)	Reportedly Engaged as Broker-Dealer (75 firms) (%)	Registered Representative (798 firms) (%)	Affiliated Activity (1,051 firms) (%)	Neither Dual nor Affiliated (4,993 firms) (%)
Financial planning	62.1	50.0	78.8	32.9	46.7
Portfolio management for individuals or small businesses	92.1	91.9	96.6	90.9	95.1
Portfolio management for investment companies	6.7	16.0	4.5	32.1	7.5
Pension consulting	24.1	20.0	30.1	18.6	15.7
Sponsor wrap-fee program	40.8	10.8	5.3	10.3	1.7
Portfolio manager for wrap-fee program	26.8	12.2	7.9	29.8	9.9

SOURCE: Activities and affiliations are from IARD data for the fourth quarter of 2006. Dual registration was determined by match in IARD and CRD data.

Table 4.10
Other Reported Business Activities, by Adviser Type

Engaged in Business	Dually Registered (478 firms) (%)	Reportedly Engaged as Broker-Dealer (75 firms) (%)	Registered Representative (798 firms) (%)	Affiliated Activity (1,051 firms) (%)	Neither Dual nor Affiliated (4,993 firms) (%)
Broker-dealer	98.3	100.0	0.0	0.0	0.0
Registered representative of a broker-dealer	8.2	52.0	100.0	0.0	0.0
Insurance broker or agent	50.0	40.0	73.8	2.9	6.3

SOURCE: Activities and affiliations are from IARD data for the fourth quarter of 2006. Dual registration was determined by match in IARD and CRD data.

Affiliations. We conclude this section by describing the activities in which the related person whom some firms identified as affiliated with them engage. Table 4.11 illustrates three that are neither dually registered nor affiliated occasionally reported on related persons, usually main observations. First, the groups of firms that reported providing many of the nonadvisory activities just discussed—dually registered, reportedly engaged as broker-dealer, and registered representative—also frequently reported affiliations with firms engaged in brokerage and other activities. Second, the firms in the affiliated-activity group frequently reported having related persons engaged in financial service activities other than just brokerage activities. Third, firms other investment advisers or insurance companies or agencies.

Table 4.11
Financial-Industry Affiliations, by Adviser Type

Related Person	Dually Registered (478 firms) (%)	Reportedly Engaged as Broker-Dealer (75 firms) (%)	Registered Representative (798 firms) (%)	Affiliated Activity (1,051 firms) (%)	Neither Dual nor Affiliated (4,993 firms) (%)
Broker-dealer, municipal- or government-securities dealer	59.8	82.7	32.5	100.0	0.0
Investment company	28.0	17.6	3.8	42.2	4.2
Other investment adviser	53.1	25.7	26.1	64.4	13.3
Banking or thrift institution	29.1	12.0	3.9	34.1	2.4
Insurance company or agency	51.0	33.3	27.4	48.0	5.9

SOURCE: Activities and affiliations are from IARD data for the fourth quarter of 2006. Dual registration was determined by match in IARD and CRD data.

Broker-Dealers

Attributes of Broker-Dealers: Fourth Quarter of 2006

The CRD data describe a heterogeneous collection of 5,224 broker-dealers listed in the database in the fourth quarter of 2006. Almost 97 percent of these firms are registered under §15(b) of the Securities Exchange Act of 1934 (48 Stat. 881). For the purpose of regulatory filings, a key defining characteristic concerns whether or not the firm clears or carries customer accounts. Generally, firms that clear or carry customer accounts file the FOCUS Part II report, whereas the remaining firms file the abbreviated Part IIA report.[5] The CRD data include several variables related to these activities. Information on the type of FOCUS report provides a convenient summary measure. Among the 5,224 broker-dealers in the CRD database, we identify 4,463 Part IIA reports and 544 Part II reports in the fourth quarter of 2006. No report was found for the remaining 217 broker-dealers. In addition, our FOCUS data include 61 broker-dealers that filed Part IIA reports but are not listed in the CRD database.

Descriptive statistics for the full set of firms in the CRD database are reported in Table C.3 in Appendix C. The table describes subsamples of firms differentiated according to the data that were available for the fourth quarter of 2006—CRD data or FOCUS report Part II or Part IIA. As discussed in Appendix A, broker-dealers report financial data for FOCUS, with much more detail provided in Part II than in Part IIA.

---

[5]   The *User Guide to Securities Industry DataBank* describes "commission introducing" firms as "broker-dealers which only 'introduce' commission business but don't carry or clear their own customer accounts," noting further that this group files Part IIA, whereas other firms file Part II (SIFMA, undated[b], p. 5). See the discussion in Appendix A for further details on filing instructions.

Balance-sheet and income statements. The FOCUS data document the great variation in size and scope of broker-dealers' operations. In Tables 4.12 and 4.13 (and in Table C.4 in Appendix C), we summarize core pieces of these data across all firms and conditional on Part II or Part IIA filing status. In a later section, we track the data over time.

The distributions of assets and ownership equity are heavily skewed, with a group of firms being vastly larger than the rest. The mean of total assets reported in the fourth quarter of 2006 is more than $1 billion, but the median is less than $500,000. The difference between mean and median ownership equity is not as vast—$32 million and $340,000, respectively—but still quite striking. As another indication of the variability across firms, note that the standard deviation is more than ten times larger than the mean for both assets and ownership equity.

Much of this variation is associated with filing status, with Part II filers tending to be vastly larger than Part IIA filers. The means of reported assets and ownership equity among Part II filers are $10 billion and $250 million, respectively, whereas the corresponding means among Part IIA filers are about $25 million and $7 million. See Table 4.14.

The quarterly income statements further document the tremendous variation across firms. The means of revenues and expenses are each about 70 times larger than the corresponding medians. As is the case with assets and ownership equity, the standard deviation is more than ten times larger than the mean for both revenues and expenses.

In terms of revenue streams, both Part II and Part IIA filers generated the lion's share of their reported commissions from exchange-traded securities. Totaling across all sources, Part II filers reported generating almost 20 times the commissions of Part IIA filers in the preceding quarter, with means of $15 million and $810,000, respectively. As reported in Table C.4 in Appendix C, a subset of both types of firms reported income from "fees for account supervision, investment advisory and administrative services" (field 3975), generating mean

Table 4.12
Balance-Sheet Items (5,068 Broker-Dealers)

Item	Mean	Standard Deviation	Minimum	Median	Maximum
Assets ($ thousands)	1,082,608	16,800,000	0.5	494	579,000,000
Ownership equity ($ thousands)	32,455	334,108	−5,518	342	10,800,000

SOURCE: FOCUS data for the fourth quarter of 2006.

Table 4.13
Income-Statement Items (5,068 Broker-Dealers)

Item	Mean ($ thousands)	Standard Deviation ($ thousands)	Minimum ($ thousands)	Median ($ thousands)	Maximum ($ thousands)
Commissions	2,337	18,233	−112	10	609,979
Revenue	22,950	306,591	−12,523	319	10,214,610
Expenses	20,736	281,331	−10,802	307	9,733,083
Income before federal taxes	2,214	29,966	−147,934	1	1,249,062

SOURCE: FOCUS data for the fourth quarter of 2006.

Table 4.14
Reported Fees for Account Supervision, Investment Advisory, and Administrative Services (field 3975) as Percentage of Total Revenue (field 4030), by Report of Advisory Services and FOCUS Filing (5,007 Broker-Dealers)

Service	All FOCUS Filers (% total revenue)	Part II Filers (% total revenue)	Part IIA Filers (% total revenue)
All firms	6.6	5.6	12.8
Firms reporting providing investment advisory services	8.2	7.0	23.3
Firms reporting not providing investment advisory services	4.1	3.0	7.8

SOURCE: Fees and revenues are from FOCUS data for the fourth quarter of 2006. Advisory services are from CRD data for the same quarter.

quarterly revenues of about $25 million and $1.8 million, respectively, among Part II and Part IIA filers reporting any such revenues.

Net income tells much the same story, with Part II filers reporting an average of about 30 or 35 times the pretax income of Part IIA filers, whether measured by the quarter or the most recent month. In terms of after-tax income, the disparity is somewhat lower. In sum, then, we observe a scale of Part II filers that dwarfs that of Part IIA filers by virtually any measure, a finding that is not too surprising.

Business activities. The CRD data document the services provided by the firms to generate these revenues. The reports of investment advisory services are of primary interest for this study. According to our CRD data from the fourth quarter of 2006, more than 20 percent of the broker-dealers reported on Form BD that they were engaged in or expected to be engaged in investment advisory services. The share among Part II filers (28 percent) exceeded that of Part IIA filers (21 percent).

We merged the FOCUS data with the CRD data to assess the share of broker-dealers' revenues that may be attributed to investment advisory services. The share of total revenues, one simple measure, seems to be relatively small. That is, among all firms, about 7 percent of total quarterly revenues were reported in field 3975, which includes *but is not limited to* investment advisory fees. Even among firms that reported being engaged in the investment advisory–service business, this share is just 8 percent.

However, further inspection of the data indicates that investment advisory fees may have accounted for a large share of revenues at smaller firms. For example, among Part IIA filers, about 13 percent of total quarterly revenues were reported in field 3975. These fees constituted almost one-quarter of all revenues reported by Part IIA filers that reported being engaged in the investment advisory business.

The CRD data describe a range of other business activities in which the broker-dealers were engaged. Form BD requires that broker-dealers report on 28 different activities. Part II filers were more likely to report engagement in all but seven activities. The largest differences between Part II and Part IIA percentages were reported for the following business activities: exchange member engaged in floor activities (25 percent for Part II filers versus 2 percent for Part IIA filers), "underwriter or selling group participant (corporate securities other than mutual funds)" (46 percent versus 21 percent), U.S. government–securities dealer (31 percent versus 7 percent), municipal-securities dealer (35 percent versus 11 percent), and trading securities for the broker-dealer's own account (46 percent versus 17 percent). In contrast, Part II filers were less likely to report being engaged in the business of mutual fund retailing (44 percent versus 54 percent) and private placement of securities (46 percent versus 50 percent), which were the two most prevalent businesses reported by Part IIA filers. In addition, more than one-third of Part IIA filers reported selling variable life insurance or annuities, whereas only one-quarter of Part II filers did so.

Affiliations. In addition to typically conducting more of these reported activities, Part II filers were also more likely to report that they directly or indirectly control, are controlled by, or are under common control with another entity engaged in the securities or investment advisory business (69 percent of Part II filers versus 38 percent of Part IIA filers). Almost 30 percent of Part II filers reported that they were directly or indirectly controlled by a bank holding company or other banking institution, whereas only 5 percent of Part IIA filers reported such an affiliation.

Civil, criminal, and regulatory enforcement. One potentially informative reporting item in the CRD database concerned past or pending experience with criminal, civil, or regulatory enforcement actions. Although the data were not sufficiently rich to provide insights on the particulars or dates of such enforcement episodes, we could consider how such reports correlated with other firm attributes.

Although we did not engage in an exhaustive analysis of this question, we used a statistical model to predict enforcement actions conditional on a number of control variables taken from FOCUS reports and CRD data. Many of these control variables themselves tend to be associated with pending or previous enforcement activity. We found that the age of the firm, for example, tends to be positively associated with reporting such experiences. This result is not surprising, since Form BD requires firms to report whether they have *ever* faced each type of charge (that is, not just during the most recent quarter). Part II filers are also more likely to face each type of enforcement action, even linearly controlling for various measures of scale. Firms that reported making interdealer markets were also more likely, conditional on other factors, to report susceptibility to enforcement activity across the board, with the exception of civil litigation.

Controlling for these and other factors, we found that brokerage firms reporting investment advisory services were generally *more* likely to report also being subject to some sort of prior or pending enforcement action. In other words, holding constant a number of scale and organizational characteristics, such brokerage firms were more likely than their non–investment advisory counterparts to have been subject to some sort of enforcement proceeding. The economic and statistical significance of this predictive effect is not uniform across all such enforcement actions, however. In particular, it appears to be most pronounced in criminal, other regulatory (including foreign and state), civil, and current pending enforcement actions but is not statistically different from zero in past enforcement actions initiated by the SEC or an SRO. See Table C.5 in Appendix C for more detailed results.

Some caution is warranted in interpreting these estimates. Although engagement in investment advisory services appears to predict at least certain types of enforcement activity, there may be multiple explanations for that finding. Notwithstanding controlling for a number of financial and nonfinancial variables, for example, we cannot rule out the possibility that broker-dealers that report dual activity (on Form BD) also have different characteristics in another important dimension not captured in the data, and it is *that* dimension that in fact causes the firm's greater susceptibility to enforcement proceedings.

Comparison of Brokerage Firms by Dual and Affiliated-Activity Classification

In this section, we provide more detailed evidence on the relationships among investment advisers and broker-dealers, this time from the broker-dealers' side. This analysis requires that we once again specify a systematic classification scheme for firms. We use variables contained in the databases we received and matches across databases to define indicators of dual and affiliated activity.

In particular, we classify each of the brokerage firms as one of five mutually exclusive and exhaustive types:

1. *Dually registered (database match):* A matching CRD number is found in our IARD database on investment advisers for the corresponding business quarter.
2. *Dually registered (Web-site match):* A matching record was found in the SEC Web site's searchable database of investment advisers—e.g., state registered (see Appendix A)—but no matching CRD number is found in our IARD database (i.e., not type 1, a database-matched dual registration).
3. *Reportedly engaged in investment advisory services business:* CRD data indicate that the firm provided investment advisory services, but we found no matching CRD number in our IARD database and no matching record in the SEC Web site's searchable database (i.e., not dually registered by either database or Web search).
4. *Affiliated activity:* CRD data indicate that the firm directly or indirectly controls, is controlled by, or is under common control with another entity engaged in the securities or investment advisory business, and the firm is not of type 1, 2, or 3 (i.e., not dually registered and not reportedly engaged in investment advisory services).
5. *Neither dual nor affiliated activity:* The firm is not of type 1, 2, 3, or 4.

As of the fourth quarter of 2006, almost half of all firms in the CRD data were of the fifth type (neither dual nor affiliated activity) and almost one-third were of the fourth type (affiliated activity). As previously discussed, about 10 percent of broker-dealers were identified as dually registered based on a database match. Another 7 percent were identified as dually registered based on a Web-site match. The remaining 4 percent of broker-dealers reported being engaged in the investment advisory business, but we found no evidence of dual registration. Detailed descriptive statistics for firms of each type are reported in Table C.6 in Appendix C.

In contrast to our data on investment advisers, the data on broker-dealers do not allow us to track the number of firms in each classification back over time. Instead, we can only track whether or not a broker-dealer falls into the dually registered (database-match) category based on matches between the FOCUS and IARD data. These shares were reported at the beginning of this chapter in Figure 4.1.

We turn our attention now to a comparison of firms across types. Some of the discussion focuses on the fourth quarter of 2006, for which we use the classification scheme detailed already. We begin with comparisons of trends using the available indicator of dual registration based on FOCUS data.

Balance-sheet and income statements. Consider first the total assets reported by broker-dealers during the sample period. As Figure 4.4 illustrates, mean reported assets tended to

Figure 4.4
Mean of Total Assets, by Year and Firm Type

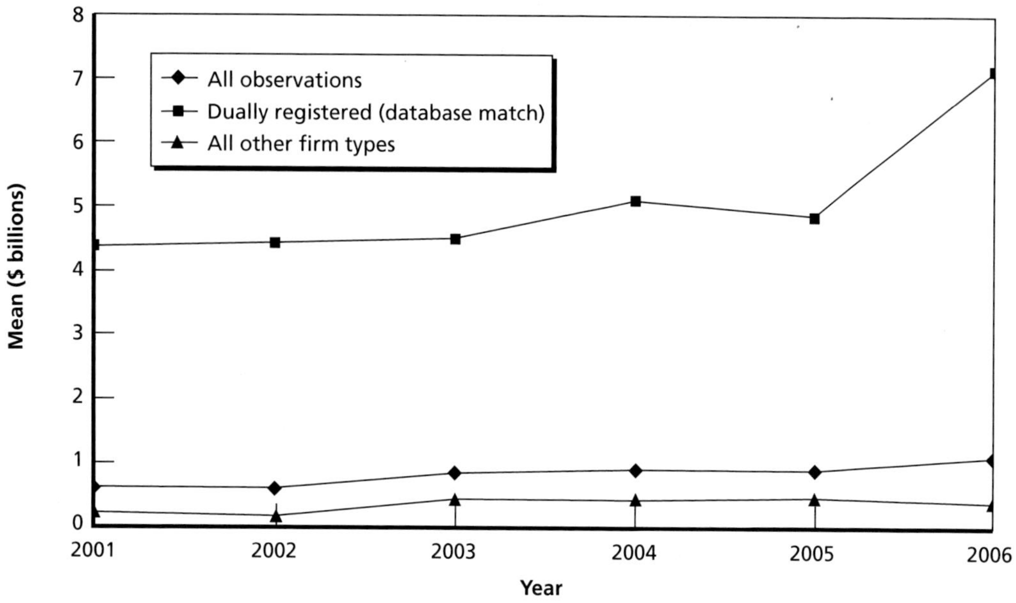

SOURCES: Assets are from FOCUS reports. Firm type was determined from IARD and FOCUS data.
RAND *TR556-4.4*

increase during the entire period for the dually registered (database-match) firms and for the other firms. What is also immediately clear is that dual registrants represent far larger operations than their respective counterparts, as measured by assets at the beginning of the period. More dramatically, this difference in size tends to magnify, approximately doubling over the period studied. Reported levels of ownership equity vary similarly.

Based on our previous results, it should come as no surprise that these dually registered firms were more likely to file FOCUS report Part II than were the other firms. As reported in Table C.6 in Appendix C, about 23 percent of dually registered (database-match) firms filed Part II in 2006, whereas only 5 percent of dually registered (Web site–match) firms did so. Among the other types, the shares filing Part II reports were 6 percent of those reportedly engaged in investment advisory business, 16 percent of affiliated-activity firms, and 5 percent of the neither dually registered nor affiliated firms.

Thus, viewed in this way, the affiliated-activity firms were more similar to the dually registered (database-match) firms than were either of the other two types that reported investment advisory services. The entries in Table 4.15 reinforce this finding. That is, firms in the dually registered (database-match) group tend to be much larger than the rest, both in total assets and in ownership equity reported in the fourth quarter of 2006. Firms in the affiliated-activity category are a distant second. When comparing means, firms reportedly engaged in investment advisory services appear to be considerable bigger than the dually registered (Web site–match) firms, but the finding is reversed when comparing medians.

Turning now to items from the income statement, the mean of total revenues varied over the period in much the same way as total assets did. Figure 4.5 and Table 5.16 depict these trends. Again, the mean for dually registered firms was much higher at the beginning of the period, and the gap grew considerably over the five years. Total expenses varied similarly,

Table 4.15
Balance-Sheet Items, by Firm Type (5,007 Broker-Dealers with Both CRD and FOCUS Report Data)

Item	Dually Registered (database match) (536 firms) ($ thousands)	Dually Registered (Web-site match) (361 firms) ($ thousands)	Reportedly Engaged in Investment Advisory Services (230 firms) ($ thousands)	Affiliated Activity (1,610 firms) ($ thousands)	Neither Dual nor Affiliated (2,270 firms) ($ thousands)
Assets					
Mean	7,081,563	4,988	513,849	943,697	12,041
Median	3,721	475	448	937	220
Ownership equity					
Mean	183,927	3,062	14,581	31,277	3,266
Median	2,019	296	271	592	159

SOURCES: Balance-sheet items are from FOCUS data for the fourth quarter of 2006. Activities and affiliations are from CRD data for the same quarter. Database-matched dual registrations were determined from match in IARD and CRD data. Web site–matched dual registrations were determined from match in SEC Web site and CRD data.

Figure 4.5
Mean of Total Revenue, by Year and Firm Type

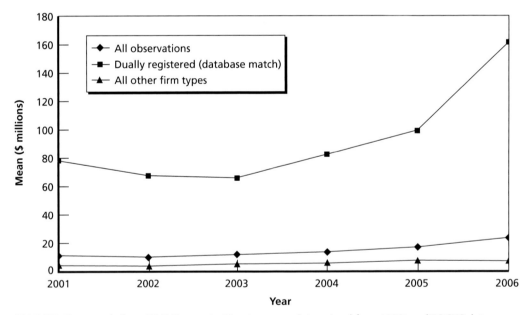

SOURCES: Revenue is from FOCUS reports. Firm type was determined from IARD and FOCUS data.
RAND TR556-4.5

yielding quite a different result for quarterly net income. As depicted in Figure 4.6, the mean of final-quarter net income among the dually registered firms fluctuated considerably, reaching a trough with losses at the end of 2002 before rebounding strongly, especially between the

Table 4.16
Income-Statement Items, by Firm Type (5,007 Broker-Dealers)

Item	Dually Registered (database match) (536 firms) ($ thousands)	Dually Registered (Web-site match) (361 firms) ($ thousands)	Reportedly Engaged in Investment Advisory Services (230 firms) ($ thousands)	Affiliated Activity (1,610 firms) ($ thousands)	Neither Dual nor Affiliated (2,270 firms) ($ thousands)
Commissions					
Mean	12,685	946	488	2,263	414
Median	405	85	12	6	0
Revenue					
Mean	160,685	3,482	13,080	13,779	1,339
Median	2,888	394	223	531	128
Expenses					
Mean	146,420	3,387	12,011	12,325	1,062
Median	2,646	392	236	497	138
Income before federal taxes					
Mean	14,266	95	1,069	1,454	277
Median	66	2	1	7	−1

SOURCES: Income-statement items are from FOCUS data for the fourth quarter of 2006. Activities and affiliations are from CRD data for the same quarter. Database-matched dual registrations were determined from match in IARD and CRD data. Web site–matched dual registrations were determined from match in SEC Web site and CRD data.

fourth quarter of 2005 and the fourth quarter of 2006. The mean reported for the final quarter of each year by the other firms grew more steadily throughout the period.[6]

Focusing again on the fourth quarter of 2006, we can see how the reports tended to vary across the five classifications of firms. The story here is much the same as for the balance-sheet items with respect to the overall size of the operations.[7] However, different income-statement items and different statistics—i.e., means and medians—give varying indications of the relative sizes of operations across classifications but for the extremely large, dually registered firms just discussed.

Business activities. The key feature that firms from the first three categories (dually registered in database or by Web-site match or reportedly engaged in advisory services) have in common is that regulatory filings indicate they are all engaged in investment advisory services. However, as reported in Table C.6 in Appendix C, 47 of the 543 dually registered (CRD database-match) firms actually did not report engagement in this business activity. Classification in any of the other four groups is determined in part by whether the firm reported investment advisory services.

---

[6] For more detailed analysis of such trends, see Appendix H.

[7] The mean of revenues among firms reportedly engaged in investment advisory services is surprisingly high, especially relative to the mean of commissions. Further inspection indicates that this result is heavily influenced by one observation with very incomplete and perhaps erroneous entries for the income-statement items in the FOCUS data.

Figure 4.6
Mean of Net Income Before Federal Taxes, by Year and Firm Type

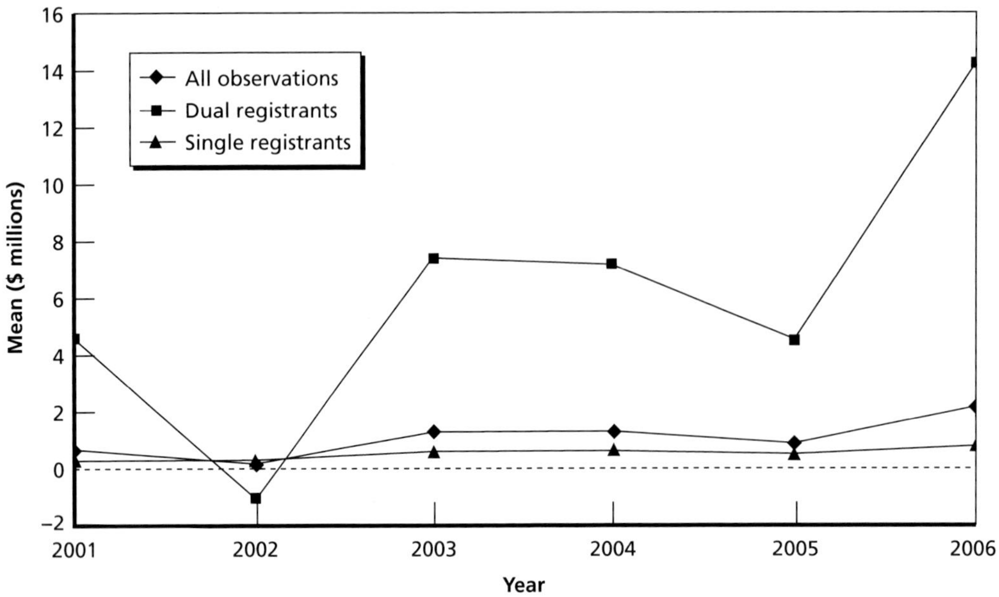

SOURCES: Net income is from FOCUS reports. Firm type was determined from IARD and FOCUS data.
RAND *TR556-4.6*

We now consider the share of broker-dealers' revenues that may be attributed to investment advisory services, based once again on revenues reported in field 3975 of the FOCUS data and the CRD business-activity data. We see striking differences in revenue shares across firm types, reported in Table 4.17. Dually registered (Web site–match) brokerage firms—that is, mostly state-registered investment advisers—report more than one-quarter of revenues in the form of fees for account supervision, investment advisory, and administrative services. The revenue shares range from just 3 to 7 percent for the other categories of firms.

Table 4.17
Reported Fees for Account Supervision, Investment Advisory, and Administrative Services (field 3975) as Percentage of Total Revenue (field 4030), by Firm Type (5,007 Broker-Dealers)

Firm	Dually Registered (database match) (536 firms) (%)	Dually Registered (Web-site match) (361 firms) (%)	Reportedly Engaged in Investment Advisory Services (230 firms) (%)	Affiliated Activity (1,610 firms) (%)	Neither Dual nor Affiliated (2,270 firms) (%)
All firms	7.0	26.4	2.7	4.6	7.4
Firms filing FOCUS report Part II	6.3	1.4	0.8	2.8	1.1
Firms filing FOCUS report Part IIA	18.3	29.3	11.9	7.9	9.6

SOURCES: Fees and revenues are from FOCUS reports for the fourth quarter of 2006. Activities and affiliations are from CRD data from the same quarter. Database-matched dual registrations were determined from match in IARD and CRD data. Web site–matched dual registrations were determined from match in SEC Web site and CRD data.

Much of this variation is associated with the type of FOCUS report filed and, thus, the size and scope of the operations. Among Part II filers, the highest revenue share is 6 percent for dually registered (database-match) firms, followed by the affiliated-activity firms with 3 percent. The other categories include a small fraction, and often a small number, of Part II filers, and these firms typically reported little if any fees in field 3975. In contrast, the smaller Part IIA filers reported revenue shares ranging from 8 percent among affiliated-activity firms to 29 percent among dually registered (Web site–match) firms.

These categories of firms also differ in the range of other services offered. As reported in Table 4.18 (excerpted from Table C.6 in Appendix C), 40 percent or more of each type reported being engaged in the following businesses: retailing corporate-equity securities over the counter, mutual fund retailing, and private placement of securities. Even these percentages vary considerably across types. Generally, the dually registered firms are the most likely to report any service, followed by the firms that were reportedly engaged in investment advisory services, then the affiliated-activity firms, and finally firms that are neither dually registered nor affiliated.

Affiliations. Affiliations with other firms are extremely common throughout the brokerage industry. All firms in the first four categories reported affiliations. Clearly, the firms in the affiliated-activity group reported affiliations with other firms engaged in the securities or investment advisory business. But so do many other firms. As reported in Table C.6 in Appendix C, more than half of the dually registered (database-match) firms also reported such an affiliation, as did 17 percent of dually registered (Web site–match) firms and 43 percent of other firms reportedly engaged in investment advisory services. Perhaps many of the affiliations in the last group are associated with the reported provision of advisory services without corresponding evidence of dual registration.

Finally, a considerable fraction of firms in all but one group—neither dual nor affiliated firms—reported being directly or indirectly controlled by a bank holding company or other banking institution. We previously found that Part II filers were much more likely to report such affiliations. Not surprisingly, these reports were most frequently given by the dually registered (database-match) firms (16 percent), followed by affiliated-activity firms (13 percent).

Conclusions

In this chapter, we have presented a range of descriptive statistics based on data provided in regulatory filings of thousands of investment advisers and broker-dealers. We have also conducted a closer analysis of the data on firms that reported offering both brokerage and advisory services or being affiliated with firms that offer the complementary service. This analysis was intended to clarify the distinctions between such firms and those that specialize solely in brokerage or advisory services.

Based on this analysis, we are able to reach some conclusions. The first one, however, concerns the limitations of what we can accomplish with the available data. We had access to extensive databases based on regulatory filings, but they were often not strictly comparable. The nature and extent of the disclosures made by each type of firm differ considerably. For example, while the FOCUS reports provide a relatively detailed picture of the financial condition of registered broker-dealers, the IARD data tend to focus primarily on organizational characteristics (such as activities and employees), with very little financial information (beyond

Table 4.18
Business Activities, by Firm Type (5,007 Broker-Dealers)

Type of Business in Which Broker-Dealer Engages	Dually Registered (database match) (536 firms) (%)	Dually Registered (Web-site match) (361 firms) (%)	Reportedly Engaged in Investment Advisory Services (230 firms) (%)	Affiliated Activity (1,610 firms) (%)	Neither Dual nor Affiliated (2,270 firms) (%)
Exchange member engaged in floor activities	14.2	3.5	1.7	6.0	3.1
Broker-dealer making interdealer markets in corporate securities over the counter	14.5	9.5	10.6	7.5	5.0
Broker-dealer retailing corporate-equity securities over the counter	78.1	81.6	64.7	47.3	39.7
Broker-dealer selling corporate-debt securities	70.0	71.4	55.3	39.2	29.2
Underwriter or selling-group participant (corporate securities other than mutual funds)	37.8	35.4	37.0	23.0	17.6
Mutual fund retailer	81.4	91.6	66.8	47.9	40.6
U.S. government–securities dealer	23.8	13.8	16.6	8.6	5.4
Municipal-securities dealer	32.4	21.6	22.6	10.3	8.3
Broker-dealer selling variable life insurance or annuities	70.9	78.6	48.5	32.5	22.0
Investment advisory services	91.3	100.0	100.0	0.0	0.0
Trading securities for own account	32.0	22.2	25.5	22.3	15.0
Networking, kiosk, or similar arrangement with insurance company or agency	9.9	4.3	3.0	1.4	0.3

SOURCES: Activities and affiliations are from CRD data for the fourth quarter of 2006. Database-matched dual registrations are determined from match in IARD and CRD data. Web site–matched dual registrations are determined from match in SEC Web site and CRD data.

reports about assets under management). Moreover, comparison across the data sets suggests that many of the filings are likely to have inaccuracies within them, which, in turn, yield discrepancies among alternative methods for identifying firms that simultaneously engage in both brokerage and advisory activities. Ultimately, then, it is difficult to make systematic and conclusive comparisons between the different types of firms.

By comparing details across databases, we noted many inconsistencies in the information reported. For example, we noted that many investment advisory firms that were not sole proprietorships reported being engaged as registered representatives of broker-dealers. Other investment advisory firms reported being engaged as broker-dealers, but we could find no evidence that they were dually registered. In most of these cases, the firms appear to be affiliated in some way with a broker-dealer with a distinct CRD number, including one investment adviser that reported having more than 1,000 employees who were registered representatives of a broker-dealer. These findings suggest that many financial service professionals themselves are confused about how they should be reporting their activities.

Nevertheless, our analysis of about 15,000 distinct firms from the fourth quarter of 2006 reveals that most of them were reportedly engaged, either directly or indirectly, as either an investment adviser or as a broker-dealer but not both. Many others were directly engaged in only one type of activity but were affiliated with a firm engaged in the other type. Finally, the remainder—a minority of firms—were directly engaged in both brokerage and advisory activities.

As the economic scope of a firm grows, it tends to offer a much fuller range of services and consequently either is affiliated with other financial service firms or conducts a significant amount of business in both the investment advisory and brokerage fields. Smaller firms, which are much more numerous, tend to provide a more limited and focused range of either investment advisory or brokerage services. Still, they frequently reported some sort of affiliation with firms providing the complementary service.

Among firms that are either dually registered or affiliated with firms that offer complementary services, the advisory and brokerage services provided may be difficult to disentangle. Some corporations may have multiple subsidiaries or business units, each registered separately as an investment adviser or broker-dealer, but our data do not identify these relationships. To complicate matters further, some solely registered investment advisory firms have employees who are registered representatives of a broker-dealer. Quite frequently, one such employee is the sole proprietor or founder of a small investment advisory firm.

Other unique aspects of the dually registered firms also warrant mention. The total population of broker-dealers has consistently shrunk over the past five years, but the total number of dually registered firms (based on an IARD-FOCUS match) has remained relatively constant (between 500 and 550 per year). Further, there has been discernible growth in the population of SEC-registered investment firms during the same period (even excluding 2006, which may be an aberrational year), the lion's share of which do not appear to operate in a dually registered fashion.

In addition, dual registrants appear more likely than other registered broker-dealers to report being subject to some sort of past or pending enforcement action. Not only is this true in the aggregate, but it appears to remain true even after attempting to control for a number of variables related to size, scale, and other organizational characteristics.

Although their raw numbers have remained somewhat constant, dual registrants have, in many ways, become much more significant. From 2001 to 2006, for example, dual registrants grew discernibly as a proportion of Form BD filers. They also got bigger, spent more, and tended to generate higher net incomes over the entire period than other firms. Much of this variation may be attributed to differences between FOCUS report Part II and Part IIA filers. The March 2008 version of this report will include more detailed analysis of such trends.

While the differences described in this chapter come through in the statistics produced based on the administrative data, it is not clear how these differences are presented to investors. What appear in the data to be affiliations between two or more registrants could be viewed by customers as a single business or as completely distinct entities. In the next chapter, we examine how these activities are portrayed to investors and what investors understand about the information they are given.

CHAPTER FIVE

Documentation and Information Provided by Firms

To better inform our description of current practices in the industry, we collected and examined business documents used by selected investment advisers and broker-dealers sampled from the complete listing of firms in the administrative databases analyzed in Chapter Four. We also conducted 34 interviews with financial professionals from brokerage and investment advisory firms. We collected this information to address the following questions:

- How do firms interact with current and prospective clients, especially with respect to the provision of services and the presentation thereof?
- How do firms operate to provide these services, including interactions with other financial service providers?
- What do firms disclose to clients about these relationships and their services?
- What are firms' perspectives on current policy issues?

The remainder of this chapter first describes the methods used in selecting firms and analyzing information from both the document collection and firm interviews. We then discuss parallel results from analysis of the documents and firm interviews and additional information obtained only through firm interviews. In an effort to illustrate the complexity of how many of these firms operate and their affiliations with other firms, we close the chapter by providing some case studies of sample firms.

Document-Collection Methodology

As noted in the introduction to Chapter Four, the unit of observation in our administrative data determines the definition of a *firm*, and that definition is maintained throughout this analysis. In practice, however, what appears to a customer to be a single company may actually be composed of multiple registrants in these databases—i.e., multiple firms. This analysis was designed to illustrate these relationships for a probability sample of firms.

Despite our numerous attempts via multiple contact methods to recruit firms to participate in this study, we received documents from only 29 sampled firms deemed eligible to participate in the study, out of a total sample size of 164 firms, and most of these submissions only partially complied with our requests. We were able to supplement the submitted documents with an extensive review of publicly available Web sites maintained by another 34 firms from the probability sample. Still, many of our findings must be seen as anecdotal. However, the sampling process ensures that these anecdotes pertain to both the largest firms and selected representatives of the remaining brokerage and investment advisory firms.

In the following sections, we summarize our methods and refer the reader to a more detailed account in Appendix D.

Document Collection and Review

We originally set a target of 75 firms from which to collect and examine business documents. The documents we sought were marketing and sales documents (e.g., brochures, flyers) advertising the firm itself, its range of services, or individual products; regulatory documents (e.g., disclosure statements, disclaimers) required by federal and state regulators and SROs; account-based documents (e.g., application forms, account agreements, transaction confirmations, account statements); and interfirm agreements and contracts among investment advisers, broker-dealers, and other financial institutions, such as mutual fund managers.

Sampling methods. We designed a sampling scheme to achieve a balance between broker-dealers and investment advisers. In June 2007, we used the available administrative data to select a probability sample of investment advisers and broker-dealers for solicitation of business documents. Our selection process for the recipient firms followed a two-step procedure. First, we stratified based on whether the firm was registered as an investment adviser or as a broker-dealer. Note that the dually registered firms with individual advisory clients are listed in both databases. Second, we chose to oversample from among the more dominant firms in the market with respect to total accounts and account holdings, but we also sought to include a sufficient number of broker-dealers and investment advisers randomly sampled from the thousands of other firms of each type. See Appendix D for more detail on the sampling method used.

Recruiting participants. Appendix E includes a copy of the document-request letter and sample checklists. The principal investigator sent letters to all 164 firms via Federal Express to individual contact persons whose names FINRA provided (in the case of registered broker-dealers) or included in the IARD database (in the case of investment advisers). The principal investigator and RAND survey staff made more than 300 follow-up phone calls. Additional calls were also made to both solicit participation in the firm interviews, described later in this chapter, and to prompt nonrespondents to submit business documents. Multiple email messages were also sent to most firms to remind them about the study and notify them of forthcoming contact attempts. We also made a request to the associations that represent broker-dealers, investment advisers, and financial planners that they post a message on their Web sites about the study and encourage all members that receive a request from RAND to participate in the study.

In addition, a second Federal Express package was sent to 47 nonresponding firms and 27 firms that were classified as giving a "soft" refusal.[1] This follow-up package included prepaid Federal Express return packaging accompanied by a letter from the office of the SEC chair stressing the importance of participating in the study, as well as a new document-request letter from the study's principal investigator that included this supplemental statement: "We understand that not all firms will have all of the items on this list, but we would appreciate you sending us what materials you have, even if this is just a new client package."

---

[1]   We characterized a refusal as "soft" if the respondent refused but did not give a concrete reason for refusal and did not express adamant refusal.

Follow-up telephone discussions and messages also included scaled-back requests of this type. These contact attempts were discontinued 12 weeks after the first letters were sent.

Response rate. Despite our numerous attempts via multiple contact methods to recruit these firms to participate in this study, we received documents from only 29 sampled firms deemed eligible to participate in the study, and most of these submissions only partially complied with our requests. Initially, we received documents from 33 firms. However, four of these firms do not work directly with individual U.S. investors and were therefore not eligible for the study. The 29 eligible firms include 18 from the sample of investment advisers and 11 from the sample of broker-dealers. (Two firms were included in both samples.)

This limited participation greatly limits our ability to extrapolate findings from the submitted sample of documents. To supplement the documentary evidence, we conducted thorough reviews of the Web sites maintained by these 29 responding firms as well as another 34 sampled firms that both maintain a public Web site and were deemed eligible to participate in the study. Almost all of the remaining firms from the original list of 164 do not maintain public Web sites or were determined to be ineligible for the study because they do not work directly with individual investors or are no longer in business as registered in the fourth quarter of 2006. See Appendix D for more information on nonresponding or ineligible firms.

After excluding the total of 66 ineligible firms,[2] the mailed-document response rate is just 29 out of 98. However, when supplemented with Web-site data collected from another 34 firms, the effective response rate is 64 percent.

Types of documents received. The 29 eligible firms that complied with the request submitted documents varying in number, size, range of topics covered, and complexity. Data were recorded for the following topics: documents returned, company background, clients, services and products, disclosures, affiliations, online accounts, modes of access, fees and commissions, account and product specifications, employees, and marketing material.

A total of 158 sets of documents corresponding to the document categories we requested were received from the 29 eligible firms. Table D.1 in Appendix D breaks down the number of investment advisory and brokerage firms that submitted documents by document type. Multiple documents were included in most sets. Every document in every set was reviewed for data extraction and further analysis. Firms that offer more than one product and service could submit marketing and sales documents and account-based documents separately for each product or service. Large firms tended to make the most voluminous submissions. Smaller companies often submitted fewer than ten documents. For instance, one large firm made an electronic submission that included almost 100 separate brochures, 34 print advertisements, and 16 disclosure documents. Another large firm also submitted hundreds of electronic documents.

About half the firms submitted such documents as account-application forms and agreements, pricing schedules, disclosure statements, and examples of business cards for investment professionals. Broker-dealers in our sample were more likely to send marketing and sales documents.[3] Investment advisers were more likely to submit samples of account-based documents.

---

[2] The final tally of ineligible firms consists of 57 firms that do not work with individual clients and nine firms that no longer exist.

[3] Most of the investment advisers we interviewed reported that they do not engage in advertising or other marketing activities.

Web data collection. As previously mentioned, we supplemented the mailed-document collection efforts by recording publicly available information from firm Web sites. Web-site data collection was attempted for 80 firms from the original sample, including the 33 firms that submitted documents and 47 firms that did not.[4] In total, Web sites were found for 73 firms, but 12 of these firms were deemed to be ineligible because they do not work with individual investors. Of the 33 firms that submitted documents, four firms do not work with individual investors, as previously stated, and two firms do not maintain a Web site, leaving us with 27 eligible firms with Web sites. Of the 47 firms that did not submit documents, five do not maintain Web sites and eight were ineligible for the study (seven firms do not work with individual investors and one firm no longer exists), leaving us with 34 eligible firms with Web sites. The 61 eligible firms with Web sites include 36 from the sample of investment advisers and 25 from the sample of broker-dealers. We reviewed approximately 1,000 pages on these Web sites and recorded data using a nearly identical protocol to that used for the business documents submitted by mail.

Table 5.1 depicts the source of the document collection for both investment advisers and broker-dealers. In sum, we have 63 firms with submitted documents or Web-site information. For two firms, we have mailed documents only, we have mailed documents and Web documents for 27 firms, and we have only Web documents for 34 firms.

Representativeness of the sample. Table 5.2 presents the breakdown of firms by size from which we collected data, either from submitted documents or from Web sites.

Our sampling scheme was designed to select a sample that is representative of the population of brokerage and investment advisory firms conditional on the stratification variables (broker-dealer or investment adviser, large or other). However, with such a small number of firms, partial compliance, and selective nonresponse, our results may be more reasonably viewed as illustrative rather than representative of the industry at large.

Table 5.1
Source of Documents Collected from Broker-Dealers and Investment Advisers

Firm Type	Mail Only	Mail + Web	Web Only	Total
Investment adviser	2	16	20	38
Broker-dealer	0	11	14	25
Total[a]	2	27	34	63

[a] Two firms are counted twice because they are dually registered and appear in both the samples of investment advisers and broker-dealers.

Table 5.2
Eligible Firms with Submitted or Web Document Data, by Size

Firm Type	Large Firms	Other Firms
Investment adviser	10	28
Broker-dealer	13	12

---

[4]   That is, we searched for Web sites from (1) all of the firms that submitted documents and (2) almost all of the firms that did not submit documents and were not yet determined to be ineligible.

Methodology for Firm Interviews

The selection of firms to be interviewed followed from the sample selection for the analysis of business documents. The RAND research team invited a total of 106 firms that had not yet been deemed ineligible as of the end of July 2007 to participate in an interview. Another 13 potentially eligible firms were not invited to participate. These firms had previously been contacted as part of the business-document request, at which point they informed us they were not willing to participate in any component of this study.

The second Federal Express package that was sent to firms regarding the document request also informed firms that we were conducting interviews as part of the study. Thank-you emails were sent to firms that had already submitted documents, and these firms were informed about the interviews in these emails. Most selected firms then received follow-up phone calls in which they were asked to participate in an interview.[5]

At the end of this effort, seven brokerage firms and nine investment advisory firms agreed to participate in the interview process. The broker-dealers include six large firms, all dually registered, and one other firm that is solely registered. In contrast, only one of the participating investment advisers, a solely registered firm, came from the sample of large firms, and only one of the other participating investment advisers is dually registered. Of the remaining 90 firms, 19 refused to participate in an interview, 21 were found to be ineligible, and 50 did not respond to our interview request (including 21 firms that had already refused to send in documents).

Given the high nonresponse rate of firms from our original probability sample, we elected to allow for a volunteer sample to help fill in gaps in knowledge. We asked association groups that represent investment advisers, broker-dealers, and financial planners to post announcements on their Web sites regarding our study and ask for volunteers to participate in the interview process. We decided to allow for a similar number of volunteers representing both broker-dealers and investment advisers. The response from the investment advisers was overwhelming, with more than 130 individuals volunteering to participate. The response from broker-dealers was much more subdued, with only eight volunteers. We cut off our interviews with volunteer investment advisers after ten to more closely align with the number of volunteer broker-dealers. Adding the volunteer sample to the firms from the probability sample, in total, we conducted 34 interviews with financial professionals from brokerage and investment advisory firms. The interviews were conducted between August and October 2007.

Interview Approach

Interviews were aimed at gaining a better understanding of how investment advisers and broker-dealers work with individual investors today. Interviewees were asked specific questions about their firm: the types of services and products offered, number and titles of financial professionals in the firm, educational requirements of financial professionals, ongoing training requirements for financial professionals, supervisory and compliance functions, and forms of compensation. Interviewees were also asked how they market their products and services and what types of disclosures they provide to investors. We also asked their views on the current

---

[5] The 27 firms that were classified as soft refusals in the document-collection portion of the study were not called about the interviews. The letters that these firms were sent instructed them to call the principal investigator if they were interested in participating in an interview.

regulatory system (i.e., separate regulatory schemes for investment advisers and broker-dealers) and asked them to identify their key policy issues.

Results from Document Collection, Web Data Collection, and Firm Interviews

We combine the information we collected from the business-document data, including submitted documents and Web-site reviews, with information gleaned from the firm interviews to get a better understanding of the following four broad topics:

- How do firms interact with current and prospective clients, especially with respect to the provision of services and the presentation thereof?
- How do firms operate to provide these services, including interactions with other financial service providers?
- What do firms disclose to clients about these relationships and their services?
- What are firms' perspectives on current policy issues?

Given the nature of interviews, we were able to explore more topics during the interviews than we could abstract from written documents, such as thoughts on current policy issues. Therefore, for each of the subtopics, we will identify sources from which we draw the information.

We then compare findings from the volunteer broker-dealers to findings from brokerage firms from the probability sample. The majority of the participating broker-dealers from the probability sample were large firms. The volunteers added more insight into those operating as independently registered representatives usually working with smaller firms or in loose networks (independent broker-dealers). For the investment advisers, responses from the volunteer firms interviewed mirrored what we heard from our participants from the probability sample.

How Firms Interact with Clients

Clientele. To be eligible for the sample, each firm must serve individual clients. As reported in Table 5.3, from documents collected and Web sites, we are able to identify nine out of the 13 (70 percent) large brokerage firms as also working with trusts or estates, whereas only one out of 12 (8 percent) other broker-dealers was identified as doing so. The corresponding percentages were 92 percent and 33 percent for institutional investors and 92 percent and 25 percent for non-U.S. investors. Thus, the larger brokerage firms appear to work with a wider range of clients than do other broker-dealers.

Table 5.3
Clients of Investment Advisers and Broker-Dealers

Clientele	Broker-Dealers			Investment Advisers		
	All	Large	Other	All	Large	Other
Trusts and estates	10	9	1	22	6	16
Institutional investors	16	12	4	27	9	18
Non-U.S. investors	15	12	3	7	7	0
Total firms	25	13	12	38	10	28

The broker-dealers from the probability sample whom we interviewed ranged in firm size but primarily represented larger firms. Some firms had only a few hundred financial representatives, while others had many thousands. The number of accounts each of these firms held ranged from about 50,000 to several million.

Representatives from about half of the firms we interviewed had no specific account minimums and were willing to work with investors with small sums. These firms reflected a long-term view of their client relationship, noting that they wanted to grow with their clients as they advanced in their careers and earned more money in the future. These firms often promoted themselves as providing broad offerings so as to be useful at any life stage. The other broker-dealers we interviewed targeted the mass affluent (e.g., more than $100,000 in investable assets) or HNW individuals. The specific dollar amounts in the categories varied across firms. For example, some firms considered HNW individuals as those with more than $5 million in investable assets.

As reported in Table 5.3, documents collected and information from Web sites tend to indicate that investment advisers at large firms also work with a wider range of clients than do those at other advisory firms. Among those with any information on clientele, about two-thirds of large firms were identified as working with trusts or estates, and three-fifths of the other firms were found to work with trusts and estates. Most investment advisers with submitted documents also indicated that they work with institutional investors, including all nine large firms with available information on clientele and 18 of the other firms.

Another difference between large investment advisory firms and other investment advisory firms arises with respect to non-U.S. investors. The available information from business documents and Web sites specifically indicates that seven of the large investment advisory firms work with foreign investors, whereas this information is not found for any of the other investment advisory firms.

Services. We reviewed the available information from the Web sites and business documents to determine which firms provide any of a number of advisory services. The types of services include cash-flow planning and budgeting; asset management and evaluation services; and tax, college, retirement, and estate planning. The results are reported in Table 5.4.

Investment management and monitoring and investment-planning and retirement-planning services are provided by most, if not all, large firms from the sample of investment advisers, as well as most large firms from the sample of broker-dealers. The finding that the large brokerage firms provide many of these advisory services should not be surprising, because all of the large firms from the sample of broker-dealers are dually registered as investment advisers.

No more than one-third of the other broker-dealers were identified as performing any of these services except for the investment, portfolio, and asset management and monitoring. Seven of the 12 other broker-dealers were identified as providing services in this category. In fact, investment-management and -monitoring services are the most commonly provided service, across all categories: Eleven of 13 large brokerage firms and 35 of 38 investment advisory firms, including all ten large firms, were also identified as providing such services.

Most brokerage firms interviewed offered a range of investment products (e.g., stocks, bonds, mutual funds, individual retirement accounts, 529 plans [named for §529 of the Internal Revenue Code]), including proprietary products. One firm specifically noted that it has no incentives for selling proprietary products.

Table 5.4
Services Provided by Investment Advisers and Broker-Dealers

Service	Broker-Dealers			Investment Advisers		
	All	Large	Other	All	Large	Other
Cash-flow planning, budgeting, and budget-management planning	10	8	2	17	6	11
Investment, portfolio, and asset management and monitoring	18	11	7	35	10	25
Investment, portfolio, and asset evaluation, review, and planning	14	10	4	25	9	16
Tax-planning strategies	8	7	1	17	6	11
Education and college planning	12	8	4	15	5	10
Retirement planning	12	8	4	24	8	16
Estate planning	13	9	4	16	3	13
Insurance and risk evaluation, planning, and analysis	7	5	2	16	4	12
Total firms	25	13	12	38	10	28

Typical services offered by most advisory firms we interviewed include asset allocation, money management, financial planning, retirement planning, college planning, and estate planning. Some firms had specific strategies for investing the funds, such as convertible securities, large cap funds, and index funds. Most of the interviewed advisers said that they develop an investment strategy based on the client's profile and risk preference.

Web sites. Whereas the set of mailed documents we reviewed constitutes a selected and clearly limited sample of documents that could have been made available by the sampled firms, we believe that the Web-site documents we reviewed constitute the entire universe of Web documents available to prospective clients of these firms. In many cases, however, current clients have password-protected access to many additional documents.

We discovered very diverse Web-site functionality. Forty firms in the sample allow customers to monitor and manage accounts online. Seven firms provide clients with an option of opening an advisory or brokerage account online. Requirements for opening such an online account vary. The most frequently mentioned requirements included bank-account information, social-security number, and valid email address.

Web sites also significantly varied in the scope and amount of the information available. Many firms also offer their clients assistance tools and information on their Web sites. Table 5.5 presents our findings for the number of the Web sites that offer assistance tools and information.

As shown in Table 5.5, we found that two-thirds of the firms in the sample offer stock and mutual fund reports on their Web sites. About half of the firms offer historical analyses and educational materials. Our findings also indicate that, among the firms with publicly available Web sites, there are no sharp differences in the share of the broker-dealers and of investment advisers that provide assistance tools online.

Marketing to investors. The advertising campaigns of the larger brokerage firms whose representatives we interviewed focused on promoting the brand name rather than any specific product or service. These campaigns often promote experience managing money and long firm

Table 5.5
Firms That Provide Assistance Tools and Information Online

Tool	Broker-Dealers' Web Sites That Offer the Tool	Investment Advisers' Web Sites That Offer the Tool
Electronic investment assistance (online chat or help)	7	3
Historical analyses	10	12
Stock or mutual fund reports or articles	16	21
Educational materials	12	17
Total Web sites	25	36

history. Some firms also focus on their broad range of services. Those that do advertise use print media more than they use radio or television. The firms that focus on HNW individuals tend not to advertise. All firms reported that their primary source for new clients was referrals from existing clients or professional referrals (e.g., accountants, lawyers). Some participants noted that it is the discount brokerage firms that tend to have the large advertising campaigns.

Few of the small investment advisers we interviewed advertised. A couple of firms did market to other professional service providers, such as accountants, brokerage firms, and banks. All firms reported getting new clients almost exclusively through referrals from existing clients or other professional service providers. A couple of these firms had loose relationships with certain banks, which was also a source of new clients.

Many of the investment advisers we interviewed commented that the advertising campaigns by financial service firms create confusion and set false expectations. They said that many of those ads are for brokerage firms but that it sounds as if they are selling advice. Many of those ads portray a close relationship (e.g., attending family wedding, walking on the beach together) that almost no client will receive, which is a setup for disappointment for the client.

Investor knowledge. Most representatives of brokerage firms reported in interviews that investors do not understand the difference between broker-dealers and investment advisers, nor do they care. Investors want their financial service needs taken care of and are not concerned with exactly how that needs to happen (e.g., might need to open both advisory and brokerage accounts). Some noted that investors may be confused because many of the advertisements indicate that the firm can do everything, meeting any financial need. Many interviewees reported that, more generally, financial knowledge among the general investing public is quite low. Financial representatives end up providing general financial education to many clients.

Among the representatives of brokerage firms whom we interviewed, those who work primarily with HNW individuals reported more financial sophistication among their clients. In fact, they reported that open access to more financial information via the Internet has resulted in savvier investors who request more complex financial solutions.

Most representatives of investment advisory firms said in interviews that they did not think that investors knew the differences between broker-dealers and investment advisers. Some thought that, if they did know about the differences, this knowledge might affect their decisionmaking. Others thought that, as long as investors were getting service they like and returns they expect, they would not care about the differences.

Like broker-dealers, most of the investment advisers' representatives whom we interviewed observed that their clients' financial knowledge was generally low. However, a couple of interviewees reported having quite savvy clients. For the most part, educating the client on financial matters was viewed as being an important part of their job.

Fees and commissions. We also assessed the presentation of information on fees and commissions. We begin by discussing findings based on information provided in collected business documents, as reported in Table 5.6. We could identify that nine out of 25 brokerage and 12 out of 38 investment advisory firms provide fee tables in their mailed documents or on their Web sites (or both). We also found that large brokerage firms in our sample more frequently provided this information than did the large investment advisory firms. In contrast, none of the other broker-dealers provided fee tables in the business documents we obtained.

Our search for explanations of commissions in business documents produced similar qualitative results. We found that nine of the large brokerage firms and three of the large investment advisory firms explained the commission structure in business documents.

Next, we tried to obtain information on the structure of fees. We could not find this information for all firms. Based on the available information, we found that the firms in the sample of broker-dealers were almost equally likely to charge fees based on (1) the percentage of assets under management, (2) the number of transactions, and (3) a flat fee, as shown in Table 5.7. This surprising result on asset-based fees arises solely from the large brokerage firms, each of which is dually registered. Most of the investment advisory firms for which we could find information charged fees based on the percentage of assets under management.

To improve our understanding of the structure of the commissions and fees, we collected detailed information for each of the various brokerage and investment accounts and services described in the collected documents, as well as on the Web sites. Overall, we found information on 31 brokerage and 124 advisory accounts and services. We collected data on

Table 5.6
Availability of Information on Fees and Commissions

Information Available	Broker-Dealers			Investment Advisers		
	All	Large	Other	All	Large	Other
Fee table	9	9	0	12	4	8
Explanation of commissions	11	9	2	8	3	5
Total firms	25	13	12	38	10	28

Table 5.7
Compensation Structures

Compensation Type	Broker-Dealers			Investment Advisers		
	All	Large	Other	All	Large	Other
Percentage of assets under management	10	10	0	18	4	14
Transaction based	10	9	1	3	3	0
Flat fee	9	9	0	11	3	8
Total firms	25	13	12	38	10	28

many different fee and commission characteristics of these accounts and services, including minimum balances to maintain the account, transaction fees, flat fees, percentages of assets under management, hourly charges, minimum annual fees, existence of other charges, and variation in fees by asset type. For example, the minimum account size ranges up to $1 million for brokerage accounts and up to $10 million for advisory accounts. We found information about the minimum annual fee for half the brokerage accounts and 51 out of the 124 advisory accounts. Among those accounts and services with this fee information, the minimum annual fee ranged between $1,250 and $6,000 for brokerage accounts and between $500 and $5,000 for advisory accounts.

All the investment advisers we interviewed charged a percentage of assets under management for managing a client's portfolio. Representatives from about half of the investment advisory firms we interviewed reported account minimums of at least $1 million. Most of the others had account minimums of $100,000 to $500,000. Only one firm did not have an account minimum. A typical fee charged to investors started at 1.25 percent for $100,000 to $1 million assets under management; 1.00 percent for $1 million to $5 million; 0.75 percent for $5 million to $10 million; and 0.25 percent for more than $10 million.

Almost all of the advisory firms whose representatives we interviewed used outside custodians, such as Charles Schwab or Fidelity Investments, to house and trade the investments. It was typical for firms to use more than one custodian because they often had clients that came to them with accounts in a different custodian from the one that the firm typically used. Advisory-firm representatives said that the firms received no fees from these custodians—that clients pay custodians directly—but that the firms could negotiate certain rates for their clients because of their volume. The custodians send out monthly statements and updated prospectuses on products to clients. In these arrangements, the investment advisers also receive the monthly statements.

Two of the advisory firms whose representatives we interviewed also acted as subadvisers on wrap-fee accounts. Under these agreements, they work for the bank or brokerage firm offering the wrap-fee program and do not interact directly with the client. As compensation, they receive a percentage of the fees charged on those accounts.

How Firms Provide Services and Affiliate with Other Firms

Dual activity and affiliations. In Chapter Four, we described the various indicators of dual and affiliated activities available in the administrative data on all broker-dealers and investment advisers. For broker-dealers, we reported that about 10 percent are dually registered in our IARD database from the fourth quarter of 2006 and another 7 percent are state registered. In our sample, we found that 16 out of 25 of the broker-dealers are dually registered in this database and another firm is state registered. This high percentage of dually registered firms is largely attributable to the probability-sampling process. All 13 firms in our sample of large brokerage firms are dually registered in IARD. For investment advisers, on the other hand, only two of the ten large investment advisory firms in our sample are dually registered as broker-dealers in CRD, as are two of the other 28 investment advisers. Thus, just more than 10 percent of the investment advisory firms in the sample are dually registered. Recall that we found about 6 percent of all investment advisers in IARD to be dually registered as broker-dealers in CRD.

During our review of the submitted documents and Web sites, we found that 11 of the 16 dually registered firms from the sample of broker-dealers and two of four from the sample of investment advisers are clearly identified as such. Of course, current clients must have access to much more information than we could review, and this dual activity may therefore be apparent to them. The same can surely be said of prospective clients with respect to most, if not all, of the firms in our sample.

Education and job titles. None of the broker-dealer representatives whom we interviewed reported specific educational requirements for their firms' financial representatives. While all firms stated that the overwhelming majority of their financial representatives had a college degree, it was not a job requirement; this allowed for hiring individuals with strong experience but no degree. Many of the firms required certifications, such as series 6 or series 7 securities licenses. Most of the firms reported that many of their financial representatives also carried advanced degrees in finance or business or certifications in accounting (e.g., CPA) or professional certifications (e.g., CFP).

Typical job titles used by employees in these large brokerage firms interviewed included financial advisor, financial consultant, financial representative, investment specialist, investment representative, and registered representative.

Some investment advisory firms whose representatives we interviewed required their financial professionals to hold at least four-year college degrees. A few firms did not require degrees, but almost all firms stated that their current professionals all had at least bachelor's degrees. Some firms required advanced degrees in business, finance, or accounting. Many professionals held additional certifications in financial planning (CFP) or as a CFA, or other securities licenses (e.g., series 65). A few firms hired only seasoned professionals with more than ten years of experience.

Typical job titles among those working in advisory firms interviewed included financial advisor, financial planner, financial analyst, investment adviser, wealth-management consultant, and portfolio manager.

We received samples of business cards from about half of the firms that sent in documents. Several of the large, dually registered broker-dealers submitted templates for business cards. Some templates listed both corporate titles (e.g., senior vice president, vice president, managing director) and such functional titles as financial consultant, registered financial associate, senior investment management specialist, financial advisor, and wealth advisory specialist. Other templates simply noted that both corporate title and functional titles would be listed. Two others noted that only high-level corporate titles would be listed; otherwise, the card would simply identify the business division. None of these templates mentioned certifications.

The other business-card submissions were made by smaller firms. One of these firms, the only broker-dealer among them, listed no titles or certifications. The investment advisory firms tended to list either corporate titles or no titles. The two exceptions each listed corporate titles and functional titles, such as portfolio manager, investment strategist, investment specialist, relationship manager, and client associate. The business cards submitted by three of these investment advisers listed certifications, such as CFA, CFP, ChFC, or personal financial specialist.

Employee compensation. From our interviews with firm representatives, we learned that compensation for individual employees (both broker-dealers and investment advisers) was more often salary plus bonus than it was pure commission. Bonuses are often based on the performance of the individual (i.e., amount of revenue generated), the performance of the individual's business unit, or firm performance.

Training. Most of those interviewed from larger brokerage firms described fairly extensive training programs. Many firms supported online training to make it as convenient as possible for the individual representatives to fit the training into their schedules. These firms reported offering continuous training on new products offered, compliance, ethics, or emerging issues in the industry. Some firms required that each representative perform a certain number of hours of training per year. This training was usually required in addition to continuing-education requirements for any licenses or certifications. Many firms expressed the need for their representatives to maintain a current base of knowledge to remain competitive and in compliance.

Given that the vast majority of the investment advisory firms whose representatives we interviewed were quite small, they did not have large in-house training programs like those we observed with the broker-dealers. It was common for these firms to provide in-house training on company policies and procedures and ethics, but most other training courses were taken from outside professional providers or through online services. Many of these firms did have yearly training requirements. One firm required 40 hours of continuing-education credits each year. Other firms strongly supported additional training, but they did not have specific requirements. Some of the smaller firms relied solely on the annual training requirements for individual certifications and licenses.

Compliance. Representatives of the larger brokerage firms whom we interviewed described a web of compliance functions starting with the individual broker, branch manager, and regional supervisors and working its way up to corporate headquarters. Technology is heavily involved in the compliance process. The sophisticated financial platforms that brokers use to conduct trades can monitor portfolios for conformance with established guidelines and clients' stated goals. A trade will get flagged if it seems misaligned. Audits are another avenue to assess the level of compliance. Branch managers conduct the oversight of daily compliance operations. Regional supervisors often oversee multiple branches for compliance. The main headquarters typically have compliance offices with dedicated compliance staff who serve as a resource to regional and branch staff and have ultimate reporting authority on firm compliance. Some of the larger firms whose representatives we interviewed have executive-level chief compliance officers with their own dedicated compliance staff.

Since most of the advisory firms whose representatives we interviewed were small in staff size, members often wore multiple hats. The firm's president or CEO was often the compliance officer as well. As such, they are responsible for reviewing trades, monitoring email traffic, logging activities, and assessing risk. Many noted that the compliance burden had increased over the past several years and that they spend more of their time on their compliance duties than they once did. They pointed out that this increased compliance burden is particularly tough on small firms.

What Firms Disclose About Their Services and Affiliations with Others

Disclosures. To better understand how firms provide disclosure information to their clients, we sought to differentiate types of disclosures that were submitted to us from those that were publicly available on the firms' Web sites. We used the following seven classifications: differences between investment advisers and broker-dealers, conflicts of interest, compensation structure, future performance, code of ethics or fiduciary oath, client duties or responsibilities, and client rights. Table E.1 in Appendix E reports the number of firms for which we identified each type of disclosure in each source of information. The possible sources were classified as one of the following: marketing brochure, product brochure, print advertisement, account agreement, pricing schedule, separate disclosure document, or Web site. Table 5.8 aggregates these numbers across all information sources.

In the submitted business documents, across all broker-dealers, the most frequently identified disclosures concerned issues of compensation—e.g., how clients compensate the firm, how other firms compensate it, and how employees are compensated. We found 28 such disclosures. In contrast, the most frequently found disclosure on the Web sites of the broker-dealers was related to future performance. We identified 13 such Web-site disclosures, which typically were phrased as follows: "Past performance is not an indication of future results."

For the sample of investment advisers, the most frequently identified disclosure in the submitted business documents concerned a code of ethics or fiduciary oath. Note that these disclosures were also frequently found among the documents submitted by large brokerage firms—that is, dually registered broker-dealers. One code of ethics was stated as follows:

> This Code of Ethics is based on the fundamental principle that firm and its employees must put client interests first. This Code of Ethics and firm's written policies and procedures contain procedural requirements that employees must follow to meet legal and regulatory requirements.

As is the case with the Web sites of firms in the sample of broker-dealers, the most frequently identified disclosure on the investment advisers' Web sites is the one concerning future performance. Three types of disclosures are of particular interest to this study: differences between investment advisers and broker-dealers, conflicts of interest, and compensation structure. We begin with disclosures on differences between investment advisers and broker-dealers. The now-vacated 2005 rule (§202[a][11]-1) prescribed that "advertisements for, and contracts, agreements, applications and other forms governing, accounts for which the broker or dealer receives special compensation" must include a statement explaining that the account is a brokerage account rather than an advisory account. As is reported in Table E.1 in Appendix E, we most frequently found this type of disclosure in the account agreements of large firms from the sample of broker-dealers, each of which is dually registered as an investment adviser. We did not find any such disclosure in the submitted documents or Web sites of any of the other

Table 5.8
Disclosures Found Across All Sources of Information

Type of Disclosure	Broker-Dealers			Investment Advisers		
	All	Large	Other	All	Large	Other
Differences between investment advisers and broker-dealers	31	31	0	13	10	3
Conflicts of interest	32	31	1	19	10	9
Compensation structure	37	32	5	18	7	11
Code of ethics or fiduciary oath	30	30	0	29	15	14
Client duties and responsibilities	29	25	4	27	14	13
Client rights	25	23	2	21	16	5
Future performance	32	26	6	17	8	9

NOTE: Entries indicate total times found. See Appendix E for disaggregated totals.

broker-dealers. We also found it in the submitted documents or Web sites of two large investment advisory firms, one of which is dually registered, as well as one other investment advisory firm that is dually registered. Note that our document collection occurred during the period after the appellate-court ruling on March 31, 2007 (*Fin. Planning Ass'n v SEC*, 375 U.S. App. D.C. 389, 2007), but before the October 1, 2007, vacature of the rule. Therefore, we cannot identify whether lack of disclosure on the difference between a brokerage and an advisory account is due to the changing regulatory landscape or standard business practices.

Disclosures on conflicts of interest may include statements indicating, for example, (1) whether the investment adviser or broker-dealer receives compensation or reimbursement for referring clients to financial service providers, (2) that the investment adviser receives transaction-based compensation or fees related to the investment products recommended to his or her clients, or (3) that the firm's interests may not always coincide with the client's interests.

Once again, disclosure on conflicts of interest was most frequently found in the account agreements submitted by large firms from the sample of broker-dealers, but it was also found in product brochures submitted by six of these 13 firms. We also found this type of disclosure on the Web site of one of the other firms from the sample of broker-dealers, and this firm is a dually registered firm.

In the sample of investment advisers, conflict-of-interest disclosures were found on the Web sites of a large, dually registered firm and four other firms, none of which is dually registered. These disclosures were rarely found among the documents submitted by firms from the sample of investment advisers.

Finally, disclosures on compensation structure may also be related to differences between investment advisers and broker-dealers and conflicts of interest, and our findings are quite similar, especially for the broker-dealers. This type of disclosure was found more frequently than the other disclosures in the account agreements of investment advisers, but still it was only found in six of ten account agreements that investment advisers submitted.

Representatives of all brokerage firms whom we interviewed reported that they did a good job in providing disclosures and recounted the numerous avenues through which disclosures are provided to each client. The disclosures aim to identify the type of account and the level of responsibility of the firm. Several of the larger firms had specific documents that discussed the products and services offered and the roles and responsibilities of the investor and the firm. They made attempts to write these booklets in plain English rather than legal language. Additionally, the individual representatives are trained to discuss the risks associated with each product.

Several of the representatives interviewed acknowledged that, regardless of how carefully they craft documentation, investors rarely read these disclosures. They expressed frustration at providing the necessary documentation but still being held responsible in arbitration hearings when investors fail to read the disclosures. They felt that investors needed to accept some amount of responsibility for their decisions. One interviewee acknowledged that a client is going to sign something that a trusted adviser asks them to sign. Clients feel that the reason they engage a professional is so that they do not have to read all the accompanying literature. Therefore, for many investors, the fact that they were given disclosures was seen as meaningless.

Many of the dually registered firms offer a broad range of products and services for clients across the economic spectrum. Inherent in offering multiple services is the issue of conflicts of interest. These firms argued in the interviews that the existence of potential conflicts of interest should not imply that such business models are unworkable. They acknowledged that conflicts should be clearly explained in disclosure statements that are customized for each service or product. They argued that offering a broad range of products and services is a result of client demand. Many investors prefer to purchase multiple services from one firm and receive one set of statements each month.

The standard set of disclosures that most of the interviewed investment advisers provided to new clients include Form ADV Part II, an account agreement that sets out the terms and conditions of the relationship, fee schedule, any conflicts of interest, and a privacy statement. Form ADV Part II is available to clients annually.

Firms' Perspectives on Policy Issues

Policy issues. Industry consolidation was a prominent theme of the interviews with broker-dealers and investment advisers. The large brokerage firms appear to be getting larger, with many financial service firms merging with banks. Some noted that consolidation is a by-product of the high cost of doing business in the industry and the need to gain economies of scale. Many cited that the regulatory-compliance burden has increased significantly over the past five years. Agencies with regulatory oversight of broker-dealers include SEC, NASD, NYSE, 50 states' attorneys general, the U.S. Department of Labor, the U.S. Department of Treasury, and insurance regulators. Each of these regulatory bodies has its own oversight and involvement as to how services are to be delivered to a single client. Participants in interviews said that these requirements can often be in conflict or even contradictory, which makes it very time-consuming (and labor-intensive) and difficult for financial service firms to resolve.

Other broker-dealers noted that the technological expense of the sophisticated financial platforms needed to trade and track trades was a hurdle for smaller firms. The cost of these platforms makes it difficult for small and medium-sized firms to stay on the cutting edge of technology. To stay competitive, they must gain greater economies of scale by merging with other firms.

Mergers are also occurring as brokerage firms attempt to offer a broader array of products and services to their clients. They no longer want to be viewed as brokers, but rather as wealth-management organizations. In addition to mergers with banks, some traditional broker-dealers have merged with various firms to be able to offer more comprehensive financial solutions to clients and to keep fees low. Examples of some of these broker-dealers' acquisitions or mergers mentioned in our interviews included combinations with advisory firms, firms with strong bond underwriting, and research firms.

Many dually registered firms that offer proprietary products stated that more work needs to be done regarding principal trades. They recognized that the SEC's Interim Rule 206(3)-3T (SEC, 2007b) adopted October 1, 2007, does provide limited relief from the principal trading restrictions of §206(3) of the Investment Advisers Act of 1940 (54 Stat. 847) for nondiscretionary advisory accounts, likely alternatives for fee-based brokerage accounts. However, they felt that this relief did not go far enough.

Most of the investment advisers interviewed felt that there should be a level playing field for those who provide financial advice, whether they are investment advisers or broker-dealers. Some thought that there should be stronger sanctions for wrongdoing. Given that this is an industry based on trust, a few bad apples can undermine an entire industry almost overnight. Adhering to the highest standards of integrity will maintain public trust and confidence in the financial service industry, but the burden of compliance should not outweigh its benefits.

Many noted that the additional compliance burden over the past five years has increased the costs of compliance to firms and therefore the costs to investors but has done little to add protection for investors. The compliance burden versus investor protection should be looked at more closely. Some interviewees noted that one cannot raise fees enough to cover these increased compliance costs and feared that smaller firms may sell to larger firms, thereby restricting consumer choice.

Some of the investment advisers interviewed expressed concern over access to advisory services. They noted that investment advisers are not currently serving many investors because these investors cannot meet the account minimums. They thought that the industry should give some thought to reaching these underserved populations that could greatly benefit from professional advice.

One investment adviser noted that, when a broker with a negative disciplinary background switches to a new brokerage firm, his or her errant history can be verified using CRD. However, that same broker could switch to being an investment adviser, and the former broker's background may not be detected. He suggested a unified database that could track individuals who jump back and forth between practicing as a registered representative and as an investment adviser.

Many advisory firms noted increased competition from banks and insurance companies in this area of investment advice. As another example of how this industry is evolving, some investment advisers noted that they no longer receive referrals from brokerage firms, which are now keeping those clients in house.

Thoughts on current regulatory structure. The regulatory structure governing broker-dealers and investment advisers is important because it affects how and what type of products and services are delivered to investors. Although every representative interviewed complained about the increasing compliance burden, all recognized the necessity to have a financial service industry that protects the investor from bad actors. Such protection is vital for ensuring public trust, and this is an industry that is based on trust. If investors lose trust in the industry, they will not invest, and there will be no industry. So not one person interviewed thought they could continue to operate without regulatory oversight. Most thought that oversight should be measured and streamlined, noting that, over the years, it has ballooned to unrealistic proportions.

Some interviewed argued that regulations on broker-dealers protect investors more than regulations on investment advisers do because of the sheer volume of rules they must follow, even though investment advisers are thought to have a higher legal standard of care (i.e., being a fiduciary).

Many of the firms interviewed thought the current two regulatory structures were outdated and do not address the realities of today's marketplace. Some felt that changes need to be made in the law that recognize three types of businesses—brokerage, advice, and planning—and that thought should be given to regulating planning. Regulatory distinctions should not be made on how the investor pays for the service but rather who makes the decision (investor or financial representative).

Some dually registered firms noted how burdensome it was to have the compliance team understand both regulatory schemes. Regulations for both investment advisers and broker-dealers can be very similar for some issues, but other issues will be completely different or even contradictory. It is both time-consuming and expensive trying to navigate two regulatory schemes. One representative from a large brokerage firm affiliated with a bank noted that the firm was moving toward discretionary management under the bank rather than through the investment adviser because of the regulatory burdens. Some argued that, if there were just one standard of care, many of the regulatory burdens could be streamlined.

Most of the advisory firms whose representatives we interviewed thought that there was a need to differentiate how broker-dealers and investment advisers are regulated. They argued that, since broker-dealers are actually selling products, the manner in which they provide advice about those very products is important. However, some suggested that there could be some regulatory overlap between broker-dealers and investment advisers regarding issues such as advertising or disclosures.

Some firms expressed concern over the SEC's lack of specific guidance attached to new rules and regulations. It leaves much up to interpretation. One dual registrant expressed frustration that the SEC allows dually registered firms but gives little to no guidance on how dual registrants should follow new rules or regulations. The implementation of a new rule or regulation can have very different implications for a dually registered firm from those for a solely registered investment adviser.

Response to appellate-court ruling. Nine of the broker-dealers we interviewed reported that the appellate-court ruling (*Fin. Planning Ass'n v SEC*, 375 U.S. App. D.C. 389, 2007) regarding the 2005 rule (§202[1][11]-1) did not affect them because they had no (or few) fee-based accounts. Three of the full-service brokerage firms had converted their fee-based accounts (estimated to be on the order of hundreds of thousands of accounts) to either brokerage or advisory accounts. Those firms lamented losing the ability to offer fee-based accounts, because many clients preferred these types of products. They argued that offering fee-based products was driven by demands in the marketplace and that the court ruling will mean that clients will pay more but have access to less. They felt that the regulatory framework should provide a competitive environment in which firms can innovate to provide solutions for individual investors.

Most investment advisers agreed with the appellate-court ruling. Only one advisory firm, a dually registered firm, offered fee-based brokerage accounts to its clients. At the time of the interview, the firm had converted almost all of those accounts to advisory accounts. It reported that many clients were not happy about having to give up their fee-based accounts. The accounts of some clients who were uncomfortable with the idea of a discretionary account were converted to brokerage accounts.

Broker-Dealers from the Volunteer Sample

As previously mentioned, broker-dealers who volunteered for interviews were primarily from firms that were independently registered representatives affiliated with smaller firms or loose networks (independent broker-dealers). This differed from the group of interviewees from the probability sample, who almost exclusively represented larger brokerage firms that are dually registered. Those operating as independently registered representatives for smaller firms or loose networks appeared to function as independent operators and could set their own standards for certain criteria. For example, even if the representatives were associated with firms that did not have account minimums, they could choose to take only clients with a certain amount of investable assets or those who did not have other brokerage relationships. Many of these independent brokers were also licensed to sell insurance.

These independent brokers often do their own advertising, such as sponsoring a Little League® team or airing radio ads. These smaller firms tend to not have the extensive training programs that the larger firms have. They rely primarily on the annual continuing-education requirements of any licenses (e.g., series 7) or any professional certifications (e.g., CFP). Some noted that mandatory training sessions tend to be very perfunctory.

Some of the smaller firms outsourced administrative functions, such as payroll or IT, as well as their compliance and training functions. Compliance for brokers affiliated with smaller firms or loose networks are usually required to generate daily reports from the unified computing system whereby the computer looks at the suitability of clients' investments. These reports are sent into the home office or the outsourced compliance supervisor to validate that the client's assets are invested correctly.

From the individual brokers' viewpoint, increased compliance measures means that they spend more time filling out paperwork but that how they interact with clients and what products they offer clients has not changed. An independent broker-dealer affiliated with a regional firm recounted a recent story of opening three accounts for a husband and wife. The compliance rules required him to fill out three forms, even though the information was exactly the same. Bigger firms have automated online forms that will populate all of the fields on the three sets of paperwork in about 15 minutes. It took him an hour and a half to fill out all the forms by hand. He noted that this is one of the reasons small firms are at a disadvantage to larger, national firms. Another individual broker at a small brokerage firm commented that the new account-agreement form used to be one page. It is now 22 pages long, and that does not even include disclosures or mutual fund expense forms.

None of the smaller broker-dealers or independent brokers had fee-based brokerage accounts; therefore, they were unaffected by the appellate-court ruling. Many of these firms were not in favor of the SEC and NASD promoting the use of fee-based accounts and felt that investors end up paying more fees in these accounts than they would in a traditional brokerage account. They felt that, if they were not making some adjustment to a client's account, they should not be able to charge for it. Many of them were traditional, commission-based brokers and felt that receiving a fee for not doing anything with the client's account just seemed wrong.

Illustrative Examples

We conclude this chapter with case studies that illustrate a range of business practices regarding dual activity and affiliations. In Chapter Four, our analysis of the administrative data reveals a number of apparent reporting problems, especially with respect to dual activity. It also documents the considerable heterogeneity of business practices across firms. A relatively small number of large firms provide a full range of services, are often affiliated with other financial service providers, and conduct an overwhelming proportion of the investment advisory and brokerage business. On the other end of the spectrum are the large number of relatively small firms that provide a limited range of either investment advisory or brokerage services but that frequently report affiliations with firms providing complementary services.

We present case studies to better illustrate the types of businesses in which these firms are engaged and the types of relationships they maintain with other firms. The administrative data that we obtained described these relationships in only a very limited way. Moreover, there appears to be some confusion about how these relationships should be reported in the regulatory filings. We attempt to paint a fuller picture by combining the administrative data with information taken from business documents, Web sites, and firm interviews.

These case studies highlight the blurring lines between investment advisers and broker-dealers. As researchers, we faced a substantial challenge when we attempted to classify firms based on reported activities and affiliations. We often needed to piece together the evidence using multiple sources of information, such as regulatory filings, business documents, Web sites, and firm interviews (see, for example, Appendix A). What became clear was that each registered firm may be involved in multifaceted relationships spanning a variety of business activities. These relationships appear to be not uncommon practices within the financial service industry. Therefore, it also seems clear that the typical retail investor faces a substantial challenge when attempting to understand the nature of the business from which he or she receives investment advisory or brokerage services. The case studies below provide examples of these business relationships.

Investment Advisers in the Registered-Representative Classification

We begin by discussing three investment advisory firms that we classified as registered-representative firms based on the IARD data. Two of these firms were included in our probability sample of investment advisers. The other firm volunteered to be included in firm interviews. All three firms are organized as corporations. Recall that, according to the Investment Adviser Association and National Regulatory Services (2006), only sole proprietorships should be eligible to report being engaged as a registered representative of a broker-dealer. Yet these reports were frequently given by investment advisory corporations with founders or other executives who are registered representatives of other firms. These three examples illustrate how this type of relationship may be portrayed to clients.

Case 1A. We begin with an investment advisory firm from the probability sample. On its Form ADV for the fourth quarter of 2006, it reported having one to five employees and around $50 million in assets under management in a total of about 300 customer accounts, all of which are discretionary. Most of the clients were individuals other than HNW individuals.

This firm reported on Form ADV that it was actively engaged in business as a registered representative of a broker-dealer. It also reported the existence of a related person that is a broker-dealer, municipal-securities dealer, or government-securities broker or dealer. A securities firm with a similar name is clearly identified in the business documents we received.

The profile page of the investment advisory firm's Web site clearly identifies the existence of a holding company for both firms. The close relationship between the two firms should be apparent to clients who receive the account agreement that the advisory firm submitted to us. Using the investment-management agreement, a client can open a brokerage account with the affiliated securities firm simply by checking a box in §4 of the agreement and signing Schedule B attached to the agreement.

Case 1B. We turn now to another investment advisory firm from the probability sample. On its Form ADV, it reported having six to ten employees and around $150 million in assets under management in a total of about 300 customer accounts, a fraction of which are non-discretionary. Most of the clients were HNW individuals, but some other individuals were clients as well. As in the first case, this investment advisory firm reported being engaged in business as a registered representative of a broker-dealer; however, it did not report the existence of a related person that is a broker-dealer, municipal-securities dealer, or government-securities broker or dealer.

This investment adviser submitted to us a six-page investment-management agreement. An item at the bottom of the first page notes that a securities firm with a dissimilar name may execute transactions through its clearing broker. The president and CEO of the advisory firm is a registered representative of the former broker-dealer.

The investment advisory firm's Web site does not make any such relationships clear, but it does include a statement on the core principles page indicating that the firm has "no incentive to increase transaction costs." We independently identified the related brokerage firm by conducting a broker search through FINRA, using the name of the individual who founded the advisory firm, now its president and CEO. The advisory firm's Web site description of this individual notes that he previously worked at several different brokerage firms, but it does not mention his current firm.

Case 1C. We now consider an investment advisory firm that volunteered for interviews. As in the previous case, this corporation reported on Form ADV being engaged in business as a registered representative of a broker-dealer, and it did not report the existence of a related person that is a broker-dealer, municipal-securities dealer, or government-securities broker or dealer. It reported having 11 to 50 employees, including six to ten employees who are registered representatives of a broker-dealer. It reported having more than $150 million in assets under management, all in nondiscretionary accounts. Most of the clients were individuals other than HNW individuals.

According to our records, this firm was identified as a broker-dealer when volunteering for the interview. During the course of the interview with a founding member of the firm, it became apparent that the firm is an investment advisory firm with individual professionals who all have securities licenses (series 6 or 7).

The firm's Web site describes six individual professionals on its management team, including the interviewee. Two of these individuals are described as "registered representative of and offers securities through" a large broker-dealer. One of these two individuals, in addition to one other member of the management team, is also described as a "registered representative of" the investment advisory firm. The description of the interviewee, who reported having a series 6 license, does not indicate any activity as a broker, which is consistent with his own comments.

Broker-Dealers in the Affiliated-Activity Classification

We now discuss two broker-dealers that we classified as affiliated-activity firms based on the CRD data. Both firms were included in our probability sample of broker-dealers. These two brokerage firms did not submit any documents and maintain no Web sites, but some information is available via the Web sites of affiliated investment advisers.

Case 2A. The first broker-dealer reported less than $50,000 in total assets on its FOCUS Part IIA report for the fourth quarter of 2006. On Form BD, this firm reported that it was not engaged in the investment advisory service business, but it did report the existence of an affiliated firm in the securities or investment advisory business. The broker-dealer did not submit any business documents, and it does not maintain a Web site. We identified the firm with which it is affiliated based on a Web search that found a Form ADV linked to the terms-of-use page on the advisory firm's Web site.

On this posted Form ADV, the advisory firm reports on its broker-dealer affiliate, but not elsewhere on the Web site. The report includes text noting that principals of the advisory firm are registered representatives of the broker-dealer, which was founded by the founder of the advisory firm. The Web site description of this individual, however, does not note his role with the broker-dealer. The Form ADV also notes that the advisory firm has entered into an agreement with the broker-dealer to pay all the broker-dealer's overhead expenses. "At its discretion," the broker-dealer may repay the advisory firm for these disbursements.

Case 2B. Finally, we consider another broker-dealer that reported less than $50,000 in total assets on its FOCUS Part IIA report. As in the previous case, this firm reported on Form BD that it was not engaged in the investment advisory service business, but it did report the existence of an affiliated firm in the securities or investment advisory business. The broker-dealer also did not submit any business documents, and it does not maintain a Web site. We identified the firm with which it is affiliated based on a Web search that found the affiliate's Web site. This affiliated investment adviser has a similar name.

The homepage of the advisory firm's Web site notes that securities are offered through the brokerage firm. The remainder of the Web site describes the range of services that the advisory firm offers. It provides links to pages describing each of six financial-planning services and four other professional services. The link to information about brokerage services is listed second in the latter group, between litigation support and accounting services.

The page about brokerage services includes the following text that describes the benefit to clients of operating a wholly owned brokerage firm: "[W]e are completely free to select the products and services that we recommend to our clients." This page also notes that this business relationship provides "our clients with the added convenience of one-stop shopping within their current personal financial relationship."

Conclusions

This analysis of business documents and firm interviews was designed to obtain a more in-depth understanding of investment advisers' and broker-dealers' business practices than is possible based solely on administrative data. Taken together, these complementary, empirical findings portray an industry composed of heterogeneous firms engaged in a variety of relationships with their clients and with other firms.

The usefulness of the business-document analysis is limited by the low response rate among selected firms and partial compliance rate among responding firms. Even with full cooperation, this type of analysis cannot mimic the experience of individual investors seeking to understand the business practices of investment advisers and broker-dealers seeking to provide services to them. Still, the submitted documents and documents available on the Web present illuminating examples of the range of products and services offered by these firms, the variety of relationships among these firms, and the manner in which these alternative offerings and relationships are presented to prospective clients. If prospective clients were exposed to the documents we received and the Web sites we reviewed, they would likely obtain a very uneven understanding about these firms. In some cases, they would face a flood of information, only some of which could possibly be processed. In other cases, they receive only a trickle of information. In any case, they would likely be left to turn to individual professionals to summarize the key aspects of the prospective relationship.

The firm interviews provided supplemental information on these and other topics. Perhaps of most use are the investment advisers' and broker-dealers' perceptions of the level of investor knowledge in general and investor understanding of the differences between investment advisers and broker-dealers in particular. The concerns they typically express about regulatory burdens are frequently weighed against the recognized need to protect unsophisticated investors.

Finally, the importance of the relationship between the investor and the individual professional was frequently discussed in the firm interviews. This relationship was said to typically be initiated based on a referral. Firm-interview participants described the industry as one based on trust. It is this relationship that we seek to understand in the next chapter discussing survey interviews and focus-group discussions with current and potential investors.

CHAPTER SIX

Investors' Level of Understanding

The preceding chapters have focused on addressing our first research question by examining current business practices of investment advisers and broker-dealers. We now turn to the second research question of what investors understand about a range of issues, including whether investors understand distinctions between broker-dealers and investment advisers. We also seek to learn about their experiences interacting with the financial service industry and their expectations of service provided by individual professionals and firms in the financial service industry. We used two main avenues to make queries of investors. We administered a large-scale, national household survey, and we conducted six intensive focus-group discussions. The focus groups complement the national survey by providing a deeper understanding of how investors interact with the financial service industry and what they do and do not understand about the nature of that relationship. Participants in both the survey and the focus groups represent a range of ages, income levels, and racial and ethnic groups. In general, responses by survey and focus-group participants tended to be quite similar.

Our results show that most survey respondents and focus-group participants do not have a clear understanding of the boundaries between investment advisers and broker-dealers. Even those who have employed financial professionals for years are often confused about job titles, types of firms with which they are associated, and the payments they make for their services. Respondents and participants also understand relatively little about the legal distinctions between investment advisers and broker-dealers. Despite this confusion, however, respondents reported that they are largely satisfied with the services they currently receive from financial professionals.

We begin with discussion of results from our household survey, and we then turn our attention to the focus-group discussions. The household survey addresses several major topics, including (1) beliefs about the differences between investment advisers and broker-dealers and (2) experience with different types of financial service providers. In the latter part of this chapter, the focus-group results amplify the results from the household survey.

Household Survey

We collected data from U.S. households via an Internet survey of investment behavior and preferences, experience with financial service providers, and perceptions of the different types of financial service providers. The survey was administered to members of the ALP, a probability sample of more than 1,000 individuals aged 18 and over, who either used their own computers or a WebTV® appliance provided by RAND to participate in the panel over the

Internet. These individuals were recruited to the ALP after participating in the monthly survey of consumers conducted by the University of Michigan's Survey Research Center (SRC). (For more detail about the ALP and the Michigan monthly survey, see Appendix F.)

The household survey was administered for six weeks, from September 26, 2007, through November 6, 2007, and, because it was conducted online, we had quick access to the results. During this time, 654 households completed the survey. Respondent age varies from 19 to 89, with an average age of 52. Eleven percent of the sample has a household income of less than $25,000; 22 percent of the sample has one greater than $25,000 but less than $50,000; 23 percent of the sample has one greater than $50,000 but less than $75,000; and 45 percent of the sample has one greater than $75,000. More than 98 percent of respondents have a high-school degree or GED. Almost 52 percent of respondents have a bachelor's degree. Forty-nine states (all except Alaska) are represented in our sample. Using the U.S. Census Bureau geographic regions, almost 22 percent of households live in the West region, almost 23 percent live in the Midwest region, 18 percent live in the Northeast region, and 37 percent live in the South region. More than half of the households who live in the South region are in the South Atlantic division of the South region. This division includes Delaware, Maryland, Virginia, the District of Columbia, West Virginia, North Carolina, South Carolina, Georgia, and Florida.

Because our participants were drawn from the ALP, they tend to have more education and income than the broader U.S. population.[1] For this reason, our results will likely overstate the levels of financial knowledge, experience, and literacy of the U.S. population at large.

The survey began with an assessment of investment experience. We then asked several questions on respondent beliefs regarding the differences between investment advisers and broker-dealers. Next, for respondents who currently use a financial service provider, we asked detailed questions about their interactions with their providers. Respondents who do not use a financial service provider were asked for the reasons that they do not use a financial service provider. The last section of the survey presented respondents with definitions of a broker and an investment adviser, including a description of common job titles, legal duties, and typical compensation. Respondents were then asked to report the likelihood of their seeking services (in general) from a broker or investment adviser, the likelihood of seeking investment advice (in particular) from a broker or investment adviser, and the degree to which they would trust investment advice from a broker or an investment adviser.

Investment Experience

Participants were determined to be "experienced" investors if they held investments outside of retirement accounts, had formal training in finance or investing, or held investments only in retirement accounts but answered positively to questions gauging their financial understanding, such as the nature and causes of increases in their investments, seeking out information about their investments when necessary, and knowing the different investment options available to them. Participants who did not meet these requirements were deemed "inexperienced" investors. We used an identical classification method to determine participation in the focus groups.

---

[1]   According to the March 2007 Current Population Survey, 85 percent of Americans aged 18 and older have at least a high-school diploma or GED, and 26 percent have at least a bachelor's degree. The distribution for U.S. household income is 22 percent with less than $25,000; 27 percent greater than $25,000 but less than $50,000; 20 percent between $50,000 and $75,000; and 31 percent greater than $75,000. See U.S. Census Bureau (2007).

In the ALP sample, about two-thirds of survey respondents are categorized as experienced investors and one-third are categorized as inexperienced investors.

Beliefs About the Differences Between Investment Advisers and Brokers

To elicit their beliefs regarding the differences between investment advisers and brokers, we presented respondents with a series of specific services and obligations and asked them to indicate which items applied to any of the following financial service professionals: (1) investment advisers, (2) brokers, (3) financial advisors or financial consultants, (4) financial planners, or (5) none of the above.[2]

Respondents tended to perceive differences between investment advisers and brokers in terms of services provided and duties and obligations. Table 6.1 summarizes the survey results. Comparing beliefs on services provided by investment advisers to services provided by brokers, respondents were more likely to say that investment advisers provide advice about securities, recommend specific investments, and provide planning services. Respondents were more likely to say that brokers rather than investment advisers execute stock transactions and earn commissions. Respondents were slightly more likely to report that investment advisers rather than

Table 6.1
Respondents' Beliefs About Financial Service Professionals

What types of financial service professionals: (Check all that apply)	Investment Advisers (%)	Brokers (%)	Financial Advisors or Financial Consultants (%)	Financial Planners (%)	None of These (%)
Provide advice about securities (e.g., shares of stocks or mutual funds) as part of their regular business	80	63	78	63	3
Execute stock or mutual fund transactions on the client's behalf	29	89	28	23	3
Recommend specific investments	83	51	72	50	2
Provide retirement planning	51	12	80	91	2
Provide general financial planning	42	13	80	88	1
Typically receive commissions on purchases or trades that the client makes	43	96	34	22	1
Are typically paid based on the amount of assets that the client holds	49	40	50	34	12
Are required by law to act in the client's best interest	49	42	59	55	19
Are required by law to disclose any conflicts of interest	62	58	57	51	18

SOURCE: ALP survey, 651 respondents.

---

[2] Between subjects, we randomly varied the order of *broker* and *investment adviser* as they appeared on the computer screen.

brokers are required to act in the client's best interest and disclose any conflicts of interest. Even though these differences are small in magnitude, they are statistically significant.

Respondents tended to believe that financial advisors and consultants are more similar to investment advisers than to brokers in terms of the services provided, compensation methods, and duties. However, as noted in Chapter Five, *financial advisor* and *financial consultant* are titles commonly used by investment adviser employees as well as broker-dealer employees. Furthermore, we present evidence below that the most common titles of financial service providers that these respondents employ are generic terms, such as *advisor* or *financial advisor*.

We replicated the analysis, summarized in Table 6.1, conditioning on age, education, income, geographic region, investment experience, and whether the respondent later reported using a financial service provider. Results are presented in Table G.1 in Appendix G. For each category, the conclusions are qualitatively similar to those drawn from the entire sample.

Characteristics of Respondents Who Use Financial Service Providers

Of those surveyed, 47 percent of respondents reported that they currently use a financial service provider for "conducting stock market and/or mutual fund transactions" and/or "advising, management, and/or planning."[3] These respondents were more likely than other respondents to be older than 40, have at least a college degree, have household income of at least $75,000, and be an experienced investor (see Table 6.2).

Of the 306 respondents who reported using a financial service provider, 73 percent reported receiving professional assistance for advising, management, or planning, and 75 percent reported receiving professional assistance for conducting stock market or mutual fund transactions. Initially, more than 48 percent of respondents reported using professional assistance for both types of services. In discussing the services they receive, respondents were given another opportunity to report whether their financial service professional provides both types of services. In response to that follow-up question, we found that more than 70 percent of the reported financial service professionals provide both types of services.

Of respondents who say that they have a financial service provider, we asked whether there is a specific person or a firm that provides these financial services. Almost 81 percent of respondents personally interact with an individual professional. Of those respondents, 31 percent personally interact with more than one individual professional. Just over one-third (35 percent) reported employing at least one firm at which they do not interact regularly with a specific person.

To better assess whether respondents have different experiences depending on whether or not they interact with a specific individual or a firm, we distinguish between these experiences when presenting the survey results.

Job Titles and Firm Types of Financial Service Providers

Respondents who reported that they use a specific person, or an individual professional, were then asked for that person's title (or brief job description). Respondents gave 449 titles for 323

---

[3] When we posed the question, "Do you currently use any professional service providers for (1) conducting stock market or mutual fund transactions or (2) advising, management, or planning?" we randomly varied the order of the services between subjects as the question appeared on the computer screen.

Table 6.2
Respondents Who Use Financial Professionals, by Respondent Characteristics

Respondent	Responding Yes (%)
All respondents	47.3
Age	
40 and older	50.3
Under 40	33.9
Education	
College degree or more	55.4
No college degree	38.8
Household income	
At least $75,000	55.0
Less than $75,000	40.7
Region	
West	48.2
Midwest	42.9
Northeast	48.7
South	49.2
Investment experience	
Experienced	59.4
Inexperienced	23.4

SOURCE: ALP survey, 647 respondents.

NOTE: Question was worded as follows: Do you currently use any professional service providers for (1) conducting stock market or mutual fund transactions or (2) advising, management, or planning?

individual professionals.[4] The vast majority (248) of these individual professionals reportedly provide both advisory and brokerage services. Respondents reported that 45 of these individual professionals provide brokerage services but not advisory services, and 34 provide advisory services but not brokerage services. Respondents reported a wide variety of titles that their financial service providers use. The most commonly listed titles and their functions are reported in Table 6.3.

The most commonly reported title is *financial adviser* or *financial advisor*, regardless of the type of service provided by the individual professional. In fact, if these titles are combined with *financial consultant* and *advisor*, they account for almost one-quarter of all listed titles. *Financial planners* were listed 44 times, and CFPs were listed 21 times. *Broker, stockbroker,* or *registered representative* was used 38 times, and *investment adviser* or *investment advisor* was used 22 times.

---

[4]   Some respondents provided more than one title for an individual professional. For example, "financial planer *[sic]*, stockbroker, insureance *[sic]* agent."

Table 6.3
Professional Titles Most Commonly Reported by Respondents

Title	All Individual Professionals	Provide Advisory Services Only	Provide Brokerage Services Only	Provide Both Types of Services
Advisor	11	1	1	9
Banker	21	2	8	11
Broker, stockbroker, or registered representative	38	0	8	30
CFP	21	3	3	15
Financial adviser or financial advisor	78	7	11	60
Financial consultant	25	2	0	23
Financial planner	44	6	1	37
Investment adviser or investment advisor	22	3	3	16
President or vice president	20	0	2	18

SOURCE: ALP survey.

NOTE: Four hundred forty-nine titles were reported. Entries indicate the number of times that the title was reported.

For any given title, the individual professional is most likely to be reported as offering both types of services. Titles for individual professionals who provide only advisory services or only brokerage services suggest some confusion on respondents' part, although these numbers are small. For example, of the 22 individual professionals with a reported title of *investment adviser* or *investment advisor*, respondents reported that three provide brokerage services only. Furthermore, recall that responses to the questions on beliefs about financial service providers indicated that respondents view financial advisors or financial consultants as being more similar to investment advisers than to brokers. However, when asked about job titles and service provided, responses indicate that financial advisors are more likely to provide brokerage services only than to provide advisory services only. Lastly, note that 26 responses were left blank or explicitly stated that the respondent did not know the individual professional's job title or job description.

Respondents who work with at least one individual professional were asked to report what kinds of firms employ the individual professionals who provides financial services to them. Respondents who do not interact with a specific person were asked to report what kinds of firms they use for financial services. Respondents were asked to check all that apply: investment advisory firm, brokerage firm, bank, or other. The order of the first two categories was randomized between subjects.

For firms that are associated with an individual professional, the most common response to the type-of-firm question is for the first two categories to be checked—that is, both investment advisory firm and brokerage firm (see Figure 6.1). We refer to these firms as *dual investment advisory–brokerage firms*. The second most common response is for the category of investment adviser to be checked but not the brokerage category to be checked. We refer to these

Figure 6.1
Types of Firms That Employ Individual Professionals

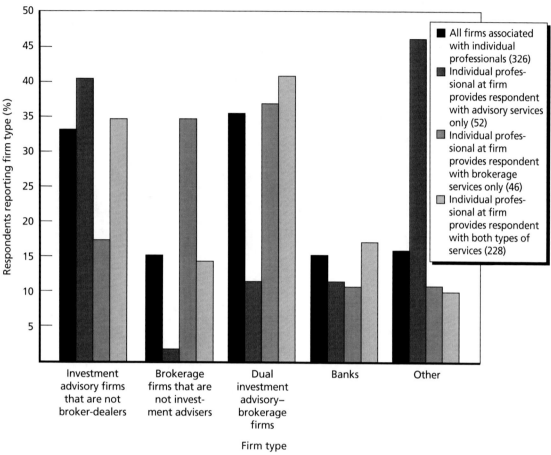

SOURCE: ALP survey.
RAND *TR556-6.1*

firms as *investment advisory firms that are not broker-dealers*. There were 52 other firm categories checked, and respondents specified 37 of them. The most commonly mentioned other type of firm was insurance firm (ten), and the second most commonly mentioned type of firm was accounting firm (seven).

For firms not associated with an individual professional, the most common response to the type-of-firm question is for the brokerage category to be checked but not the category for investment advisers to be checked. We refer to these firms as *brokerage firms that are not investment advisers*. The second most common is investment advisory firms that are not broker-dealers (see Figure 6.2).

Experiences with Financial Service Providers

We asked respondents detailed follow-up questions on the first individual professional or the first reported firm that is not associated with an individual professional. The frequency distributions for these first individual professionals are similar to those for all individual professionals reported. Likewise, for the first firm reported, the frequency distribution of firm types is

Figure 6.2
Types of Firms Used That Are Not Associated with Individual Professionals

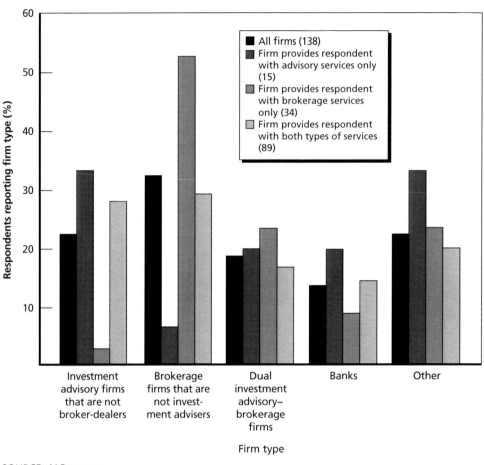

SOURCE: ALP survey.
RAND *TR556-6.2*

similar to those for all firms reported. For further details on the frequency distributions, see Appendix G.

We received detailed responses on 246 individual professionals and 85 firms. When comparing the professionals and firms about which respondents gave us detailed information, we found that the firms are less likely to provide both advisory and brokerage services, according to our respondents. Of the 246 individual professionals about whom respondents gave us detailed information, 12 percent provide advisory services only, 11 percent provide brokerage services only, and 76 percent provide both types of services. Of the 85 firms about which respondents give us detailed information, 18 percent provide advisory services only, 29 percent provide brokerage services only, and 53 percent provide both types of services.

Methods of payment for financial services. We asked respondents what methods of payment they make for advisory or brokerage services: commission, rate (hourly, monthly, or annual), flat fee, a fee determined by a percentage of assets, or other. Figure 6.3 presents the results. The most commonly reported compensation method to individual professionals for brokerage services is commission (37 percent), and the most commonly reported compensation method for advisory services is a fee determined by percentage of assets (35 percent). When asked to estimate their annual expenditure for the different types of services, the answers from respondents whose individual professional provides advisory services range from $0 to $30,000, with an average of $1,374. Answers from respondents whose individual professional provides brokerage services range from $0 to $21,500, with an average of $1,131. However, the median annual expenditure on advisory services from individual professionals is $125, and the median annual expenditure on brokerage services from individual professionals is $200. The large difference between average and median expenditure indicates that a small proportion of respondents reported paying a large amount for these services. Indeed, 10 percent of the responses on annual expenditure for advisory services from an individual professional are greater than or equal to $3,000. Likewise, 10 percent of the responses on annual expenditure for brokerage services are at least $2,400.

Responses to the questions on methods of payment suggest that many respondents are confused about the methods of payment or the type of firm with which their individual professional is associated. For example, 84 respondents indicated that they receive advisory services (either alone or in conjunction with brokerage services) from an investment advisory firm that is not also a brokerage firm. Of these respondents, 19 percent reported that they pay for these advisory services based on a percentage fee, and 22 percent indicated that they pay commission for advisory services. However, recall from Chapter Four that 97 percent of SEC-registered

Figure 6.3
Methods of Payment to Individual Professionals for Financial Services

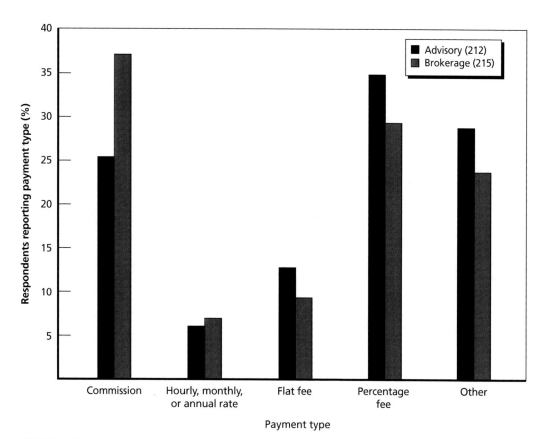

SOURCE: ALP survey.

RAND *TR556-6.3*

investment advisers that are not registered broker-dealers reported that they are compensated by asset-based fees, and only 10 percent reported that they receive commissions.[5]

Finally, 14 respondents did not answer the estimated annual expenditure question for advisory services, and 41 reported that they pay $0. For brokerage services, 18 respondents did not answer the estimated annual expenditure question, and 34 reported that they pay $0.

For firms, as opposed to individual professionals, respondents reported the most common form of compensation for brokerage services was commission and, for advisory services, was other (see Figure 6.4). Of the 28 other responses, 16 had further explanations. The most common explanations for the other responses were that the respondent does not pay for the service (six responses) or does not know what he or she pays for the service (four responses).

When asked to estimate their annual expenditures for the different types of services provided by firms rather than directly from individual professionals, the answers from respondents with firms providing advisory services ranged from $0 to $5,700, with an average of $278. The answers from respondents with firms providing brokerage services ranged from $0 to $8,000, with an average of $476. For advisory services, eight respondents did not answer

Figure 6.4
Methods of Payment to Firms for Professional Services

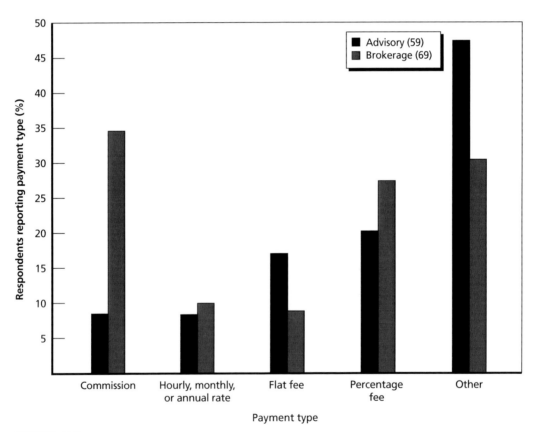

SOURCE: ALP survey.

---

[5]   An alternative explanation for this inconsistency could be if the firms that our respondents use are state-registered rather than SEC-registered firms, and state-registered firms are less likely than SEC-registered firms to charge asset-based fees.

the estimated annual expenditure question, and 21 reported that they pay $0. For brokerage services, five respondents did not answer the estimated annual expenditure question, and 14 reported that they pay $0.

How respondents located their financial service provider. Regardless of the types of services received, the most common way in which respondents found their current individual professional is by referral from a friend or family. The second most common way is by professional referral (see Table 6.4).

When asked about how respondents found the current firm that they employ for financial services, the most common response was other. Of the 32 other responses, there were 19 explanations. The most frequently mentioned explanation (six responses) was that the respondent found the firm through their place of work. The second most common method was by referral from a friend or family (see Table 6.5).

Length of relationship and satisfaction with financial service provider. In general, respondents reported that they have been working with the current individual professional for several years. When respondents were asked how long they have been working with their

Table 6.4
Methods of Locating Individual Professionals

Method	All Responses (239) (%)	Advisory Service Only (30) (%)	Brokerage Service Only (29) (%)	Both Types of Services (180) (%)
Professional referral	30.5	23.3	13.8	34.4
Referral from friend or family	45.6	43.3	34.5	47.8
Mailing	3.3	6.7	0.0	3.3
Print ad	3.8	0.0	6.9	3.9
Television ad	0.8	0.0	3.4	0.6
Internet	1.3	0.0	6.9	0.6

SOURCE: ALP survey.

Table 6.5
Methods of Locating Financial Service Firms

Method	All Responses (83) (%)	Advisory Service Only (14) (%)	Brokerage Service Only (25) (%)	Both Types of Services (44) (%)
Professional referral	18.1	14.3	12.0	22.7
Referral from friend or family	28.9	28.6	28.0	29.5
Mailing	2.4	0.0	0.0	4.5
Print ad	10.8	7.1	8.0	13.6
Television ad	6.0	0.0	4.0	9.1
Internet	8.4	0.0	12.0	9.1
Other	36.1	50.0	44.0	27.3

SOURCE: ALP survey.

current individual professional, 34 percent reported more than ten years, 26 percent reported five to ten years, 32 percent reported one to five years, and 8 percent reported less than one year. For respondents who receive only advisory services and for respondents who receive both types of services from their individual professional, the most common length of relationship is more than ten years. Ten respondents who receive only brokerage services reported that the length of the relationship is between one and five years, and nine respondents who receive only brokerage services reported that the length of the relationship is more than ten years (see Table 6.6).

Table 6.6
Length of Time with Same Individual Professional and Customer Satisfaction

Survey	All Responses (239) (%)	Advisory Service Only (30) (%)	Brokerage Service Only (29) (%)	Both Types of Services (180) (%)
About how long have you been doing business with this individual?				
Less than one year	7.5	20.0	6.9	5.6
1–5 years	31.8	23.3	34.5	32.8
5–10 years	26.4	20.0	27.6	27.2
More than 10 years	34.3	36.7	31.0	34.4
I am very satisfied with the service that I receive from this individual.				
Strongly disagree	7.1	0.0	6.9	8.3
Disagree	2.1	3.3	3.4	1.7
Neither agree nor disagree	15.9	26.7	10.3	15.0
Agree	41.4	43.3	62.1	37.8
Strongly agree	33.5	26.7	17.2	37.2
I trust that this individual acts in my best interest.				
Strongly disagree	7.1	0.0	3.4	8.9
Disagree	2.5	6.7	6.9	1.1
Neither agree nor disagree	15.1	26.7	17.2	12.8
Agree	35.1	33.3	51.7	32.8
Strongly agree	40.2	33.3	20.7	44.4
I believe that this individual provides me with a valuable service.				
Strongly disagree	7.5	0.0	6.9	8.9
Disagree	1.7	0.0	6.9	1.1
Neither agree nor disagree	11.7	20.0	17.2	9.4
Agree	41.0	53.3	51.7	37.2
Strongly agree	38.1	26.7	17.2	43.3

SOURCE: ALP survey.

Most respondents are satisfied with their individual professionals. At least 70 percent of respondents reported that they agree or strongly agree with the statements: I am very satisfied with the service that I receive from this individual; I trust that this individual acts in my best interest; I believe that this individual provides me with a valuable service. This same result holds true when we condition on the type of service provided, with one minor exception: Sixty-nine percent of respondents whose individual professional provides only brokerage services reported that they are being provided with a valuable service.

Respondents who have been working with their individual professional for at least ten years expressed even greater satisfaction: Seventy-eight percent agreed or strongly agreed that they were very satisfied with the service that they receive, 83 percent agreed or strongly agreed that their individual professional acts in their best interest, and 82 percent agreed or strongly agreed that they are being provided with a valuable service.

When we examined the length of the relationship with the current firm, we found a similar pattern to that we found with individual professionals. In general, as shown in Table 6.7, respondents reported that they have been working with the current firm for several years. Overall, 42 percent of respondents reported that they have been working with their current firm for more than ten years. For respondents who receive advisory services or both types of services from a firm, the most common length of the relationship is more than ten years. For respondents who receive brokerage services only, the most common length of relationship is between five and ten years.

As we found with the results on individual professionals, respondents tended to be satisfied with their firms. At least 70 percent of respondents reported that they agreed or strongly agreed with these statements: I am very satisfied with the service that I receive from this firm; I trust that this firm acts in my best interest; I believe that this firm provides me with a valuable service. When we condition on the type of service provided, one category in which respondents indicate a lower level of satisfaction is the degree to which they trust that the firm that provides brokerage services acts in their best interest. In this case, only 48 percent of respondents agreed or strongly agreed with the statement.

We found that respondents who have been working with their firm for at least ten years tended to express even greater satisfaction: Eighty-six percent agreed or strongly agreed that they are very satisfied with the service that they receive, 77 percent agreed or strongly agreed that their individual professional acts in their best interest, and 83 percent agreed or strongly agreed that they are being provided with a valuable service.

We also asked respondents two open-ended questions: "What do you like about the service that you receive from this individual professional?" and "What do you dislike about the service that you receive from this individual professional?" Respondents reported what they liked about 235 individual professionals. Of these professionals, 30 provide advisory services, 27 provide brokerage services, and 178 provide both types of services.

We coded comments by broad categorizations. The most common types of positive comments are presented in Table 6.8. Examples of comments that are categorized as accessibility or attentiveness are, "She makes certain she stays updated on any changes I have made in the direction of my financial future," and "this person is available when I need him." Comments are coded as relationship or personality if the respondent said that he or she likes the individual professional's personality or that he or she feels like the relationship is a good one. For example, comments might include that the individual professional is "personable" or "friendly" or that the respondent feels that he or she receives "personalized service." Comments that cited

Table 6.7
Length of Time with Same Firm and Customer Satisfaction

Survey	All Responses (83) (%)	Advisory Service Only (14) (%)	Brokerage Service Only (25) (%)	Both Types of Services (44) (%)
About how long have you been doing business with this firm?				
Less than one year	7.2	7.1	12.0	4.5
1–5 years	25.3	21.4	28.0	25.0
5–10 years	25.3	7.1	32.0	27.3
More than 10 years	42.2	64.3	28.0	43.2
I am very satisfied with the service that I receive from this firm.				
Strongly disagree	7.2	7.1	4.0	9.1
Disagree	1.2	0.0	4.0	0.0
Neither agree nor disagree	19.3	21.4	24.0	15.9
Agree	38.6	35.7	32.0	43.2
Strongly agree	33.7	35.7	36.0	31.8
I trust that this firm acts in my best interest.				
Strongly disagree	6.0	7.1	4.0	6.8
Disagree	2.4	0.0	8.0	0.0
Neither agree nor disagree	31.3	28.6	40.0	27.3
Agree	31.3	35.7	20.0	36.4
Strongly agree	28.9	28.6	28.0	29.5
I believe that this firm provides me with a valuable service.				
Strongly disagree	7.2	7.1	4.0	9.1
Disagree	1.2	0.0	0.0	2.3
Neither agree nor disagree	19.3	21.4	20.0	18.2
Agree	34.9	28.6	36.0	36.4
Strongly agree	37.3	42.9	40.0	34.1

SOURCE: ALP survey.

that the individual professional is knowledgeable or "knows her business" were coded as positive comments on expertise. Some examples of comments that are categorized as understands, listens, or explains are "She asks pertinent questions about my lifestyle and goals," and "He knows and understands my needs, knows of my family and understands how I feel about my investments and what I need or want in life for me and my family."

The comments indicate that personal service is very important in an individual professional who provides financial services. The most common positive comments are related to

Table 6.8
Most Common Positive Comments About Individual Professionals

Positive Comment	All	Advisory	Brokerage	Both
Accessibility or attentiveness	80	6	9	65
Relationship or personality	74	8	7	59
Expertise	63	7	7	49
Understands, listens, or explains	41	7	1	33
Acts in my best interest	29	2	2	25
Performance	24	1	2	21
Honesty and integrity	22	5	5	12
Trust	10	1	0	9
Cost	8	2	1	5
Available products, options, or services	8	0	0	8

SOURCE: ALP survey.

NOTE: Two hundred thirty-five respondents reported positive comments. Entries indicate the number of times that the comment was reported.

personal service: accessibility and attentiveness; relationship and personality; and understands, listens, and explains.

We received far fewer negative comments. Respondents reported what they dislike about 109 individual professionals. Of these individual professionals, 14 provide advisory services to the respondent, 18 provide brokerage services, and 77 provide both types of services. We coded the negative comments in the same way as the positive comments. The most common negative comments are presented in Table 6.9.

As with the positive comments, the most common type of negative comment discusses lack of accessibility or attentiveness, such as "lack of contact" or "doesn't call me frequently enough." The second most common type of negative comment cites high fees or expensive service as a cause for dislike of the service received from the individual professional. Another common negative comment is that the individual professional does not act in the respondent's best interest. Examples of such comments are "I don't think he has my interests at heart. He is trying to make money for himself," or "often tries to sell securities that the brokerage firm is pushing."

When we asked respondents what they liked and disliked about the firm that provides their financial services, respondents reported many more positive comments than negative comments, as they did with individual professionals (see Table 6.10). Respondents gave positive comments on 79 firms and negative comments on 24 firms. Of the firms with positive comments, 25 provide only brokerage services to the respondent, 14 provide only advisory services, and 40 provide both types of services. Of the firms with negative comments, six provide brokerage services, five provide advisory services, and 13 provide both.

Like the positive comments about individual professionals, the most commonly reported positive comments about firms are related to accessibility and attentiveness. However, unlike the positive comments on individual professionals, cost is the second most commonly reported positive comment.

Table 6.9
Most Common Negative Comments About Individual Professionals

Negative Comment	All	Advisory	Brokerage	Both
Lack of accessibility or attentiveness	38	4	6	28
Cost	10	1	4	5
Does not act in my best interest	9	1	2	6
Lack of expertise	6	1	1	4
Performance	6	0	0	6
Relationship or personality	4	2	0	2
Lack of trust	3	0	1	2
Does not understand, listen, or explain	3	1	0	2
Dislike of the individual professional's firm	3	0	0	3

SOURCE: ALP survey.

NOTE: One hundred nine respondents reported negative comments. Entries indicate the number of time that the comment was reported.

Table 6.10
Most Common Positive Comments About Financial Service Firms

Positive Comment	All	Brokerage	Advisory	Both
Accessibility or attentiveness	25	7	6	12
Cost	12	4	0	8
Expertise	11	3	4	4
Online features, such as email	9	3	3	3
Relationship or personality	8	1	2	5
Performance	7	2	1	4
The firm itself	4	1	2	1
Reliability	4	1	0	3
Available products, options, or services; broad based	4	1	1	2
Honesty or integrity	3	0	1	2

SOURCE: ALP survey.

NOTE: Seventy-nine respondents reported positive comments. Entries indicate the number of times that the comment was reported.

Again, we found that the most commonly reported negative comments about firms are related to accessibility or attentiveness, as reported in Table 6.11. Negative comments about firms also reported disappointment in the level of expertise and in the online features of the firm.

Table 6.11
Most Common Negative Comments About Financial Service Firms

Negative Comment	All	Brokerage	Advisory	Both
Lack of accessibility or attentiveness	7	1	1	5
Lack of expertise	3	2	1	0
Online features, such as email	3	1	0	2

SOURCE: ALP survey.

NOTE: Twenty-four respondents reported negative comments. Entries indicate the number of times that the comment was reported.

Reasons Not to Use a Financial Service Provider

We asked respondents who reported that they do not use a financial service provider for the reasons that they do not employ one. For respondents who use a financial service provider only for advisory services, we asked why they do not use a financial service provider for brokerage services. Likewise, for respondents who use a financial service provider for brokerage services only, we asked why they do not use a financial service provider for advisory services. The results are summarized in Table 6.12.

Respondents were given the following five specified choices for why they might not employ a financial service provider, in addition to an other category, and asked to choose all that apply: no money for investments; too expensive; too hard to choose one; do not need assistance with financial decisions; or had one and did not like him, her, or the firm.

For respondents who do not use a financial service provider at all, the most common specified reason (47 percent) is "no money for investments." For respondents who do not use a financial service provider for brokerage services, the most common specified reason (36 percent) is "no money for investments." For respondents who do not use a financial service provider for advisory services, the most common reason (18 percent) is that the respondent does not "need assistance with [his or her] financial decisions."

We replicated the analysis for respondents who do not currently use a financial service provider, conditioning on age, education, income, geographic region, and investment

Table 6.12
Reasons Given for Not Using a Financial Professional

Reason	Brokerage and Advisory Services	Brokerage Services	Advisory Services
No money for investments (%)	47.1	35.5	17.6
Too expensive (%)	13.2	9.7	20.6
Too hard to choose one (%)	6.2	0.0	2.9
Do not need assistance with financial decisions (%)	21.5	12.9	52.9
Had one and did not like him, her, or the firm (%)	8.2	0.0	11.8
Observations	340	31	34

SOURCE: ALP survey.

experience.[6] For each category, the most common reason to not use a financial service provider is "no money for investments," except for respondents in households with income greater than $75,000, respondents who live in the Northeast region, and respondents who are characterized as experienced investors. For these respondents, the most common reason not to use a financial service provider is not needing help with financial decisions.

Relative Inclination to Seek Services from Brokers or Investment Advisers

The last section of the survey presented all respondents with definitions of *broker* and *investment adviser*, including a description of common job titles, legal duties, and typical compensation. We first asked respondents: "On a scale from 0 to 100, what do you think is the percent chance that you will seek (or continue to seek) services from a [broker/investment adviser] in the next five years?" For respondents who reported a positive probability, we followed up with a question on investment advice: "On a scale from 0 to 100, what do you think is the percent chance that you will seek (or continue to seek) investment advice from a [broker/investment adviser] in the next five years?" Lastly, we ask respondents to rate the degree to which they agree with the following statement: "I would trust investment advice from a [broker/investment adviser]."

Answers, as shown in Table 6.13, indicate that respondents were roughly equally likely to seek services in general and investment advice in particular from investment advisers and brokers. On average, respondents were equally likely to seek services, in general, from investment advisers and brokers (37.1 percent versus 36.6 percent),[7] but the median response is slightly higher for services from an investment adviser (25 percent versus 20 percent). Almost 29 percent of respondents reported a 0 percent chance that they will seek services from a broker, and 28 percent of respondents reported a 0 percent chance that they will seek services from an investment adviser. Among respondents who reported a positive probability that they will seek services, in general, from a broker or investment adviser, the median response indicates an equal willingness to seek investment advice from investment advisers and brokers (50 percent), whereas the average response indicates a slightly greater willingness to seek services from an investment adviser (51.9 percent versus 47.7 percent).[8] Of respondents who reported a positive probability of seeking services from a broker, 4 percent, or 16 respondents, reported a 0 percent chance of seeking investment advice from a broker. Of those respondents who reported a positive probability seeking services from an investment adviser, only one respondent reported a 0 percent chance of seeking investment advice from an investment adviser.

Types of Assistance That Respondents Would Like with Financial Matters

We asked all respondents, "what kind of professional assistance with financial matters would you find most helpful at this point in your life?" with the following options: asset management, college-saving planning, debt consolidation or management, developing a budget and saving plan, estate planning, executing stock or mutual fund transactions, general financial planning, investment advising, retirement planning, or other. A majority of respondents (62 percent) would like assistance with retirement planning. Many respondents would also like assistance

---

[6]   The complete results are in Table G.3 in Appendix G.

[7]   These means are not significantly different from one another at any conventional levels of statistical significance.

[8]   These means are not significantly different from one another at any conventional levels of statistical significance.

Table 6.13
Inclination to Seek Future Services from Investment Advisers and Brokers

Survey	Investment Adviser			Broker		
	Mean (%)	Median (%)	n	Mean (%)	Median (%)	n
Percent chance of seeking *services* from [investment adviser/broker] in the next five years	37.1	25	634	36.6	20	637
Percent chance of seeking *investment advice* from [investment adviser/broker] in the next five years	51.9	50	454	47.7	50	458
I would trust investment advice from [investment adviser/broker] (1 = strongly disagree, 5 = strongly agree)	3.4	3	635	3.1	3	637

SOURCE: ALP survey.

with investment advising (41 percent), financial planning (38 percent), and estate planning (35 percent).

We replicated the analysis conditioning on age, education, income, geographic region, investment experience, and whether the respondent reported using a financial service provider.[9] Across all groups, the most commonly selected option is "retirement planning." Across all groups, the second most common is "investment advising," except for respondents who live in the West region, respondents who do not have a college degree, respondents who did not report using a financial service provider, or respondents who are classified as inexperienced. For the first three of those groups, the second most commonly selected option is "general financial planning." For the last group, those respondents classified as inexperienced, the second most commonly selected option is "developing a budget and savings plan."

Focus Groups

Focus groups allow for interactive discussion of the topics and allow moderators to follow up on beliefs and understanding behind responses. Although focus-group participants are not nationally representative and data collected during focus groups are qualitative in nature, this method often provides researchers with important evidence on the more nuanced issues surrounding topics. Indeed, we believe that we gained a greater understanding about some of the beliefs regarding views of the financial service industry. Moreover, evidence suggests similarities to the broader population represented in the ALP.

We begin with a brief discussion of our methodology. Next, we present general impressions from the focus groups on the financial service industry. We then describe participants' financial decisionmaking and experience with financial service providers. Lastly, we examine some of the perceived differences between investment advisers and broker-dealers.

---

[9] Complete results are in Table G.4 in Appendix G.

Methods

We conducted six focus groups of ten to 12 participants each, representing both experienced and inexperienced investors. As with survey respondents, focus-group participants were determined to be experienced investors if they held investments outside of retirement accounts, had formal training in finance or investing, or held investments only with retirement accounts but answered positively to questions eliciting their self-assessed financial understanding, such as the nature and causes of increases in their investments, seeking out information about their investments when necessary, and knowing the different investment options available to them. Participants who did not meet these requirements were deemed inexperienced investors.

The 67 participants ranged from 22 to 77 years of age, with two-thirds of participants older than 40. The mix of racial and ethnic background includes 44 white but not Hispanic, 18 black, 2 Hispanic, and 3 Asian participants. The focus groups were held in one of two locations (Alexandria, Virginia, and Fort Wayne, Indiana) in September and October 2007. We employed the services of outside firms to recruit our participants. For the Virginia focus groups, we used a recruiting firm that maintains a database of approximately 17,000 individuals from the Washington, D.C., metropolitan area, including northern Virginia and parts of Maryland. For the Indiana focus groups, we used a local recruiting firm that maintains a database of approximately 35,000 individuals, mainly from Allen County, Indiana, with a small percentage (9–10 percent) of individuals who reside in counties immediately adjacent to Allen County.

Each location included two groups of experienced investors and one group of inexperienced investors. The approximate ratio of two-thirds experienced investors and one-third inexperienced investors is similar to the ratio among the ALP respondents. We asked them a range of questions about their level of understanding and their own experience with the financial service industry. We also presented them with sample advertisements from both broker-dealers and investment advisers and asked what types of products and services and levels of interaction they expected from each.

Investment Experience

Almost all participants held investments in retirement accounts, primarily through their employer. Many had investments outside of retirement accounts, primarily in mutual funds, and some held individual stocks and annuities. A few individuals who are particularly uncertain about what to do with their money have put their savings into money-market accounts (MMA) and certificates of deposit (CDs). These participants felt that they had received poor financial advice in the past and were unsure how to invest it, so they went with the perceived security of MMAs and CDs.

Participant age ranged from 22 to 77 years, and investment experience ranged from two years to 40 years. The vast majority of participants described their level of financial knowledge as low, including many who had been investing for several years. About 10 percent of participants considered their level of financial knowledge to be good or advanced. Participants attributed their lack of knowledge to having little interest in finances, lack of time to learn and keep up, and the fact that financial literature is complicated and confusing. Some mentioned that there is a lot of conflicting information available and that they are not sure which sources to trust.

General Impressions of the Financial Service Industry

When asked about their general views of the financial service industry, participants tended to say that the industry is complicated. As with any industry, they feel that there are both honest and dishonest individuals within the financial service industry. Some noted that recent corporate scandals, such as those at WorldCom and Enron, have led the public to view the financial service industry with more skepticism. It is an industry based on trust, and many participants noted that they did not trust the industry.

Many of those with investments acknowledged that they were unsure what they were being charged for the investments they currently hold. They believe that there are hidden fees and that investment professionals will not provide them with certain information unless they specifically ask for it. They believe that one must know the right questions to ask or be at a disadvantage. When asked about financial service advertisements that they may have seen, participants reported that they believe that advertisements for investment professionals try to make people think that it is easy to get started and that the company will work for its clients to help them attain a certain lifestyle.

Participants most frequently cited the following reasons they see as to why people fail to invest:

- They think that it is necessary to have a large amount of disposable income to invest.
- They have no money to invest.
- They fear losing their money in investments.
- They lack knowledge about investing.
- They see the financial service industry as too complex to navigate.

Investor Decisionmaking and Experience with Financial Service Professionals

Sources of information. Participants reported getting information about financial products and services from a variety of sources, including the Internet, friends and family, financial magazines, television, prospectuses, presentations at work, and financial service professionals (including advisers, accountants, insurance agents, and their bank).

Choosing an investment professional. Roughly half of participants reported that they currently use a financial service provider. Those who have investments but do not use a financial service provider explained that they trusted themselves as much as they trusted a professional with their money.

Trust of the individual financial service professional was the most cited feature of what investors would be looking for in a financial service provider. Trust of the individual professional was cited as more important than trust of the firm for which that individual works. Many participants had a preference for older, established firms, because it shows staying power and the ability to ride out hard times. The majority of participants currently working with a financial service provider found that provider through personal or professional referral. When we asked participants who do not currently use a financial service provider how they would find one if they chose to employ one in the future, referral was the most common response.

Participants felt that the personal relationship is very important and would like an individual who is accessible. Though the majority of those who use a financial service provider were happy with the relationship and the service, several participants did note that they were not satisfied primarily due to lack of personal interaction. These comments are similar to those reported by ALP respondents. Many had gone years without hearing from their financial service provider, but some recognized that they were partly responsible for this lack of communication. Others noted that their financial service provider did not seem to do much.

Participants were asked what they like about their relationship with their financial service provider, if they currently use one; otherwise, they were asked what they would seek in a relationship with a financial service provider if they were to employ one. Some participants preferred a very hands-off relationship with their financial service provider. They stated that they had neither the inclination nor the time to follow the markets and were happy to turn that job over to a professional. Other participants thought that they would like to be a partner in their financial decisions and have a say in what is done with their money. However, these participants tended to realize that there is much about the financial service industry that they do not know or understand, so it is important to have a financial service provider who will take the time to educate them about the market and the various products available. Many participants felt that, because their assets were too modest, they would not be of interest to the majority of financial service providers to spend the necessary amount of time to work with and educate them.

Contact with investment professionals. Some participants said that they would prefer to communicate with an individual professional via the phone, while others cited preference for face-to-face meetings and others preferred email communication. Participants felt that, in an ideal relationship, they would want to meet with their representative more frequently at first (monthly) and then on a quarterly or semiannual basis after they felt more comfortable in the relationship. Participants who feel fairly knowledgeable about their investments wanted less contact with their investment professional. These participants felt that receiving quarterly statements in the mail was enough contact.

Desired services. Of those who were looking for professional help, all cited retirement planning as a needed service. They considered retirement planning to involve not only saving for retirement but also determining how the funds should be spent and invested during retirement. The other desired services that participants mentioned most were education planning, insurance planning, and estate planning. A few participants noted needing help with budget planning and saving to buy a house.

Participants were divided over whether it is better to have all of their investments handled by one firm or to have several firms helping them. Participants cited convenience as an advantage to having one firm: The individual professional would be able to see the whole financial picture and better advise the client and reduce the amount of paperwork to track. Other participants wanted to spread their investments across a couple of firms, believing that this would reduce their risks. They also noted that some firms specialize in certain types of investments and that it may be better to play to the strengths of certain firms. Still others preferred the idea of entrusting some of their money to financial service providers but also investing a portion of their money on their own.

Perceived Differences Between Investment Advisers and Brokers

Focus-group participants displayed some confusion regarding the role of investment advisers and brokers, as we observed with ALP respondents. Focus-group discussion helped illuminate the sources of confusion. We begin with a discussion of participants' initial beliefs regarding the differences between investment advisers and broker-dealers. Next, we will describe their reactions to sample advertisements from investment advisers and broker-dealers. We then explore participants' inclination to seek services in general and investment advice in particular from investment advisers and broker-dealers. Lastly, we will describe some further reactions to investment advisers' and broker-dealers' marketing materials.

Initial beliefs regarding the differences between investment advisers and brokers. To assess participant levels of understanding regarding the roles of various financial service professionals, we administered a short questionnaire. The questionnaire was given before detailed discussion on the distinction between investment advisers and brokers to capture their understanding coming into the focus-group session and not reflect anything they might learn during the focus-group session. The questionnaire is similar to the first section of survey questions on financial service providers administered to ALP respondents: Participants were presented with a series of specific services and obligations and were asked to indicate which items applied to the following financial service professionals: investment advisers, brokers, financial advisors, financial consultants, financial planners, or none of the above. Table 6.14 provides the results of that questionnaire.[10]

Focus-group responses were quite similar to those of the household survey. Comparing beliefs on services provided by investment advisers to services provided by brokers, participants were more likely to say that investment advisers provide advice about securities, recommend specific investments, and provide planning services. Participants were more likely to say that brokers rather than investment advisers execute stock transactions and earn commissions. Participants responded similarly that investment advisers and brokers are required to act in the client's best interest. Participants were more likely to say that brokers rather than investment advisers are required to disclose any conflicts of interest.

We note some key differences between these responses from focus-group participants and responses from survey respondents. Responses indicate that a much smaller share of focus-group participants (5 percent) believe that investment advisers receive commissions than survey respondents did (43 percent). Focus-group participants were more likely to report that both investment advisers and brokers are required to act in the client's best interest (64 percent and 63 percent, respectively) than did ALP respondents (49 percent and 42 percent, respectively). Furthermore, focus-group participants were more likely than survey respondents to report that brokers are required to disclose any conflicts of interest. In fact, focus-group participants were more likely to report that brokers, rather than investment advisers, must disclose conflicts, whereas ALP respondents were more likely to report that investment advisers must disclose conflicts.

Initial reactions to investment advisers' and broker-dealers' advertisements. The first set of advertisements that we presented to focus-group participants were general advertisements from actual firms taken from magazines. Any identifying information or marks were stripped from the advertisements. The firm A advertisement on brokerage services stressed the importance of building a relationship with one's financial consultant based on trust. The advertisement further described the expertise of its financial consultants and its research tools (with fine print detailing that the research tools provide general, not personal, advice). The advertisement specifically mentioned mutual funds and stocks. The firm B advertisement, taken from an investment advisory firm, stressed the importance of careful planning so that the reader's estate will be left to his or her beneficiaries rather than to the IRS. This advertisement also

---

[10] Table F.4 in Appendix F provides a breakdown of questionnaire responses by age, education, location, investment experience, and whether the participant has a financial service provider.

Table 6.14
Participants' Beliefs About Financial Service Professionals

What types of financial service professionals: (check all that apply)	Investment Advisers (%)	Brokers (%)	Financial Advisors or Consultants (%)	Financial Planners (%)	None of These (%)
Provide advice about securities (e.g., shares of stocks or mutual funds) as part of their regular business	85	61	76	63	0
Execute stock or mutual fund transactions on the client's behalf	27	84	22	18	0
Recommend specific investments	93	46	67	46	0
Provide retirement planning	39	12	81	91	0
Provide general financial planning	33	16	79	91	0
Typically receive commissions on purchases or trades that the client makes	5	96	43	33	0
Are typically paid based on the amount of assets that the client holds	51	57	45	19	6
Are required by law to act in the client's best interest	64	63	58	57	18
Are required by law to disclose any conflicts of interest	60	70	61	72	18

SOURCE: Focus-group survey, 67 participants.

highlighted the firm's experience and expertise. The advertisement specifically mentioned philanthropy, asset management, and sophisticated wealth-transfer strategies.

In discussing what appealed to them about firm A, many participants mentioned that they liked the trust message and that the advertisement implied that all of its employees are well trained. A commonly mentioned dislike of the firm was the fine print detailing that the research tools are not personal advice.

In discussing what they found appealing about firm B, many participants mentioned that they believed that firm B has a lot of expertise and that they think that they could benefit from its services, such as asset management. However, given the tone of the advertisement, many participants also thought that they do not have enough money to be a client at firm B.

Inclination to seek services from investment advisers or brokers. Participants were presented with fact sheets on investment advisers and brokers. The information on the fact sheets included the same information as the descriptions given to ALP survey respondents: definitions of *broker* and *investment adviser*, including a description of common job titles, legal duties, and typical compensation. Even after being presented with fact sheets, participants were confused by the different titles. They noted that the common job titles for investment advisers and broker-dealers are so similar that people can easily get confused over the type of professional with which they are working. Some participants said they knew which type of investment professional they have, but most did not.

Participants expressed interest in the fact that brokers have to be certified and investment advisers do not. Several interpreted this to mean that advisers were not as qualified as the brokers.

Some did not understand such terms as *fiduciary* and whether fiduciary was a higher standard than suitability. Some participants did not think that the legal requirements for either investment advisers or brokers were stringent enough. Several participants mentioned that, if an investment adviser made a costly mistake with a client's money, they thought that it would be extremely difficult to prove that the adviser was not acting in what he or she perceived to be the client's best interest. Other participants did not like that brokers had to recommend products that were suitable for them. They thought that *suitable* was too vague a term and that it was not clear how the broker would determine suitability. Many participants also noted that investment advisers have to disclose conflicts of interest while brokers do not.

Further Reactions to Investment Advisers' and Broker-Dealers' Marketing Materials. Last, after discussion of differences between investment advisers and brokers, we presented participants with two more sets of marketing materials. These materials were adapted from documents that we collected in our business-document collection. All identifying details were stripped from the materials.

The first set of materials was marketing pamphlets from firm C, a dually registered firm, and firm D, an investment advisory firm. These pamphlets gave more detail than did the initial set of advertisements. The firm C pamphlet detailed the firm's experience, expertise, wide range of services, and size. This pamphlet also mentioned that firm C works with clients regardless of their amount of assets and included a disclaimer that it generally works as a broker-dealer, except in a few instances, in which the client will be told in writing that it is acting as an investment adviser. Specifically mentioned services and products included financial planning, retirement planning, estate planning, and various investment products, including annuities, mutual funds, stocks, and options. The firm D pamphlet detailed the firm's experience and expertise, as well as the personal service that clients receive from the firm. The firm D pamphlet specified a $100,000 minimum and discussed its fee structure. Firm D offered only a discretionary account.

Some participants favored firm C, citing the lack of account minimum and wide range of services. Some of these participants said that they would prefer firm D but that the account minimum was a barrier. Regarding firm D, some respondents did not like the notion of a discretionary account. They preferred more interaction and would want to give specific direction to their financial professional. On the other hand, many respondents liked the personal-relationship aspect of firm D. Many participants stated they believe that they would have a long-term relationship with a firm like firm D, if only they had enough assets.

Several participants noted the irony that, to enlist an investment adviser, one has to have what the participants considered to be a high account minimum, although there are many people with not much in investable assets who really need the advice.[11] Many focus-group participants found the brokerage advertisements to be more in their ballpark in terms of account minimums and fees, although almost all respondents presumed that it would involve advice. They liked the concept of directing a broker but felt that they were not knowledgeable enough to provide good instruction.

The last set of materials was taken from the same dually registered firm, firm E, but one pamphlet detailed brokerage services and the other detailed advisory services. Again, we heard that brokerage services were more appealing in terms of cost and lack of account minimum—trades for firm E started at $12.95 per trade, and the fee for advisory services was a one-time $250 fee, and the pamphlet mentioned that advisory services are "only appropriate for investors with $100,000 or more in investable assets." However, all participants felt that the advisory services described in the pamphlet would be valuable to them.

Differences Between the Experienced and Inexperienced Groups

The inexperienced group noted that often they did not understand the terminology used by the financial service industry. They often felt that professionals talk over them, which causes them to feel even less knowledgeable. In such instances, people do not feel comfortable asking questions about or even talking about money, so they avoid the topic altogether. In general, they felt that financial-management issues are discussed in esoteric terms. They felt that financial information should be presented in terms of more practical concepts. Some in these groups also struggled with some basic financial distinctions, such as differences between stocks and mutual funds.

Other Comments

At the end of each focus-group session, we asked participants whether they had anything else that they wanted to discuss. Most groups cited a lack of financial knowledge across the general public as a serious problem. Some suggested that financial education should be mandatory in schools. Others suggested that, to get financial aid in college, a financial-education course should be required. They noted that many young people are entering the workforce with large amounts of debt and zero financial knowledge. Others expressed a desire for retirement accounts not tied to one's job, and others expressed concern about medical insurance after retirement.

Conclusion

Overall, we found that many survey respondents and focus-group participants do not understand key distinctions between investment advisers and broker-dealers—their duties, the titles they use, the firms for which they work, or the services they offer. Yet they tend to have relatively long-term relationships with their financial service professionals, and they expressed high

---

[11] Recall that participants in the firm interviews expressed a similar concern.

levels of satisfaction with their services. This satisfaction was often reported to arise from the personal attention the investor receives. We do not have evidence on how levels of satisfaction vary with the actual financial returns arising from this relationship. In fact, focus-group participants with investments acknowledged uncertainty about the fees they pay for their investments, and survey responses also indicate confusion about fees.

In general, the roles of broker-dealers and investment advisers are confusing to most survey respondents and focus-group participants. Answers from survey respondents and focus-group participants indicated that they have a general sense of the difference in services offered by brokers and by investment advisers but that they are not clear about their specific legal duties. Furthermore, answers indicated that respondents and participants view financial advisors and financial consultants as being more similar in terms of services and duties to investment advisers than to brokers. However, regardless of the type of service (advisory or brokerage) received from the individual professional, the most commonly cited titles are generic titles, such as advisor, financial advisor, or financial consultant. Focus-group participants shed further light on this confusion when they commented that the interchangeable titles and "we do it all" advertisements made it difficult to discern broker-dealers from investment advisers.

Survey respondents indicated that they are about equally likely to seek services or investment advice from a broker or from an investment adviser. Comments from focus-group participants may illuminate these results. Like survey respondents, focus-group participants were about equally likely to seek services from an investment adviser or a broker but for different reasons. The compensation structures, disclosure requirements, and legal duties make investment advisers appealing. However, account minimums, industry certification, and costs make brokers appealing. Even though we made attempts to explain fiduciary duty and suitability in plain language, focus-group participants struggled to understand the differences between the standards of care. Furthermore, even after explaining to them that a fiduciary duty is generally a higher standard of care, focus-group participants expressed doubt that the standards are different in practice.

Despite their confusion, however, most respondents and participants expressed satisfaction with their financial service providers. The most commonly cited reasons for survey respondens' satisfaction were the professional's attentiveness and accessibility, which were mentioned even more often than expertise. Although focus-group members also mentioned these qualities, they more often mentioned trust. Finally, respondents and participants often indicated that they recognize the value of investment advice. Those who currently receive investment advice often reported that they find the service to be valuable. Many of those who do not currently receive investment advice expressed a desire to receive these services but are concerned that their relatively low amount of investable assets makes it difficult to find these valuable services.

CHAPTER SEVEN

Conclusions

This report provides a factual description of the current state of the investment adviser and broker-dealer industries. Specifically, the report addresses two primary questions:

- What are the current business practices of broker-dealers and investment advisers?
- Do investors understand the differences between and relationships among broker-dealers and investment advisers?

Based on a large-scale empirical inquiry of the broker-dealers and investment advisers, we have characterized the current industry along a number of dimensions—including size, level of assets, clientele, nature of services and fees, and disclosures—to identify the distinctions between investment advisers and broker-dealers. We also gave special attention to the dual registrations and firm affiliations that may make it more difficult to distinguish among the services and practices of the two categories of financial professionals. For other perspectives, we examined business documents and Web sites to identify how firms present themselves to their clients and compared these documents with administrative data on file for these firms. We administered a large-scale, national household survey and conducted intensive focus-group discussions to gauge understanding of distinctions between the different types of financial service providers. We summarize our key findings in this chapter.

Our review of the regulatory and legal environment for broker-dealers and investment advisers suggests that current laws and regulations are based on distinctions between the two types of financial professionals that date back to the early 20th century and that these distinctions appear to be eroding today. Recently, the SEC attempted to clarify the boundaries between broker-dealers and investment advisers—namely in the 2005 rule, "Certain Broker-Dealers Deemed Not to Be Investment Advisers" (SEC, 2005); however, the ruling was challenged and eventually overturned. Most of the stakeholders we interviewed expressed concern that the business practices of investment advisers and broker-dealers have become increasingly similar, especially with the introduction of fee-based brokerage programs, and that investors understand little about their differences. They pointed to recent marketing practices that emphasize both types of service and the use of generic titles, such as *financial advisor* and *financial consultant*, for both types of professionals. Academic studies and media and trade reports confirm that the industry is becoming increasingly complex and intertwined and that investors do not operate with a clear understanding of the different functions and fiduciary responsibilities of their financial professionals.

To analyze whether this is indeed the case, we conducted empirical analyses to address the nature of the industry on the one hand and the nature of investor understanding on the other. Our industry analyses began with presentation of a range of descriptive statistics based on data provided in regulatory filings of thousands of investment advisers and broker-dealers. We also conducted a closer analysis of the data on firms that report offering both brokerage and advisory services or are affiliated with firms that offer the complementary service. This analysis was intended to clarify the distinctions between such firms and those that specialize solely in brokerage or advisory services.

To provide a more in-depth look at current practices in the industry, we collected and examined business documents used by selected investment advisers and broker-dealers sampled from the complete listing of firms in the administrative databases analyzed. We also conducted 34 interviews with financial professionals from brokerage firms and investment advisory firms.

To analyze what investors understand regarding the distinction between investment advisers and broker-dealers, we administered a nationwide survey with 654 respondents and conducted six intensive focus groups with 67 participants in Fort Wayne, Indiana, and Alexandria, Virginia. The household survey addresses several major topics on financial service providers, including (1) beliefs about the differences between investment advisers and broker-dealers, (2) experience with different types of financial service providers, and (3) inclination toward employing the services of investment advisers and broker-dealers. The focus-group discussions involved in-depth exploration of these topics, as well as reactions to various financial service marketing materials.

What Are the Current Business Practices of Broker-Dealers and Investment Advisers?

The nature of the administrative data made it difficult to identify the business practices of broker-dealers and investment advisers with any certainty. While the data sets to which we had access were extensive, they were often not strictly comparable. The type and extent of the disclosures made by each type of firm are exceedingly different. Therefore, direct comparisons between the industries are relatively sporadic and unsystematic. Furthermore, by comparing details across databases, we also noted many inconsistencies in the information reported. These findings suggest that many financial service professionals themselves are confused about how they should be reporting their activities.

In addition, among firms that are either dually registered or affiliated with firms that offer complementary services, the advisory and brokerage services provided are difficult to disentangle. Corporations may have multiple subsidiaries or business units, each registered separately as an investment adviser or broker-dealer, but our data do not identify these relationships. To complicate matters further, some solely registered investment advisory firms have employees who are registered representatives of a broker-dealer. Quite frequently, one such employee is the sole proprietor or founder of a small investment advisory firm.

Despite these challenges, however, the portrait of the financial service industry that emerges from the data is extremely heterogeneous in terms of firm size, services offered, activities of affiliated firms, and nearly every other dimension we examined. This variation is true of investment advisers and broker-dealers, as well as across these industries. Our analysis of about 15,000 firms from the fourth quarter of 2006 reveals that most of them were reportedly engaged, either directly or indirectly, as either an investment adviser or as a broker-dealer but not both. Many others were directly engaged in only one type of activity but were affiliated with a firm engaged in the other type. Finally, the remainder—a minority of firms—were directly engaged in both brokerage and advisory activities.

As a firm's economic scope grows, it engages (unsurprisingly) in a much fuller range of services and consequently is either affiliated with other financial service firms or conducts a significant amount of business in both the investment advisory and brokerage fields. Smaller firms, which are much more numerous, tend to provide a more limited and focused range of either investment advisory or brokerage services. Still, they frequently reported some sort of affiliation with firms providing the complementary service.

While the differences described here come through in the statistics produced based on the administrative data, it is not clear how these differences are presented to investors. What appear in the data to be affiliations between two or more registrants could be viewed by customers as a single business or as completely distinct entities.

With our business-document collection and firm interviews, we examined how these activities are portrayed to investors and what investors understand about the information they are given. Although the business-document analysis is limited by the low response rate among selected firms and partial compliance rate among responding firms, the submitted documents and documents available on the Web provide illuminating examples of the range of products and services offered by these firms, the variety of relationships among these firms, and the manner in which these alternative offerings and relationships are presented to prospective clients. If prospective clients were exposed to the documents we received and the Web sites we reviewed, they would likely obtain a very uneven understanding about these firms. In some cases, they would face a flood of information, only some of which could possibly be processed. In other cases, they receive only a trickle of information. In any case, they would likely be left to turn to individual professionals to summarize the key aspects of the prospective relationship.

The firm interviews provide supplemental information on these and other topics. Perhaps of most use are the investment advisers' and broker-dealers' perceptions of the level of investor knowledge in general and investor understanding of the differences between investment advisers and broker-dealers in particular. The concerns they typically express about regulatory burdens are frequently weighed against the recognized need to protect unsophisticated investors. Interview participants reported that investors rarely read the disclosures they provide, regardless of how digestible they make these documents. They acknowledged that their business relationships with clients are built on trust rather than investor understanding of the services and responsibilities involved and that it is crucial for the financial service industry to maintain that foundation of trust.

Do Investors Understand the Differences Between and Relationships Among Broker-Dealers and Investment Advisers?

Given the growing complexity of the financial service market, we were not surprised to find that many survey respondents and focus-group participants did not understand key distinctions between investment advisers and broker-dealers—their duties, the titles they use, the firms for which they work, or the services they offer. Yet they tended to have relatively long-term relationships with their financial service professionals, and they expressed high levels of satisfaction with their services.

In general, the roles of broker-dealers and investment advisers are confusing to most survey respondents and focus-group participants. Beliefs reported by survey respondents and focus-group participants indicated that they have a general sense of the difference in services offered by brokers and by investment advisers but that they are not clear about their specific legal duties. Furthermore, these reports indicate that respondents and participants are unclear on the role of financial professionals who use generic titles, such as *financial advisor* and *financial consultant*.

Survey respondents indicated that they are about equally likely to seek services or investment advice from a broker as from an investment adviser. Comments from focus-group participants may illuminate these results. Like survey respondents, focus-group participants were about equally likely to seek services from an investment adviser or a broker, but for different reasons. The compensation structures, disclosure requirements, and legal duties make investment advisers appealing. However, account minimums, industry certification, and costs make brokers appealing. From the firm interviews, the investment advisers themselves expressed concern that there is a population of investors with a relatively low amount of investable assets who would like investment advice but do not meet the account minimums of most investment advisory firms.

We made attempts in our focus-group discussions to explain fiduciary duty and suitability in plain language, but participants struggled to understand the differences between the standards of care. Even after explaining to them that a fiduciary duty is generally a higher standard of care, focus-group participants expressed doubt that the standards are different in practice.

Despite their confusion, most respondents and participants expressed satisfaction with their own financial service providers. This satisfaction was often reported to arise from the personal attention the investor receives. We do not have evidence on how levels of satisfaction vary with the actual financial returns arising from this relationship. In fact, focus-group participants with investments acknowledged uncertainty about the fees they pay for their investments, and survey responses also indicate confusion about fees.

Overall, we found that the industry is very heterogeneous, with the thousands of firms taking many different forms and offering many different combinations of services and products. Partly because of this diversity of business models and services, investors typically fail to distinguish broker-dealers and investment advisers along the lines defined by federal regulations. Despite their apparent confusion about titles, duties, and fees, investors expressed high levels of satisfaction with the services they receive from their own financial service providers.

Today's investment adviser and broker-dealer industries are complex, heterogeneous industries. Regulating these industries presents many challenges. We hope that the information provided in this report will contribute to this important effort.

Descriptions of Regulatory Filings, Data Sets, and Use of the Data to Identify Dual and Affiliate Activity

Investment Advisers: Form ADV Data

In March 2007, the SEC Division of Investment Management provided us with IARD data for the fourth quarter of 2006, as well as quarterly data for each quarter from the fourth quarter of 2001 through the fourth quarter of 2005. Recall from Chapter Two that regulatory disclosures by investment advisory firms are made through Form ADV, which contains two parts. Part I contains general information about the nature and size of the adviser's business and disciplinary history within the firm (pertaining to either the company or individual employees). Part II of the form contains less structured data and includes disclosures about potential conflicts of interest.

Form ADV is the Uniform Application for Investment Adviser Registration. The investment adviser uses Form ADV to (1) register with the SEC, (2) register with one or more state securities authorities, and (3) amend those registrations. See SEC (2006).

The data set we used includes almost all of the information reported in Part IA of Form ADV. Part IA data include responses to a number of questions about the adviser, its business practices, the *persons* who own and control the adviser, and the *persons* who provide investment advice on its behalf.

Requested data from Part II of Form ADV were not electronically available, nor were requested quarterly data for the years 1999 and 2000 or for the first three quarters of 2006. Data for the first three quarters of 2006 were subsequently provided in August 2007, but these data include only a subset of the Part IA information: (1) identifying information, (2) registration information, and (3) total assets under management.

For the quarters with complete data—i.e., 2001–2006, excluding the first three quarters of 2006—the data describe a total of 150,195 reports. The data set begins with 7,614 advisers in the fourth quarter of 2001. The number falls to 7,560 in the first quarter of 2002 and then increases each quarter, reaching 10,484 in the fourth quarter of 2006. The biggest year-to-year increase occurs in the fourth quarter of 2006—an increase of 1,400 observations from the fourth quarter of 2005.

As described in the 2006 *Evolution Revolution* report (Investment Adviser Association and National Regulatory Services, 2006, p. 4), much of the growth in 2006 "is attributable to new registrations pursuant to SEC rule changes requiring that certain previously unregistered hedge-fund managers register as investment advisers by February 1, 2006." And indeed, the data we received for the first quarter of 2006 include a total of 10,274 advisers, indicating that most of the increase in registrants during this one-year period did occur in the first quarter. During 2006, however, a court decision invalidated the SEC rule requiring registration of hedge funds (*Goldstein v SEC*, 371 U.S. App. D.C. 358, 2006). According to the 2007 *Evolution Revolution* report (National Regulatory Services and Investment Adviser Association, 2007), more than 700 hedge funds deregistered.

The IARD data we received pertain to firms that have applied for SEC registration. Many advisory firms complete Form ADV and register with state regulators but not the SEC and therefore are not included in these data. Eligibility for registration with the SEC is determined based on responses to items 2.A(1) through 2.A(11) on Form ADV. Among the 150,195 advisers in the database, 85 percent of the records indicate that the adviser has "assets under management of $25 million (in U.S. dollars) or more" (language from SEC, 2006). Among the remaining 23,092 adviser reports, all but 1,211 select at least one of the other eligibility criteria. Of the 1,211 that remain, 1,032 indicate that they "are no longer eligible to remain registered with the SEC." (language from SEC, 2006).

Broker-Dealers: Form BD and FOCUS Report Data

Form BD Data

In May 2007, FINRA sent us a file containing CRD data that describe Form BD information for 5,117 broker-dealers from the fourth quarter of 2006. Recall from Chapter Two that Form BD, the Uniform Application for Broker-Dealer Registration (SEC, 2007a), requires information on the broker-dealer; its business practices; persons, firm, and organizations that are controlled, controlling, or under common control; and criminal, civil, and other actions. The data we received include identifying and contact information; SEC-registration information; legal status; and information concerning business practices, business activities, and related persons.

Subsequently, in July 2007, FINRA sent us a new file containing CRD data on 5,086 broker-dealers. These data also were represented to pertain to the fourth quarter of 2006. The data include identifying and contact information, SEC-registration information, legal-status and firm-formation information, and information on business activities, as well as criminal-, regulatory-, and civil-action disclosures.

We have not been able to determine definitively why there were differences in the two data transfers. Nevertheless, the differences were rather small: Both data sets include significantly overlapping information. Identifying, registration, legal status, and business-activity information is included in both files. A total of 4,979 firms are included in both files, another 138 were included in only the file received in May, and 107 were in only the July file.

FOCUS Report Part II and Part IIA Data

In July 2007, FINRA provided us with FOCUS report data for quarterly and monthly reports from January 1999 through December 2006. The records for quarterly reports are dated March, June, September, and December. As described in Chapter Two, broker-dealers are required to file the FOCUS report either monthly or quarterly. It constitutes the basic financial and operational report required of those brokers or dealers subject to any minimum net capital requirement set forth in Rule 15c3-1 (FINRA, 2004). The report is filed with the regulatory organization designated as the examining authority for the broker or dealer.

The requirements about filing a periodic FOCUS report are articulated in SEC Rule 17a-5 (17 C.F.R. 240.17a-5), which states (in relevant part, and with emphasis provided):

a. Filing of monthly and quarterly reports.

(1) This paragraph (a) shall apply to every broker or dealer registered pursuant to section 15 of the Act.

(2) . . .

(ii) Every broker or dealer subject to this paragraph (a) who *clears transactions or carries customer accounts* shall file Part II of Form X-17A-5 within 17 business days after the end of the calendar quarter and within 17 business days after the date selected for the annual audit of financial statements where said date is other than a calendar quarter. *Certain of such brokers or dealers shall file Part IIA in lieu thereof if the nature of their business is limited* as described in the instructions to Part II of Form X-17A-5.

(iii) Every broker or dealer who *does not carry nor clear transactions nor carry customer accounts* shall file Part IIA of Form X-17A-5 within 17 business days after the end of each calendar quarter and within 17 business days after the date selected for the annual audit of financial statements where said date is other than the end of the calendar quarter.

(iv) Upon receiving written notice from the Commission or the examining authority designated pursuant to section 17(d) of the Act, *a broker or dealer who receives such notice shall file monthly,* or at such times as shall be specified, Part II or Part IIA of Form X-17A-5 and such other financial or operational information as shall be required by the Commission or the designated examining authority.

Thus, with some exceptions, the rule essentially channels clearing firms and those that carry customer accounts on their books into Part II, leaving firms that neither clear nor carry customer accounts (a category that includes many introducing brokers that originate customer contacts) to be channeled into Part IIA.[1]

As noted in Rule 17a-5 (17 C.F.R. 240.17a-5), Part II filers are generally required to file on a quarterly basis. However, Part II is filed monthly by those firms that receive written notice pursuant to Rule 17a-5(a)(2)(iv) that they have exceeded parameters set by the self-regulators. See SEC (2002).

Part IIA is also generally filed on a quarterly basis but must be filed monthly by those firms that receive written notice pursuant to Rule 17a-5(a)(2)(iv) that they have exceeded parameters set by the self-regulators.

The main sections of the FOCUS report include a statement of financial condition describing assets, liabilities, and ownership equity; computation of net capital; statement of income or loss; and computation for determination of reserve requirements. The Part II reports contain a

---

[1] Introducing brokers may deal directly with clients but then pass off all trades to a clearing broker-dealer who ultimately executes them. See, e.g., Rule 17a-5(c)(1)(i) (describing introducing brokers) (SEC, 2002). In some cases, a large corporate family systematically separates its introducing brokers from its clearing and carrying operations through different affiliates. For instance, Fidelity Investments has historically used a special vehicle, Fidelity Brokerage Services LLC, as an introducing broker. See Weiss (2007).

Other subsections of Rule 17a-5 and alternative industry sources appear to corroborate this description. See, e.g., Rule 17a-5(c) (exempting introducing brokers from the requirement of furnishing statements to the SEC so long as such introducing brokers do not hold funds or securities for their clients but are merely pass-through agents) (SEC, 2002); see also B/D Solutions Consulting (undated).

number of line items in these sections that are not included in the Part IIA reports. The Part II reports also contain several supplemental sections.

The FOCUS data we received include nearly all of the financial and operational information provided in the main sections of the FOCUS report. The main sections of the FOCUS report include a statement of financial condition describing assets, liabilities, and ownership equity; computation of net capital; statement of income or loss; and computation for determination of reserve requirements. We also received some supplemental information provided in Part II reports.

The data describe a total of 281,040 reports. The data set begins with 1,853 monthly filers in January 1999. The quarterly data begin with 5,482 reports in March 1999, with two of these reports labeled *M* (for monthly). The number of reports filed increased each quarter until it reached 5,639 in September 2000. The number decreases in 21 of the next 25 quarters, falling to 5,068 in December 2006.

Overall, about 18 percent of the data pertain to Part II reports (as opposed to Part IIA reports). However, Part II reports constitute a much smaller share of quarterly filings (when all firms submit reports) and a declining share from 1999 to 2006. For March 1999, almost 14 percent of the data pertain to Part II reports. The share fell below 11 percent in 2002 and stays in the range of 10.6 percent to 11.0 percent thereafter.

Identification of Firms Engaged in Dual or Affiliated Broker-Dealer and Investment Advisory Activity

Each of these databases contains information about either investment advisers (IARD data) or broker-dealers (CRD and FOCUS data). We used this information set to identify firms engaged in dual or affiliated investment advisory and broker-dealer activity. This task was facilitated by the fact that all three data sets use the same unique firm identifier, the CRD number, which can be used to match firms across data sets. All registered broker-dealers who complete a FOCUS report also complete Form BD. Dually registered broker-dealers also complete Form ADV. However, many of these dually registered firms are registered with state regulatory agencies but not the SEC, because the firm does not have assets under management of at least $25 million and does not meet any of the other eligibility criteria. As described in this section, we attempted to identify state-registered firms via the SEC's searchable, Web-based database (SEC, undated).

Identification Based on Dual Registration

We begin with a restrictive definition of dual activity, whereby firms are classified according to whether the CRD number appears in both the CRD database and the IARD database that we received. As shown in Table A.1, which focuses on the most recent data from each of the three data sets, we found 543 firms listed in both databases at the end of 2006, or about 10 percent of broker-dealers and 5 percent of investment advisers.

We know that this definition is overly restrictive, because broker-dealers may be state registered and not included in our IARD database. Soon after the first electronic filings were submitted to the IARD, the National Regulatory Services and the Investment Counsel Association of America issued the 2001 *Evolution Revolution* report (National Regulatory Services and Investment Counsel Association of America, 2001), which estimated that upward of two-

Table A.1
Dually Registered Firms, by Source of Dual-Registration Determination

CRD Number	All firms	CRD	IARD	SEC Web Site Match (not IARD)		
				SEC Registered	State Registered	Formerly SEC Registered
In CRD	5,224	5,224	543	26	336	8
In IARD	10,484	543	10,484	0	0	0

thirds of registered investment advisers were state registered. To identify broker-dealers who are state-registered investment advisers, we used Form BD information on investment advisory services to initiate searches in November 2007. As shown in Table A.1, we found 370 matches based on CRD number. Of these, 336 are state-registered firms, and another 26 are SEC registered. We also identified eight that we describe as formerly SEC registered, because the Web site entry states: "THIS INVESTMENT ADVISER IS NO LONGER REGISTERED WITH THE SEC AND IS NOT REQUIRED TO UPDATE ITS FORM ADV. THE INFORMATION SHOWN IS FOR HISTORICAL PURPOSES AND YOU SHOULD NOT PRESUME IT IS CURRENTLY ACCURATE" (SEC, undated). Using this information together with matches in our IARD database, we found that 17 percent of broker-dealers are (or were) dually registered.

We also attempted to find name and address matches for the 235 firms that reported investment advisory services on Form BD but were not matched based on CRD number. For many of these firms, we identified what seem to be affiliated investment advisors with distinct CRD numbers.

Note that, using this procedure, matching broker-dealers to state-registered advisers is possible only when the brokerage firm reports on Form BD that it is engaged in (or expects to be engaged in) business providing investment advisory services that account for at least 1 percent of revenue. If the broker-dealer does not make such a report, then no search was conducted. It is somewhat reassuring that 91 percent of IARD-database matches reported such a business activity; therefore, these omitted matches may be few in number.

We also conducted a complementary search protocol for investment advisory firms that reported, on Form ADV, being engaged in broker-dealer activity. Among the unmatched cases in the IARD data from the fourth quarter of 2006, 89 investment advisers reported being so engaged. We conducted a CRD-number broker search on the FINRA Web site and identified nine additional matched firms, each of which was classified as inactive. We also conducted a broker-name search, using firm name or contact-person name and address, and found another 36 matches to broker-dealers with distinct CRD numbers. We found possible matches for many of the remaining 44 firms that reported engagement in business as a broker-dealer on Form ADV.

Finally, we also took an alternative approach to identifying dually registered broker-dealers. Rather than matching CRD data to IARD data, we matched FOCUS data to IARD data. As is the case with the Form BD filings, FOCUS filers submit reports using the CRD number, which allows us to match up a FOCUS filing in any quarter with a corresponding Form ADV record in the IARD database.

Using this protocol yields a slightly smaller number of matched firms than that obtained by matching CRD and IARD data in the fourth quarter of 2006. In particular, we identified 536 of the 543 firms that were matched using CRD data instead. Though perhaps less inclusive, this alternative approach proves advantageous for our analysis of firms from 2001 to 2006, because we have both FOCUS data and IARD data throughout this period.

Identification Based Solely on Form ADV Data

The IARD data we received contain several variables that are indicative of some form of engagement in broker-dealer activity.

Item 6 requests information about other business activities of the advisory firm. The box for Item 6.A(1) should be checked if the firm is "actively engaged in a business as a . . . Broker-Dealer" (language from SEC, 2006). Our records indicate that this box was checked in 5.9 percent of the reports. Investment Adviser Association and National Regulatory Services (2006) used this variable to identify advisory firms that are dually registered as broker-dealers. As noted, 91 percent of CRD-IARD–matched firms checked this box, as do 89 percent of the firms that are not matched.

The box for Item 6.A(2) should be checked if the firm is "actively engaged in a business as a . . . Registered representative of a broker-dealer" (language from SEC, 2006). This box was checked in 8.9 percent of the reports. According to Investment Adviser Association and National Regulatory Services (2006), this box should be checked only if the firm is organized as a sole proprietorship, but only 3.4 percent of the firms in the database reported this form of organization. The 2006 report reaches the following conclusion based on this discrepancy: "Most of the advisers checking this response did not understand the question. It is likely that these other advisers have employees who are registered representatives of a broker-dealer" (Investment Adviser Association and National Regulatory Services, 2006, p. 19).

In fact, we conducted broker-name and -address searches on the FINRA Web site to determine the manner in which these investment advisory firms are related to broker-dealers. First, we searched for 74 sole proprietorships that reported on Form ADV that (1) they work with individual clients and (2) they are engaged in business as a registered representative of a broker-dealer. We found that 69 of these sole proprietors are registered representatives of some other firm, typically a large firm (e.g., Cambridge Investment Research, Raymond James Financial Services) with a matching business address reported on the Web site. We did not definitively identify the other five individuals.

Second, we searched for a random sample of 78 (out of 784) firms other than sole proprietorships that reported on Form ADV that (1) they work with individual clients and (2) they are engaged in business as a registered representative of a broker-dealer. The results here are strikingly similar to the results for sole proprietorships but for the fact that searches based on contact name were less successful. Rather, we often needed to conduct searches using the name of the firm's founder or other leading executive whom we found listed on the firm's Web site. In the end, we found broker-name and business-address matches for 58 (out of 78 possible) individuals working as registered representatives of some other firm with a distinct CRD number. We identified another 12 individuals working for some other firm at a different address in the same city. We did not definitively locate a broker from any of the remaining eight firms in our random sample. However, these findings indicate that, as is the case with sole proprietorships, the great majority of these 784 investment advisory firms are led by individuals engaged as broker-dealers at the same physical address.

A final source of Form ADV information on broker-dealer activity concerns activity by affiliates. Item 7 requests information about related persons, who are defined as "all of your *advisory affiliates* and any *person* that is under common *control* with you" (SEC, 2006). The box for Item 7.A(1) should be checked if the firm has "a *related person* that is a . . . broker-dealer, municipal securities dealer, or government securities broker or dealer" (SEC, 2006). Our records indicate that this box was checked in almost one-quarter of the reports.

Identification Based Solely on Form BD Data

The CRD data we received contain two variables that are indicative of possible engagement in investment advisory activity. The clearest indicator comes from item 12, which requests information about all business activities of the broker-dealer other than any "category that accounts for (or is expected to account for) less than 1% of annual revenue from the securities or investment advisory business" (SEC, 2006). The category for item 12.S reads "Investment advisory services" (SEC, 2006). Our records indicate that this box was checked in more than 20 percent of the reports.

In addition, item 10.A asks: "Directly or indirectly, does *applicant control*, is *applicant controlled* by, or is *applicant* under common *control* with, any partnership, corporation, or other organization that is engaged in the securities or investment advisory business?" (SEC, 2006). Our records indicate that the "Yes" response box was checked in more than 40 percent of the reports. Note that these reported affiliations do not distinguish between investment advisory and securities affiliates. This distinction is made in explanations of responses reported in Schedule D of Form BD; however, we did not receive data describing these responses.

Identification Based Solely on FOCUS Data

The FOCUS report data contain one variable that is indicative of possible engagement in investment advisory activity. The income or loss statement includes the following line item (field 3975): "Fees for account supervision, investment advisory and administrative services" (SEC, 2002). The field 3975 instructions for Part IIA filers are as follows:

> Report fees for services to individual and corporate customers. The amount to be included as administrative services, however, shall be limited to fees charged to investment companies and periodic payment plans and other than investment advisory services. (SEC, 2002)

Part II filers are not given specific instructions for this line item.

According to a FINRA executive, fees for account supervision may include wrap fees, and fees for administrative services may include, for example, annual account fees and inactivity fees. This field may also include 12b-1 fees,[2] but such fees may instead be included in a preceding line on the FOCUS report: "Revenue from sale of investment company shares" (SEC, 2002).

According to our records, 14 percent of reports include a nonzero entry for field 3975, 22 percent are zero, and the remaining 64 percent have nothing entered. Reports of zero indicate no revenue from investment advisory services. Nonzero reports indicate that the firm may have received such revenue. It is not clear how to interpret the missing values. As noted in the analy-

---

[2]   These 12b-1 fees are paid by mutual fund out of fund assets to cover distribution expenses and, sometimes, shareholder service expenses. They are named for the SEC rule that authorizes a fund to pay them.

sis of the FOCUS data, much revenue seems to be excluded from the itemized reports, being reported instead only in the "Total revenue" line item (field 4030) (SEC, 2002).

Other Retail Providers of Financial Services

Mutual Fund Direct Purchase

A leading investor-protection advocate argues that most small investors could act without brokers, using no-load mutual funds, and they would be better off using fee-only financial advisors (Smith, 2003). Bergstresser, Chalmers, and Tufano (2006) assessed the costs and benefits of brokers to individual investors in the mutual fund industry. They quantified the benefits investors enjoy in exchange for the higher costs they incur when buying funds through the broker channel, and they found no substantial, tangible benefits to investors. For instance, distribution fees and loads are higher for brokered funds than for direct funds. They also calculated that the underperformance (lower, risk-adjusted returns) of brokered funds implies a cost to investors of $5.5 billion per year for equity funds, $3.3 billion for bond funds, and $120 million for money-market funds. They concluded that any benefits from fund brokerage must be along less tangible dimensions, nonetheless raising the question of whether fund-distribution channels at all improve the welfare of households.[1]

According to the Investment Company Institute (2005), the share of funds acquired via professional financial advisors declined from 90 percent to 58 percent between 1970 and 2003, but they still function as the dominant channel for investors. The balance is made up of direct fund purchases, retirement-plan contributions, and discount-broker purchases. Purchases through discount brokers or "mutual fund supermarkets" have emerged as a category in 2000 that held a 7 percent share as of 2003. Direct fund purchases, while jumping from 10 percent in 1970 to 28 percent in 1980, came back to 15 percent as of 2003. Purchase behavior does not seem to vary by age, experience with mutual fund investing, or asset size. However, the extent of adviser use declines with formal education.

Services by Banks

With the passage of the Financial Modernization Act of 1999 (P.L. 106-102), banks have become more involved in the financial service industry (Al Mamun, Hassan, and Lai, 2004;

---

[1] They focused on the following measurable potential benefits to fund consumers: (1) assistance in selecting funds that are harder to find or evaluate, (2) access to lower-cost funds, (3) access to higher-performance funds, (4) superior asset allocation via tailoring fund choices, and (5) attenuation of behavioral investor biases. They analyzed a sample of roughly 10,400 share classes in about 4,500 funds with total assets of $3.8 trillion from 1996 to 2002 with biennial intervals. Brokered distribution is the dominant form, accounting for 66 percent of the funds and 53 percent of the assets. In terms of costs, their calculations indicate $15.2 billion in loads and 12b-1 fees (in addition to internal fund costs of $23.8 billion) in 2002.

Alexander, Jones, and Nigro, 2001). For example, banks may offer proprietary mutual funds directly to customers or proprietary funds through unaffiliated distributors. In fact, most large banks offer brokerage services (Kehrer and Houston, 2003).

Commenting on the bank acquisitions of regional brokerage firms in 2000, Kehrer (2001) noted a catalyzing factor: the downturn in the stock market that softened prices of brokerage operations to very attractive levels. However, even without the more attractive prices, acquiring a brokerage operation has many advantages. Bank-owned brokerage firms have much higher profit margins than do nonbank brokerage firms (28 percent versus 14 percent, pretax, as of 1999). A bank-owned brokerage firm has ready access to existing clients, which lowers marketing costs, and, due to easy customer access, representatives are paid less, which lowers compensation costs. Bank-owned brokerage firms also focus on higher-margin products, such as annuities and funds, as opposed to stocks and bonds. Moreover, the bank-owned brokerage firm is reported to offer a narrower product selection with less research, all of which reduces expenses. The article notes that the major contribution of a brokerage operation to a bank comes from leveraging existing sales forces, customers, and assets. Kehrer drew attention to a common model, in which the bank's own brokers focus on middle-market retail customers and the acquired brokerage firm's representatives target a more affluent clientele. While sales forces and brands might be separate, back offices are typically consolidated.

The Financial Modernization Act (P.L. 106-102) also allowed brokerage firms to do business within banks. Some recent examples illustrate the trend: A major financial holding company started putting offices of its brokerage subsidiary inside the branches of its commercial-banking subsidiary in 2006; a large financial conglomerate opened an office in New York City, combining brokerage and banking services for ultra-HNW clients in 2006; in the branches of another major national bank, the securities subsidiary of the bank has branches, but they are segregated from the teller lines. In 2005, 23 local banks around the nation signed up to have representatives of a large brokerage firm located in their branches (Pessin, 2006a).

Services by Accountants

A 2002 survey of 1,685 CPAs found that 17 percent of CPAs offered investment services to clients and that 49 percent planned to do so before 2005 (Bowen, 2002). It is not clear from the report whether such CPAs are also registered as investment advisers or are partnering with investment advisers for investment services. CPAs saw the provision of such services as a component of better client service. A definite majority, 61 percent, cited competitive pressure as a reason and perceived investment services as an opportunity to tap into a new market. The article also notes that, in "almost all surveys of wealthy investors," CPAs obtain the highest rank in terms of trust.

APPENDIX C

Attributes of Investment Advisers and Broker-Dealers

Table C.1
Attributes of Investment Advisers

Adviser Attribute	Form ADV Item	All Advisory Firms (10,484 observations) (%)	Advisory Firms with Individuals as Clients (%)			
			All (7,395 observations)	No HNW Clients (197 observations)	Only HNW Clients (1,244 observations)	Both HNW and non-HNW (5,954 observations)
Form of organization						
Corporation	3A	50.5	57.2	53.3	43.5	60.2
LLC	3A	38.1	33.7	31.5	46.7	31.0
LLP	3A	1.3	0.8	1.0	0.9	0.8
Partnership	3A	4.1	2.4	1.0	4.6	1.9
Sole proprietorship	3A	3.4	4.6	9.6	1.7	5.0
All employees						
1 to 10	5A	49.6	54.4	58.9	41.5	57.0
11 to 50	5A	19.7	19.4	10.2	21.0	19.4
51 to 100	5A	21.5	18.3	15.7	25.9	16.7
101 to 250	5A	6.5	5.3	10.2	9.6	4.2
251 to 500	5A	1.0	0.9	2.0	1.0	0.9
501 to 1,000	5A	0.7	0.7	2.0	0.6	0.7
>1,000	5A	0.9	0.9	0.5	0.4	1.1
Employees who perform investment advisory functions						
0	5B1	1.7	1.3	4.6	1.0	1.2
1 to 10	5B1	65.7	70.5	66.0	59.7	72.9
11 to 50	5B1	15.0	13.7	10.2	18.6	12.8
51 to 100	5B1	13.3	10.3	10.7	16.2	9.0
101 to 250	5B1	3.3	2.9	7.1	4.3	2.5
251 to 500	5B1	0.5	0.6	0.0	0.2	0.7

Table C.1—Continued

Adviser Attribute	Form ADV Item	All Advisory Firms (10,484 observations) (%)	Advisory Firms with Individuals as Clients (%)			
			All (7,395 observations)	No HNW Clients (197 observations)	Only HNW Clients (1,244 observations)	Both HNW and non-HNW (5,954 observations)
501 to 1,000	5B1	0.2	0.3	0.5	0.0	0.4
>1,000	5B1	0.3	0.4	0.5	0.0	0.5
Employees who are registered representatives of a broker-dealer						
0	5B2	63.9	61.9	64.0	72.0	59.8
1 to 10	5B2	22.8	23.9	19.8	17.1	25.4
11 to 50	5B2	4.9	4.9	5.1	3.6	5.1
51 to 100	5B2	5.3	5.5	5.6	5.5	5.5
101 to 250	5B2	1.9	2.3	3.6	1.4	2.4
251 to 500	5B2	0.5	0.6	1.0	0.2	0.7
501 to 1,000	5B2	0.3	0.3	0.5	0.0	0.4
>1,000	5B2	0.5	0.6	0.5	0.2	0.7
Compensation						
Assets under management	5E1	95.4	97.2	87.3	95.0	98.0
Hourly	5E2	32.8	43.6	27.9	14.0	50.3
Subscription	5E3	1.7	1.7	4.1	1.2	1.7
Fixed	5E4	40.4	49.8	42.6	32.2	53.7
Commissions	5E5	9.5	12.9	13.2	4.0	14.7
Performance	5E6	32.7	20.4	17.8	51.3	14.0
Other	5E7	9.7	8.9	12.2	9.5	8.7
Assets under management						
Supervision or management of securities portfolios	5F1	96.0	97.8	86.8	95.8	98.6
Advisory activities						
Financial planning	5G1	35.8	49.2	25.5	16.5	56.8
Portfolio management for individuals or small businesses	5G2	71.3	94.4	79.6	82.9	97.3
Portfolio management for investment companies	5G3	13.6	10.7	20.8	21.5	8.1

Table C.1—Continued

Adviser Attribute	Form ADV Item	All Advisory Firms (10,484 observations) (%)	Advisory Firms with Individuals as Clients (%)			
			All (7,395 observations)	No HNW Clients (197 observations)	Only HNW Clients (1,244 observations)	Both HNW and non-HNW (5,954 observations)
Pension consulting	5G5	15.4	18.2	23.4	10.9	19.6
Publication of periodical or newsletters	5G7	6.8	8.5	9.6	4.9	9.2
Sponsor wrap-fee program	5I1	4.4	6.0	3.6	1.8	6.9
Portfolio management for wrap-fee program	5I2	10.0	13.6	6.6	12.6	14.1
Other business activities						
Broker-dealer	6A1	5.9	7.4	11.7	3.5	8.0
Registered representative of broker-dealer	6A2	8.9	11.8	9.6	2.6	13.9
Futures-commission merchant, commodity-pool operator, or commodity-trading advisor	6A3	4.4	2.6	3.6	7.4	1.6
Real-estate broker, dealer, or agent	6A4	0.8	0.9	1.5	0.6	0.9
Insurance broker or agent	6A5	11.8	16.3	12.2	1.8	19.4
Bank	6A6	0.5	0.6	1.5	0.2	0.6
Sell products or provide services other than investment advice to advisory clients	6B3	24.4	30.3	30.5	13.9	33.7
Affiliations						
Broker-dealer, municipal-securities dealer, or government-securities broker-dealer	7A1	25.7	22.4	29.9	26.7	21.3

Table C.1—Continued

Adviser Attribute	Form ADV Item	All Advisory Firms (10,484 observations) (%)	Advisory Firms with Individuals as Clients (%)			
			All (7,395 observations)	No HNW Clients (197 observations)	Only HNW Clients (1,244 observations)	Both HNW and non-HNW (5,954 observations)
Investment company (including mutual funds)	7A2	15.2	11.2	22.4	18.6	9.3
Other investment adviser (including financial planner)	7A3	32.5	24.6	35.2	34.2	22.3
Futures-commission merchant, commodity-pool operator, or commodity-trading advisor	7A4	9.6	5.5	8.1	12.2	4.0
Banking or thrift institution	7A5	11.2	8.9	16.2	13.5	7.7
Insurance company or agency	7A8	17.2	17.4	21.3	10.9	18.6
Pension consultant	7A9	6.0	5.3	7.6	5.1	5.3
Real-estate broker or dealer	7A10	5.3	3.8	4.1	5.0	3.6
Sponsor or syndicate of limited partnership	7A11	14.3	9.5	10.7	18.6	7.5
Discretion						
Determine broker-dealer for client-account transactions	8C3	67.2	60.7	56.3	78.9	57.1
Recommend broker-dealer to clients	8D	68.1	77.7	55.3	58.8	82.3
Receive nonexecution products or services from broker-dealer	8E	59.5	59.8	43.7	62.9	59.6

Table C.1—Continued

Adviser Attribute	Form ADV Item	All Advisory Firms (10,484 observations) (%)	Advisory Firms with Individuals as Clients (%)			
			All (7,395 observations)	No HNW Clients (197 observations)	Only HNW Clients (1,244 observations)	Both HNW and non-HNW (5,954 observations)
Custody						
Related persons have custody of client cash or bank account	9B1	20.3	14.7	9.1	20.9	13.6
Related persons have custody of client securities	9B2	19.6	13.9	8.6	19.8	12.9
Related person with custody is a registered broker-dealer	9C	3.4	3.1	2.5	2.8	3.1
Registration						
SEC registered	2A1–2A11	99.0	99.1	95.4	99.4	99.1
$25 million in assets as a basis for SEC registration	2A1	87.5	92.6	66.5	87.9	94.4
Foreign registration	1L	7.7	4.8	9.7	13.0	3.0
Clientele						
Individuals: no HNW	5D1, 5D2	1.9	2.7	100.0	0.0	0.0
Individuals: only HNW	5D1, 5D2	11.9	16.8	0.0	100.0	0.0
Individuals: HNW and non-HNW	5D1, 5D2	56.8	80.5	0.0	0.0	100.0
No individuals	5D1, 5D2	29.5	0.0	0.0	0.0	0.0
Possible hedge fund						
Yes	5D6, 7B	27.4	15.9	12.2	41.2	10.8

SOURCE: IARD data from fourth quarter of 2006.

Table C.2
Attributes of Investment Advisers, by Indicators of Dual Activity

Adviser Attribute	Form ADV Item	Dually Registered (478 advisers) (%)	Reportedly Engaged as Broker-Dealer (75 advisers) (%)	Registered Representative (798 advisers) (%)	Affiliated Activity (1,051 advisers) (%)	Neither Dual nor Affiliated (4,993 advisers) (%)
Form of organization						
Corporation	3A	79.3	74.7	62.3	55.4	54.4
LLC	3A	17.6	14.7	26.7	36.5	36.0
LLP	3A	0.2	0.0	0.9	0.1	1.0
Partnership	3A	2.3	2.7	1.1	4.3	2.2
Sole proprietorship	3A	0.4	5.3	8.6	0.2	5.2
All employees						
1 to 10	5A	15.9	52.0	65.2	23.0	63.0
11 to 50	5A	11.7	14.7	21.4	16.5	20.5
51 to 100	5A	31.0	25.3	11.9	34.4	14.5
101 to 250	5A	18.8	4.0	1.4	19.4	1.7
251 to 500	5A	5.2	0.0	0.0	3.8	0.1
501 to 1,000	5A	6.1	1.3	0.1	1.7	0.1
>1,000	5A	11.3	1.3	0.0	1.1	0.0
Employees who perform investment advisory functions						
0	5B1	1.0	1.3	1.9	1.0	1.2
1 to 10	5B1	30.1	69.3	78.8	37.0	80.1
11 to 50	5B1	12.8	12.0	13.2	19.5	12.7
51 to 100	5B1	25.7	13.3	5.4	28.7	5.6
101 to 250	5B1	13.8	1.3	0.8	12.0	0.4
251 to 500	5B1	6.5	0.0	0.0	1.2	0.0
501 to 1,000	5B1	4.4	0.0	0.0	0.4	0.0
>1,000	5B1	5.6	1.3	0.0	0.2	0.0
Employees who are registered representatives of a broker-dealer						
0	5B2	0.6	5.3	2.4	21.8	86.6
1 to 10	5B2	23.4	66.7	80.8	39.2	11.0
11 to 50	5B2	12.8	12.0	10.8	12.2	1.5
51 to 100	5B2	26.4	13.3	5.4	17.7	0.8
101 to 250	5B2	17.6	1.3	0.6	7.2	0.1
251 to 500	5B2	6.5	0.0	0.0	1.1	0.0

Table C.2—Continued

Adviser Attribute	Form ADV Item	Dually Registered (478 advisers) (%)	Reportedly Engaged as Broker-Dealer (75 advisers) (%)	Registered Representative (798 advisers) (%)	Affiliated Activity (1,051 advisers) (%)	Neither Dual nor Affiliated (4,993 advisers) (%)
501 to 1,000	5B2	4.8	0.0	0.0	0.2	0.0
>1,000	5B2	7.9	1.3	0.0	0.6	0.0
Compensation						
Assets under management	5E1	97.3	96.0	97.7	97.5	97.1
Hourly	5E2	45.8	41.3	66.5	29.0	42.8
Subscription	5E3	1.0	2.7	1.8	2.4	1.6
Fixed	5E4	55.6	42.7	59.9	47.5	48.3
Commissions	5E5	50.4	36.0	47.7	9.9	4.0
Performance	5E6	12.3	25.3	8.4	38.5	19.1
Other	5E7	14.0	5.3	9.1	13.6	7.5
Assets under management						
Supervision or management of securities portfolios	5F1	96.2	97.3	98.7	97.0	98.0
Advisory activities						
Financial planning	5G1	62.1	50.0	78.8	32.9	46.7
Portfolio management for individuals or small businesses	5G2	92.1	91.9	96.6	90.9	95.1
Portfolio management for investment companies	5G3	6.7	16.0	4.5	32.1	7.5
Pension consulting	5G5	24.1	20.0	30.1	18.6	15.7
Publication of periodical or newsletters	5G7	8.6	9.3	10.5	8.8	8.1
Sponsor wrap-fee program	5I1	40.8	10.8	5.3	10.3	1.7
Portfolio management for wrap-fee program	5I2	26.8	12.2	7.9	29.8	9.9
Other business activities						
Broker-dealer	6A1	98.3	100.0	0.0	0.0	0.0

Table C.2—Continued

Adviser Attribute	Form ADV Item	Dually Registered (478 advisers) (%)	Reportedly Engaged as Broker-Dealer (75 advisers) (%)	Registered Representative (798 advisers) (%)	Affiliated Activity (1,051 advisers) (%)	Neither Dual nor Affiliated (4,993 advisers) (%)
Registered representative of broker-dealer	6A2	8.2	52.0	100.0	0.0	0.0
Futures-commission merchant, commodity-pool operator, or commodity-trading advisor	6A3	7.9	4.0	0.5	6.5	1.6
Real-estate broker, dealer, or agent	6A4	0.6	8.0	3.6	0.4	0.4
Insurance broker or agent	6A5	50.0	40.0	73.8	2.9	6.3
Bank	6A6	0.6	2.7	1.0	1.3	0.3
Sell products or provide services other than investment advice to advisory clients	6B3	73.6	48.0	66.7	24.0	21.4
Affiliations						
Broker-dealer, municipal-securities dealer, or government-securities broker-dealer	7A1	59.8	82.7	32.5	100.0	0.0
Investment company (including mutual funds)	7A2	28.0	17.6	3.8	42.2	4.2
Other investment adviser (including financial planner)	7A3	53.1	25.7	26.1	64.4	13.3
Futures-commission merchant, commodity-pool operator, or commodity-trading advisor	7A4	13.4	5.3	1.9	24.5	1.3
Banking or thrift institution	7A5	29.1	12.0	3.9	34.1	2.4

Table C.2—Continued

Adviser Attribute	Form ADV Item	Dually Registered (478 advisers) (%)	Reportedly Engaged as Broker-Dealer (75 advisers) (%)	Registered Representative (798 advisers) (%)	Affiliated Activity (1,051 advisers) (%)	Neither Dual nor Affiliated (4,993 advisers) (%)
Insurance company or agency	7A8	51.0	33.3	27.4	48.0	5.9
Pension consultant	7A9	14.2	5.3	7.4	13.8	2.3
Real-estate broker or dealer	7A10	8.8	12.0	3.9	10.8	1.8
Sponsor or syndicate of limited partnership	7A11	20.5	10.7	3.8	34.0	4.1
Discretion						
Determine broker-dealer for client-account transactions	8C3	56.7	68.0	37.1	76.0	61.6
Recommend broker-dealer to clients	8D	72.6	73.3	78.4	75.3	78.6
Receive nonexecution products or services from broker-dealer	8E	39.3	38.7	44.6	65.7	63.2
Custody						
Related persons have custody of client cash or bank account	9B1	22.6	6.7	7.5	33.8	11.3
Related persons have custody of client securities	9B2	19.9	6.7	6.6	33.6	10.5
Related person with custody is a registered broker-dealer	9C	10.3	1.3	3.9	13.8	0.0
Registration						
SEC registered	2A1–2A11	99.2	96.0	98.5	99.3	99.1
$25 million in assets as a basis for SEC registration	2A1	89.7	78.7	94.2	90.8	93.2
Foreign registration	1L	6.3	12.2	0.5	14.7	3.2

Table C.2—Continued

Adviser Attribute	Form ADV Item	Dually Registered (478 advisers) (%)	Reportedly Engaged as Broker-Dealer (75 advisers) (%)	Registered Representative (798 advisers) (%)	Affiliated Activity (1,051 advisers) (%)	Neither Dual nor Affiliated (4,993 advisers) (%)
Clientele						
Individuals: no HNW	5D1, 5D2	3.8	8.0	1.9	3.5	2.4
Individuals: only HNW	5D1, 5D2	7.1	17.3	3.5	28.0	17.5
Individuals: HNW and non-HNW	5D1, 5D2	89.1	74.7	94.6	68.5	80.1
No individuals	5D1, 5D2	0.0	0.0	0.0	0.0	0.0
Possible hedge fund						
Yes	5D6, 7B	12.6	10.7	5.3	33.7	14.3

SOURCE: IARD data are from fourth quarter of 2006. Dual registration was determined by match in IARD and CRD data.

Table C.3
Attributes of Broker-Dealers

Broker-Dealer Attribute	Form BD Item	FOCUS Field	All Broker-Dealers with Form BD Available (5,224 broker-dealers) (%)	All Broker-Dealers with Form BD or FOCUS Report Available (%)			
				Form BD and Part IIA (4,463 broker-dealers)	Form BD and Part II (544 broker-dealers)	Form BD Only (217 broker-dealers)	FOCUS Report Only (61 broker-dealers)
Form of organization							
Corporation	3A		63.0	62.9	69.7	48.4	—
LLC	3A		32.3	32.5	23.7	49.3	—
Partnership	3A		3.1	2.9	5.3	1.8	—
Sole proprietorship	3A		0.7	0.8	0.4	0.0	—
Other	3A		0.9	1.0	0.9	0.5	—
Carrying, clearing, and introducing							
Hold or maintain funds or securities or clear for another broker-dealer[a]	6		2.8	0.6	19.7	7.1	—
Refer or introduce customers to another broker-dealer[a]	7		47.3	48.4	40.6	39.3	—

Table C.3—Continued

Broker-Dealer Attribute	Form BD Item	FOCUS Field	All Broker-Dealers with Form BD Available (5,224 broker-dealers) (%)	All Broker-Dealers with Form BD or FOCUS Report Available (%)			
				Form BD and Part IIA (4,463 broker-dealers)	Form BD and Part II (544 broker-dealers)	Form BD Only (217 broker-dealers)	FOCUS Report Only (61 broker-dealers)
Customer accounts, funds, or securities held or maintained by other person, firm, or organization[a]	8C		37.9	38.6	30.9	42.0	—
FOCUS Part IIA report available		Form	85.4	100.0	0.0	0.0	100.0
FOCUS Part II report available		Form	10.4	0.0	100.0	0.0	0.0
Carry own customer accounts[b]	40, 41		6.2	0.6	52.4	0.0	—
Business activities							
Exchange member engaged in exchange commission business other than floor activities	12A		2.9	1.1	14.0	12.0	—
Exchange member engaged in floor activities	12B		5.1	2.3	25.0	13.8	—
Broker or dealer making interdealer markets in corporate securities over the counter	12C		7.4	5.6	22.6	5.5	—
Broker or dealer retailing corporate-equity securities over the counter	12D		50.2	49.0	66.0	36.4	—
Broker or dealer selling corporate-debt securities	12E		40.8	39.1	60.1	25.8	—

Table C.3—Continued

Broker-Dealer Attribute	Form BD Item	FOCUS Field	All Broker-Dealers with Form BD Available (5,224 broker-dealers) (%)	All Broker-Dealers with Form BD or FOCUS Report Available (%)			
				Form BD and Part IIA (4,463 broker-dealers)	Form BD and Part II (544 broker-dealers)	Form BD Only (217 broker-dealers)	FOCUS Report Only (61 broker-dealers)
Underwriter or selling-group participant (corporate securities other than mutual funds)	12F		23.5	21.3	45.6	15.2	—
Mutual fund underwriter or sponsor	12G		6.4	5.9	11.4	2.8	—
Mutual fund retailer	12H		52.0	54.0	44.3	29.0	—
U.S. government–securities dealer	12I.1		9.4	6.8	31.1	8.3	—
U.S. government–securities broker	12I.2		32.8	31.5	47.4	24.9	—
Municipal-securities dealer	12J		13.0	10.7	34.9	5.5	—
Municipal-securities broker	12K		34.3	33.8	45.2	18.0	—
Broker or dealer selling variable life insurance or annuities	12L		35.6	37.6	26.3	19.4	—
Solicitor of time deposits in a financial institution	12M		8.1	7.3	15.4	4.1	—
Real-estate syndicator	12N		3.4	3.7	1.5	0.9	—
Broker or dealer selling oil and gas interests	12O		6.7	7.3	3.5	3.2	—
Put-and-call broker or dealer or option writer	12P		31.1	30.5	39.2	23.5	—

Table C.3—Continued

Broker-Dealer Attribute	Form BD Item	FOCUS Field	All Broker-Dealers with Form BD Available (5,224 broker-dealers) (%)	All Broker-Dealers with Form BD or FOCUS Report Available (%)			
				Form BD and Part IIA (4,463 broker-dealers)	Form BD and Part II (544 broker-dealers)	Form BD Only (217 broker-dealers)	FOCUS Report Only (61 broker-dealers)
Selling securities of only one issuer or associate issuers (other than mutual funds)	12Q		1.4	1.4	1.7	0.9	—
Selling securities of nonprofit organizations (e.g., churches, hospitals)	12R		2.3	1.6	8.3	0.9	—
Investment advisory services	12S		21.1	20.8	27.9	8.8	—
Selling tax shelters or limited partnerships in primary distributions	12T.1		20.9	22.3	11.8	16.6	—
Selling tax shelters or limited partnerships in the secondary market	12T.2		4.5	4.1	6.6	5.5	—
Non–exchange member arranging for transactions in listed securities by member	12U		27.0	27.4	26.3	21.2	—
Trading securities for own account	12V		20.1	17.2	46.1	13.4	—
Private placements of securities	12W		49.9	50.3	46.0	52.5	—
Selling interests in mortgages or other receivables	12X		5.9	4.7	17.1	4.1	—

Table C.3—Continued

Broker-Dealer Attribute	Form BD Item	FOCUS Field	All Broker-Dealers with Form BD Available (5,224 broker-dealers) (%)	All Broker-Dealers with Form BD or FOCUS Report Available (%)			
				Form BD and Part IIA (4,463 broker-dealers)	Form BD and Part II (544 broker-dealers)	Form BD Only (217 broker-dealers)	FOCUS Report Only (61 broker-dealers)
Networking, kiosk, or similar arrangement with bank, saving bank or association, or credit union	12Y.1		5.1	4.6	10.3	1.8	—
Networking, kiosk, or similar arrangement with insurance company or agency	12Y.2		2.1	1.9	4.8	0.0	—
Affiliations							
Control, controlled by, or under common control with another engaged in securities or investment advisory business[a]	10A		41.3	37.7	69.3	49.1	—
Control, controlled by, or under common control with bank[a]	10B		7.7	5.1	28.7	9.8	—
Registration							
Registered as broker-dealer under §15(b)[c]	2A		96.9	96.8	97.8	96.3	—
Registered under §15(b) and government-securities broker[c]	2B		0.2	0.0	0.4	4.0	—
Registered solely as government-securities broker under §15(c)[d]	2C		34.8	32.8	54.3	22.7	—

Table C.3—Continued

SOURCE: Part II, Part IIA, and carrying or clearing data are from FOCUS reports from fourth quarter of 2006. All other attributes are from CRD from the fourth quarter of 2006.

[a] Data available for 5,117 broker-dealers.

[b] Data available for 5,068 broker-dealers.

[c] This refers to §15(b) of the Securities Exchange Act of 1934 (48 Stat. 881), which deals with municipal securities.

[d] This refers to §15(c) of the Securities Exchange Act of 1934 (48 Stat. 881), which deals with government-securities brokers and dealers.

Table C.4
Summary Statistics for FOCUS Filers

Characteristic	Reporting	All Filers ($ thousands)		Part II Filers ($ thousands)		Part IIA Filers ($ thousands)	
		Mean	Standard Deviation	Mean	Standard Deviation	Mean	Standard Deviation
Total population of firms	5,068	5,068	—	544	—	4,524	—
Assets							
Cash	5,068	4,917	81,900	37,900	247,000	956	5,359
Total assets	5,068	1,080,000	16,800,000	9,880,000	50,500,000	24,300	412,000
Ownership equity							
Sole-proprietor equity	297	172	832	27	170	262	1,040
Partnership: limited-partnership equity	1,432	21,300	190,000	89,200	397,000	11,100	132,000
Total corporate equity	5,068	26,500	319,000	216,000	944,000	3,680	45,800
Total ownership equity	5,068	32,500	334,000	246,000	966,000	6,736	82,900
Commissions							
On exchange transactions	1,915	2,281	16,300	11,600	39,100	595	4,189
On OTC transactions	229	2,900	8,874	3,074	9,109	—	—
On listed options	1,150	462	2,825	1,834	5,745	154	1,368
On all other securities	2,413	2,507	12,300	10,200	27,600	1,236	6,273
Total commissions	5,068	2,337	18,200	15,000	51,800	810	5,400

Table C.4—Continued

Characteristic	Reporting	All Filers ($ thousands)		Part II Filers ($ thousands)		Part IIA Filers ($ thousands)	
		Mean	Standard Deviation	Mean	Standard Deviation	Mean	Standard Deviation
Other revenues							
Fees from account supervision or investment advisory and administrative services	1,349	5,678	41,300	24,500	95,400	1,852	11,000
Revenue from research services	134	506	4,352	560	4,578	—	—
Total revenue	5,068	23,000	307,000	183,000	919,000	3,738	21,800
Expenses							
Clerical or administrative employees' expenses	439	22,400	109,000	23,000	110,000	—	—
Registered representative's compensation	424	22,400	86,400	23,100	87,600	—	—
Salaries and other employment costs for general partners and voting stockholder officers	2,050	493	3,246	1,368	5,824	387	2,761
Total expenses	5,068	20,700	281,000	166,000	844,000	3,240	18,600
Income							
Income before federal taxes	5,068	2,214	30,000	16,500	87,600	498	7,570
Income after federal income tax and extraordinary items	5,068	1,811	23,500	12,800	67,600	490	7,394
Monthly income	5,068	697	11,400	5,235	33,300	151	3,042
Reserve requirements							
Total credits	557	875,000	5,830,000	896,000	5,900,000	—	—
Aggregate debit items	557	618,000	4,200,000	633,000	4,250,000	—	—
Total §15(c)(c)(3) debits[a]	557	599,000	4,070,000	614,000	4,120,000	—	—

Table C.4—Continued

SOURCE: Financial data are from FOCUS reports for the fourth quarter of 2006. All other attributes are from CRD data for the same quarter.

[a] This refers to §15(c)(c)(3) of the Securities Exchange Act of 1934 (48 Stat. 881), which deals with certain sanctions for violations for not registering as a government-securities broker when needed.

Table C.5
Probit Analysis of Criminal, SEC, Other Regulatory, SRO, Civil, or Pending Legal Enforcement

Characteristic	Coefficient					
	Criminal	SEC	Other Regulatory	SRO	Civil	Pending
Part II	0.42563	0.2614	0.19432	0.13593	0.4844	0.44295
	0.001	*0.001*	*0.005*	*0.062*	*0*	*0*
Total revenues	1.4E-09	1.2E-09	−3E-10	1.8E-08	2.5E-09	−7E-10
	0.524	*0.663*	*0.906*	*0.006*	*0.286*	*0.699*
Total expenses	−1E-09	1.2E-08	1.6E-08	1.1E-09	−2E-09	1.5E-09
	0.579	*0*	*0*	*0.879*	*0.506*	*0.458*
Firm age	−0.0102	0.01815	0.01986	0.02629	0.01103	0.00179
	0.026	*0*	*0*	*0*	*0*	*0.457*
Cash	−1E-09	3.8E-09	−6E-10	2.2E-08	5.5E-09	−2E-10
	0.273	*0.026*	*0.725*	*0*	*0*	*0.644*
Total assets	1.8E-12	−9E-12	−8E-12	1.7E-11	3.7E-12	−4E-12
	0.731	*0.024*	*0.033*	*0.498*	*0.324*	*0.235*
Exchange member, nonfloor activities	−0.0835	0.33866	0.12909	0.114	0.19765	0.37109
	0.747	*0.009*	*0.283*	*0.392*	*0.217*	*0.008*
Exchange member, floor activities	0.3923	0.21523	−0.0028	0.48125	−0.083	0.04805
	0.175	*0.228*	*0.987*	*0.013*	*0.694*	*0.795*
Interdealer market maker	0.34121	0.17186	0.35998	0.66738	0.02669	0.29112
	0.028	*0.067*	*0*	*0*	*0.828*	*0.003*

Table C.5—Continued

Characteristic	Coefficient					
	Criminal	SEC	Other Regulatory	SRO	Civil	Pending
Retailing corporate securities over the counter	-0.1823	-0.103	0.34677	0.60536	-0.2552	-0.1723
	0.144	*0.105*	*0*	*0*	*0.002*	*0.023*
Non-exchange member arranging transactions	0.05137	0.0836	0.03784	-0.0237	0.1469	0.23704
	0.697	*0.216*	*0.472*	*0.647*	*0.098*	*0.002*
Investment advisory services	0.21673	0.00027	0.18996	0.05293	0.2151	0.14369
	0.06	*0.997*	*0*	*0.29*	*0.006*	*0.042*
Constant	-2.1327	-1.6546	-1.2963	-1.0719	-1.9697	-1.7084
	0	*0*	*0*	*0*	*0*	*0*
N	4,931	4,931	4,931	4,931	4,931	4,931
Log likelihood	-366.64	-1,510.6	-2,523.9	-2,789	-845.33	-1,098.4
Pseudo r-squared	0.066	0.1726	0.1309	0.1713	0.135	0.0643

SOURCE: Financial data are from FOCUS reports from the fourth quarter of 2006. All other attributes are from CRD for the same quarter.

NOTE: Coefficient estimates in shaded cells are statistically different from 0 at the 5 percent significance level. Numbers in italics are p-values.

Table C.6
Attributes of Broker-Dealers, by Indicators of Dual Activity

Broker-Dealer Attribute	Form BD Item	FOCUS Field	Dually Registered (Database Match) (543 broker-dealers) (%)	Dually Registered (Web-Site Match) (370 broker-dealers) (%)	Reportedly Engaged as Investment Adviser (235 broker-dealers) (%)	Affiliated Activity (1,656 broker-dealers) (%)	Neither Dual Nor Affiliated Activity (2,420 broker-dealers) (%)
Form of organization							
Corporation	3A		78.5	78.4	74.9	58.3	59.2
LLC	3A		18.0	17.3	19.1	36.4	36.3
Partnership	3A		2.8	2.2	2.1	4.1	2.7
Sole proprietorship	3A		0.2	1.6	3.4	0.0	0.9
Other	3A		0.6	0.5	0.4	1.2	1.0
Carrying, clearing, and introducing							
Hold or maintain funds or securities or clear for another broker-dealer[a]	6		9.4	2.5	0.9	3.9	0.6
Refer or introduce customers to another broker-dealer[a]	7		68.5	73.2	56.5	46.0	38.3
Customer accounts, funds, or securities held or maintained by another person, firm, or organization[a]	8C		59.1	62.0	47.0	36.8	28.9
FOCUS Part IIA report available		Form	75.3	92.4	91.5	81.5	88.8
FOCUS Part II report available		Form	23.4	5.1	6.4	15.8	5.0
Carry own customer accounts[b]		40, 41	15.5	2.5	5.2	8.4	3.2
Business activities							
Exchange member engaged in exchange commission business other than floor activities	12A		6.8	1.1	0.4	3.8	1.9

Table C.6—Continued

Broker-Dealer Attribute	Form BD Item	FOCUS Field	Dually Registered (Database Match) (543 broker-dealers) (%)	Dually Registered (Web-Site Match) (370 broker-dealers) (%)	Reportedly Engaged as Investment Adviser (235 broker-dealers) (%)	Affiliated Activity (1,656 broker-dealers) (%)	Neither Dual Nor Affiliated Activity (2,420 broker-dealers) (%)
Exchange member engaged in floor activities	12B		14.2	3.5	1.7	6.0	3.1
Broker or dealer making interdealer markets in corporate securities over the counter	12C		14.5	9.5	10.6	7.5	5.0
Broker or dealer retailing corporate-equity securities over the counter	12D		78.1	81.6	64.7	47.3	39.7
Broker or dealer selling corporate-debt securities	12E		70.0	71.4	55.3	39.2	29.2
Underwriter or selling-group participant (corporate securities other than mutual funds)	12F		37.8	35.4	37.0	23.0	17.6
Mutual fund underwriter or sponsor	12G		12.9	1.1	7.7	13.4	0.7
Mutual fund retailer	12H		81.4	91.6	66.8	47.9	40.6
U.S. government–securities dealer	12I.1		23.8	13.8	16.6	8.6	5.4
U.S. government–securities broker	12I.2		61.0	61.4	49.4	32.1	21.1
Municipal-securities dealer	12J		32.4	21.6	22.6	10.3	8.3
Municipal-securities broker	12K		72.9	70.3	52.3	29.3	21.9

Table C.6—Continued

Broker-Dealer Attribute	Form BD Item	FOCUS Field	Dually Registered (Database Match) (543 broker-dealers) (%)	Dually Registered (Web-Site Match) (370 broker-dealers) (%)	Reportedly Engaged as Investment Adviser (235 broker-dealers) (%)	Affiliated Activity (1,656 broker-dealers) (%)	Neither Dual Nor Affiliated Activity (2,420 broker-dealers) (%)
Broker or dealer selling variable life insurance or annuities	12L		70.9	78.6	48.5	32.5	22.0
Solicitor of time deposits in a financial institution	12M		22.7	21.4	14.5	6.2	3.4
Real-estate syndicator	12N		4.1	5.1	3.8	2.2	3.8
Broker or dealer selling oil and gas interests	12O		14.2	9.5	8.1	4.7	5.9
Put-and-call broker or dealer or option writer	12P		56.2	55.7	41.3	27.9	22.9
Selling securities of only one issuer or associate issuers (other than mutual funds)	12Q		1.1	1.1	0.9	2.0	1.2
Selling securities of nonprofit organizations (e.g., churches, hospitals)	12R		7.4	4.1	5.1	1.3	1.2
Investment advisory services	12S		91.3	100.0	100.0	0.0	0.0
Selling tax shelters or limited partnerships in primary distributions	12T.1		33.3	30.0	23.8	17.1	19.1
Selling tax shelters or limited partnerships in the secondary market	12T.2		14.2	9.2	6.0	2.8	2.6

Table C.6—Continued

Broker-Dealer Attribute	Form BD Item	FOCUS Field	Dually Registered (Database Match) (543 broker-dealers) (%)	Dually Registered (Web-Site Match) (370 broker-dealers) (%)	Reportedly Engaged as Investment Adviser (235 broker-dealers) (%)	Affiliated Activity (1,656 broker-dealers) (%)	Neither Dual Nor Affiliated Activity (2,420 broker-dealers) (%)
Non–exchange member arranging for transactions in listed securities by member	12U		33.5	40.0	33.6	29.6	21.2
Trading securities for own account	12V		32.0	22.2	25.5	22.3	15.0
Private placements of securities	12W		47.0	42.2	57.4	45.8	53.9
Selling interests in mortgages or other receivables	12X		15.3	9.7	8.9	5.7	3.1
Networking, kiosk, or similar arrangement with bank, saving bank or association, or credit union	12Y.1		19.2	15.7	6.0	3.5	1.3
Networking, kiosk, or similar arrangement with insurance company or agency	12Y.2		9.9	4.3	3.0	1.4	0.3
Affiliations							
Control, controlled by, or under common control with another engaged in securities or investment advisory business[a]	10A		54.0	17.2	43.1	100.0	0.0
Control, controlled by, or under common control with bank[a]	10B		16.2	9.8	8.6	12.6	1.8
Registration							
Registered as broker-dealer under §15(b)	2A		99.3	97.8	94.5	97.1	96.2

Table C.6—Continued

Broker-Dealer Attribute	Form BD Item	FOCUS Field	Dually Registered (Database Match) (543 broker-dealers) (%)	Dually Registered (Web-Site Match) (370 broker-dealers) (%)	Reportedly Engaged as Investment Adviser (235 broker-dealers) (%)	Affiliated Activity (1,656 broker-dealers) (%)	Neither Dual Nor Affiliated Activity (2,420 broker-dealers) (%)
Registered under §15(b) and government-securities broker	2B		0.0	0.0	0.0	0.4	0.0
Registered solely as government-securities broker under §15(c)	2C		66.1	61.5	50.9	34.1	22.5

SOURCES: Part II, Part IIA, and carrying or clearing data are from FOCUS reports from the fourth quarter of 2006. All other attributes are from CRD for the same quarter. Database-matched dual registrations are determined from match in IARD and CRD data. Web-based dual registrations are determined from match in SEC Web site and CRD data.

[a] Data are available for 5,117 broker-dealers.

[b] Data are available for 5,068 broker-dealers.

Additional Detail on Sampling Method of Document Collection

Document Collection and Review

We originally set a target of 75 firms from which to collect and examine business documents. We designed a sampling scheme to achieve a balance between broker-dealers and investment advisers. We oversampled the largest firms that dominate the market with respect to total accounts and account holdings, but we also sought to include a sufficient number of broker-dealers and investment advisers randomly sampled from the thousands of other firms of each type.

The documents we sought were marketing and sales documents (e.g., brochures, flyers) advertising the firm itself, its range of services, or individual products; regulatory documents (e.g., disclosure statements, disclaimers) required by federal and state regulators and SROs; account-based documents (e.g., application forms, account agreements, transaction confirmations, account statements); and interfirm agreements and contracts among investment advisers, broker-dealers, and other financial institutions, such as mutual fund managers.

Sampling Methods

In June 2007, we used the available administrative data to select a stratified sample of investment advisers and broker-dealers for solicitation of business documents. Our selection process for the recipient firms followed a two-step procedure. First, we stratified based on whether the firm is registered as an investment adviser or as a broker-dealer. Note that the dually registered firms with individual advisory clients are listed in both databases.

Second, we chose to oversample from among the more dominant firms in the market. At the time of sample selection, we did not yet have data on total capitalization from the FOCUS reports. However, the *Expanded Securities Industry DataBank* (see SIFMA, undated[a]) includes a quarterly report of the largest 25 brokerage firms, ostensibly based on net capitalization as measured in the FOCUS report. We used these rankings to identify the registered broker-dealers that appear in the list any time from the fourth quarter of 2001 through the fourth quarter of 2006 and selected those that were included in the CRD database in the fourth quarter of 2006. We used an analogous procedure for investment advisers. In particular, we drew on the IARD data to identify the top 25 firms each quarter according to assets under management, on a quarterly basis, since 2001. These large firms were sampled with probability 1. To reach the target of 75 total firms, accounting for potential nonresponse and ineligibility, the remaining firms in each database were sampled at a rate of almost 1 percent, yielding a sample size of 164. This total includes two large, dually registered firms included in both the sample of investment advisers and the sample of broker-dealers.

Request Letters

A copy of the document-request letter sent to advisory firms is included in Figure D.1. Cover letters sent to brokerage firms were the same, except that the first sentence in the second paragraph read: "As a part of the effort to assess current practices in the industry we would like to collect and examine business documents used in conjunction with your retail *brokerage* services" (emphasis added). Figures D.2 and D.3 are sample checklists that were included in document requests to investment advisory firms and brokerage firms, respectively.

The principal investigator sent the letters via Federal Express to individual contact persons whose names were provided by FINRA (registered broker-dealers) or included in the IARD database (investment advisers). The principal investigator and RAND survey staff made more than 300 follow-up phone calls. Additional calls were also made both to solicit participation in the firm interviews and to prompt nonrespondents to submit business documents. Multiple email messages were also sent to most firms to remind them about the study and notify them of forthcoming contact attempts.

In addition, a second Federal Express package was sent to 47 nonresponding firms and 27 firms that were classified as giving a soft refusal.[1] This follow-up package included prepaid Federal Express return packaging accompanied by a letter from the office of the SEC chair, stressing the importance of participating in the study, as well as a new document-request letter from the principal investigator of the study that included this supplemental statement: "We understand that not all firms will have all of the items on this list, but we would appreciate you sending us what materials you have, even if this is just a new client package."

Follow-up telephone discussions and messages also included scaled-back requests of this type. These contact attempts were discontinued 12 weeks after the first letters were sent.

Response Rate

Despite our numerous attempts via multiple contact methods to recruit these firms to participate in this study, we received documents from only 29 sampled firms deemed eligible to participate in the study, and most of these submissions complied only partially with our requests. Initially, we received documents from 33 firms. However, four of these firms do not work directly with individual U.S. investors and were therefore not eligible for the study. The 29 eligible firms include 18 from the sample of investment advisers and 11 from the sample of broker-dealers. (Two firms were included in both samples.)

This limited participation greatly limits our ability to extrapolate findings from the submitted sample of documents. To supplement the documentary evidence, we conducted thorough reviews of the Web sites maintained by these 29 responding firms as well as another 34 sampled firms that both maintain a public Web site and were deemed eligible to participate in the study. Almost all of the remaining firms from the original list of 164 do not maintain public Web sites or were determined to be ineligible for the study because they do not work directly with individual investors or are no longer in business as registered in the fourth quarter of 2006.

---

[1] We characterized a refusal as soft if the respondent refused but did not give a concrete reason for refusal and did not express adamant refusal.

Figure D.1
Sample Cover Letter Sent to Investment Advisory Firms for Business-Document Collection

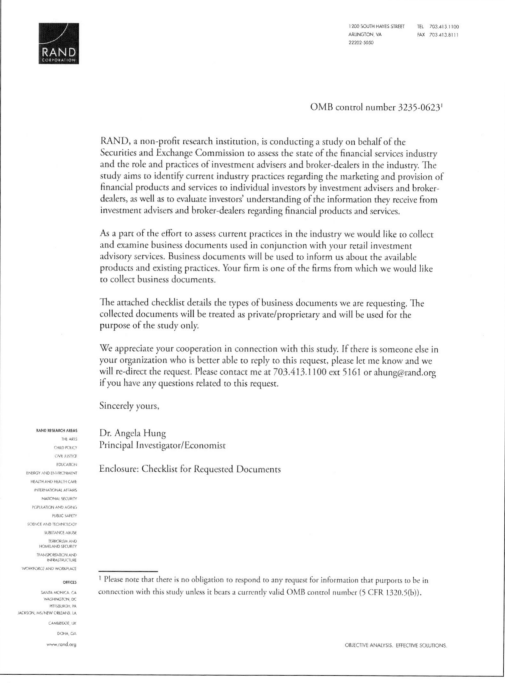

Among the 131 firms that did not send documents, 48 firms refused to participate, 21 firms never responded to numerous contact efforts, nine firms were determined to be no longer in business and thus ineligible, and an additional 53 firms were labeled as ineligible because they do not work directly with individual U.S. investors. We discovered that these firms were ineligible via follow-up calls and by examining firm Web sites.

Figure D.2
Sample Checklist Enclosed in Investment Advisory Document-Request Letter

OMB control number 3235-0623[1]

The RAND Corporation Study: Checklist for Requested Documents

Name of Firm: _____   Contact Person: _____

Firm Address: _____   Phone Number: _____

_____   Email: _____

_____

	Included in package	Item does not exist	If item exists, but it is not included in package, please provide reason.
General marketing brochures for your firm	☐	☐	
Brochures for **investment advisory** services and products	☐	☐	
Print advertisements in media	☐	☐	
Video recordings of television advertisements	☐	☐	
Examples of business cards for registered **investment advisers**	☐	☐	
Examples of business cards for any other person at the firm who comes into direct contact with individual investors	☐	☐	
Pricing schedules (fees, commissions, minimums, various charges)	☐	☐	
Disclosure statements, disclaimers and prospectuses that are typically provided to **investment advisory** clients	☐	☐	
Account application form	☐	☐	
Account agreement	☐	☐	
Sample account statement for **advisory** clients	☐	☐	
Sample trade confirmation forms	☐	☐	
Sample bills or invoices to clients	☐	☐	
Contracts or agreements between your firm and other financial service providers such as mutual fund companies or **brokerage firms**	☐	☐	
Examples of contracts or agreements between your firm and affiliated firms	☐	☐	
Examples of contracts or agreements between your firm and affiliated independent professionals.	☐	☐	
Examples of contracts or agreements between your firm and employed investment professionals	☐	☐	
Supervisory and compliance manuals	☐	☐	
Training material for associated persons of **investment advisers** relating to the marketing, sale and delivery of financial products, accounts, programs and services to individual investors	☐	☐	

[1] Please note that there is no obligation to respond to any request for information that purports to be in connection with this study unless it bears a currently valid OMB control number (5 CFR 1320.5(b)).

Among the 57 total ineligible firms deemed ineligible because they do not directly work with individual investors,[2] 26 are investment advisers and had reported on Form ADV that

---

[2] Recall that four firms that sent documents and 53 firms that did not send documents were deemed ineligible because they do not work with individual clients, giving us a total of 57 firms that were deemed ineligible on the basis of not work-

Figure D.3
Sample Checklist Enclosed in Broker-Dealer Document-Request Letter

OMB control number 3235-0623[1]

The RAND Corporation Study: Checklist for Requested Documents

Name of Firm: _____ Contact Person: _____

Firm Address: _____ Phone Number: _____

_____ Email: _____

_____

	Included in package	Item does not exist	If item exists, but it is not included in package, please provide reason.
General marketing brochures for your firm	☐	☐	
Brochures for **brokerage** services and products	☐	☐	
Print advertisements in media	☐	☐	
Video recordings of television advertisements	☐	☐	
Examples of business cards for registered representatives.	☐	☐	
Examples of business cards for any other person at the firm who comes into direct contact with individual investors	☐	☐	
Pricing schedules (fees, commissions, minimums, various charges)	☐	☐	
Disclosure statements, disclaimers and prospectuses that are typically provided to **brokerage** clients	☐	☐	
Account application form	☐	☐	
Account agreement	☐	☐	
Sample account statement for **brokerage** clients	☐	☐	
Sample trade confirmation forms	☐	☐	
Sample bills or invoices to clients	☐	☐	
Contracts or agreements between your firm and other financial service providers such as mutual fund companies or **investment adviser firms**	☐	☐	
Examples of contracts or agreements between your firm and affiliated firms	☐	☐	
Examples of contracts or agreements between your firm and affiliated independent professionals.	☐	☐	
Examples of contracts or agreements between your firm and employed investment professionals	☐	☐	
Supervisory and compliance manuals	☐	☐	
Training material for associated persons of **broker dealers** relating to the marketing, sale and delivery of financial products, accounts, programs and services to individual investors	☐	☐	

---

[1] Please note that there is no obligation to respond to any request for information that purports to be in connection with this study unless it bears a currently valid OMB control number (5 CFR 1320.5(b)).

RAND *TR556-D.3*

individuals are among their clientele. Follow-up phone calls to these firms revealed that any work with individual investors occurs either indirectly (e.g., investors purchase the funds that they manage) or is restricted to extremely wealthy individuals who are institutional in size.

---

ing with individual clients.

After excluding the total of 66 ineligible firms,[3] the mailed-document response rate is just 29/98. However, when supplemented with Web-data collection from another 34 firms, the effective response rate is 64 percent.

Nonresponding or Ineligible Firms

Among the 131 firms that did not send documents, 48 firms refused to participate, 21 firms never responded to numerous contact efforts, nine firms were determined to be no longer in business and thus ineligible, and an additional 53 firms were labeled as ineligible because they do not work directly with individual U.S. investors. We discovered that these firms were ineligible via follow-up calls and by examining firm Web sites.

Among the 57 total ineligible firms deemed ineligible because they do not directly work with individual investors,[4] 26 are investment advisers and had reported on Form ADV that individuals are among their clientele. Follow-up phone calls to these firms revealed that any work with individual investors occurs either indirectly (e.g., investors purchase the funds that they manage) or is restricted to extremely wealthy individuals who are institutional in size.

Types of Documents Received

The 29 eligible firms that complied with the request submitted documents varying in number, size, range of topics covered, and complexity. All documents were reviewed by RAND staff members who completed a document-collection data form for each firm. Data were recorded for the following topics: documents returned, company background, clients, services and products, disclosures, affiliations, online accounts, modes of access, fees and commissions, account and product specifications, employees, and marketing material. The data form concludes with a section in which other important or clarifying text may be added.

As described in Table D.1, we received 158 sets of documents corresponding to the document categories we requested. Multiple documents were included in most sets. Every individual document in every set was reviewed for data extraction and further analysis. Firms that offer more than one product and service could submit marketing and sales documents and account-based documents separately for each product or service. For instance, one large firm made an electronic submission that included almost 100 separate brochures, 34 print advertisements, and 16 different disclosure documents. Another large firm also submitted hundreds of electronic documents.

About half the firms submitted such documents as account-application forms and agreements, pricing schedules, disclosure statements, and examples of business cards for investment professionals. Broker-dealers in our sample were more likely to send marketing and sales documents. Investment advisers were more likely to submit samples of account-based documents.

The submitted packages varied significantly in the number and size of the documents. Large firms tended to make the most voluminous submissions. Smaller companies often submitted fewer than ten documents.

---

[3] The final tally of ineligible firms consists of 57 firms that do not work with individual clients and nine firms that no longer exist.

[4] Recall that four firms that sent documents and 53 firms that did not send documents were deemed ineligible as they do not work with individual clients, giving us a total of 57 firms that were deemed ineligible on the basis of not working with individual clients.

Table D.1
Types of Documents Submitted

Document Type	Investment Advisory Firms Submitting	Brokerage Firms Submitting
Any	18	11
General marketing brochures	5	8
Brochures for specific products	5	7
Print ads in media	1	4
Video recordings of TV ads	1	4
Examples of business cards for investment professionals	8	7
Examples of business cards for other personnel	2	6
Pricing schedules	9	7
Disclosure statements	8	8
Account-application form	4	6
Account agreement	10	7
Sample account statement	8	7
Sample trade-confirmation forms	5	7
Sample bills or invoices to clients	7	3
Contracts or agreements between firm and other parties	0	5
Examples of contracts or agreements between firm and affiliated firms	1	5
Examples of contracts or agreements between firm and affiliated independent professionals	2	5
Supervisory and compliance manuals	3	4
Training materials	1	5

Web-Site Document Collection

As previously mentioned, we supplemented the mailed-document collection efforts by recording publicly available information from firm Web sites. Web-data collection was attempted for 80 firms from the original sample, including the 33 firms that submitted documents and 47 firms that did not. In total, Web sites were found for 73 firms, but 12 of these firms were deemed to be ineligible because they do not work with individual investors. Of the 33 firms that submitted documents, four firms do not work with individual investors, and two did not maintain a Web site. Of the 47 firms that did not submit documents, five did not maintain Web sites, and eight were ineligible for the study (seven firms do not work with individual investors and one firm no longer exists). The 61 eligible firms with Web sites include 36 from the sample of investment advisers and 25 from the sample of broker-dealers. We reviewed approximately 1,000 pages on these Web sites and recorded data using a nearly identical protocol to that used for the business documents submitted by mail.

Representativeness of the Sample

The breakdown of firms from which we collected data, either from submitted documents or from Web sites, is presented in Table D.2.

Although our sampling scheme was designed to select a sample that is representative of the population of brokerage and investment advisory firms conditional on the stratification variables (investment adviser or broker-dealer, large or other), with such a small number of total firms, random sampling within strata can yield a sample that does not appear to be representative. Standard statistical tests indicate that our random samples of (not large) broker-dealers and investment advisers would appear to be representative of the larger population if analyzed by a researcher who was unaware of the actual sampling process.

Of more concern may be the effects of the stratification based on firm size with respect to dual registration. All of the large brokerage firms in our sample are registered with the SEC as investment advisers, whereas only about 10 percent of the broker-dealer population is SEC registered as an investment adviser. Further, 20 percent of the large investment advisory firms in our sample are registered broker-dealers and included in our CRD database. This latter share is more comparable to, but still much greater than, the 6 percent of all investment advisory firms that are dually registered in the CRD.

Finally, when the response rate is relatively low, one must be cautious before extrapolating from sample statistics to the population from which it was drawn. We therefore focus more attention on what we can learn about the firms on which we obtained information, noting that these firms cover a wide range of the attributes described with the population data analyzed in Chapter Four.

Table D.2
Eligible Firms with Submitted or Web Document Data

Firm Type	Large Firms	Other Firms
Investment adviser	10	28
Broker-dealer	13	12

Disclosures by Type and Information Source

Table E.1
Disclosure by Type and Source

Type of Disclosure	Broker-Dealers			Investment Advisers		
	All	Large	Other	All	Large	Other
Total	25	13	12	38	10	28
Disclosure types that appear in the general marketing brochure						
Differences between investment advisers and broker-dealers	5	5	0	2	2	0
Conflicts of interest	2	2	0	3	2	1
Compensation structure	3	2	1	3	2	1
Code of ethics or fiduciary oath	2	2	0	2	1	1
Client duties and responsibilities	1	1	0	1	1	0
Client rights	2	2	0	2	2	0
Future performance	5	5	0	2	1	1
Disclosure types that appear in the product brochure						
Differences between investment advisers and broker-dealers	5	5	0	1	1	0
Conflicts of interest	6	6	0	1	1	0
Compensation structure	7	7	0	2	1	1
Code of ethics or fiduciary oath	4	4	0	2	2	0
Client duties and responsibilities	5	5	0	2	2	0
Client rights	3	3	0	3	3	0
Future performance	5	5	0	1	1	0
Disclosure types that appear in the print advertisement						
Differences between investment advisers and broker-dealers	2	2	0	0	0	0
Conflicts of interest	0	0	0	0	0	0
Compensation structure	0	0	0	0	0	0

Table E.1—Continued

Type of Disclosure	Broker-Dealers			Investment Advisers		
	All	Large	Other	All	Large	Other
Code of ethics or fiduciary oath	7	7	0	7	3	4
Client duties and responsibilities	0	0	0	0	0	0
Client rights	0	0	0	0	0	0
Future performance	0	0	0	0	0	0
Disclosure types that appear in the account agreement						
Differences between investment advisers and broker-dealers	8	8	0	3	2	1
Conflicts of interest	9	9	0	4	2	2
Compensation structure	8	8	0	6	2	4
Code of ethics or fiduciary oath	7	7	0	7	3	4
Client duties and responsibilities	9	9	0	14	4	10
Client rights	7	7	0	9	4	5
Future performance	4	4	0	4	1	3
Disclosure types that appear in the pricing schedule						
Differences between investment advisers and broker-dealers	0	0	0	0	0	0
Conflicts of interest	1	1	0	1	1	0
Compensation structure	1	1	0	0	0	0
Code of ethics or fiduciary oath	0	0	0	0	0	0
Client duties and responsibilities	0	0	0	0	0	0
Client rights	0	0	0	0	0	0
Future performance	0	0	0	0	0	0
Disclosure types that appear in the separate disclosure document						
Differences between investment advisers and broker-dealers	6	6	0	3	3	0
Conflicts of interest	8	8	0	5	3	2
Compensation structure	9	8	1	2	2	0
Code of ethics or fiduciary oath	4	4	0	4	3	1
Client duties and responsibilities	6	5	1	3	2	1
Client rights	6	6	0	4	4	0
Future performance	5	5	0	2	1	1
Disclosure types that appear on the Web site						
Differences between investment advisers and broker-dealers	5	5	0	4	2	2

Table E.1—Continued

Type of Disclosure	Broker-Dealers			Investment Advisers		
	All	Large	Other	All	Large	Other
Conflicts of interest	6	5	1	5	1	4
Compensation structure	9	6	3	5	0	5
Code of ethics or fiduciary oath	6	6	0	7	3	4
Client duties and responsibilities	8	5	3	7	5	2
Client rights	7	5	2	3	3	0
Future performance	13	7	6	8	4	4
Total disclosures found in all sources						
Differences between investment advisers and broker-dealers	31	31	0	13	10	3
Conflicts of interest	32	31	1	19	10	9
Compensation structure	37	32	5	18	7	11
Code of ethics or fiduciary oath	30	30	0	29	15	14
Client duties and responsibilities	29	25	4	27	14	13
Client rights	25	23	2	21	16	5
Future performance	32	26	6	17	8	9

American Life Panel

The ALP is an Internet panel of more than 1,000 respondents aged 18 and older. The survey is administered by the RAND Roybal Center for Financial Decision Making, which is supported by the National Institute on Aging. Respondents in the panel either use their own computer to log on to the Internet or a WebTV (now MSN TV®) device, which allows them to access the Internet using their television and a telephone line. The technology allows respondents who did not have previous Internet access to participate in the panel and furthermore use the Internet appliances for browsing the Web or using email.

About once a month, respondents receive an email with a request to visit the ALP URL and fill out questionnaires on the Internet. Typically, an interview will not take more than 30 minutes. Respondents are paid an incentive of about $20 per 30 minutes of interviewing (and proportionately less if an interview is shorter).

The respondents in the ALP are recruited from among individuals aged 18 and older who are respondents to the monthly survey of the SRC. Responses to the monthly survey are used to produce the widely reported Index of Consumer Sentiment and the Index of Consumer Expectations, the latter of which is a component of U.S. Department of Commerce's Index of Leading Economic Indicators. Each month, SRC staff interview approximately 500 households, of which 300 households are a random-digit-dial (RDD) sample and 200 are re-interviewed from the RDD sample surveyed six months previously.

SRC screens monthly survey respondents. It asks those aged 18 or older whether they have Internet access and, if yes, whether they would be willing to participate in Internet surveys (with approximate response categories "no, certainly not," "probably not," "maybe," "probably," "yes, definitely"). If the response category is anything other than "no, certainly not," respondents are told that the University of Michigan is undertaking a joint project with RAND. They are asked whether they would object to SRC sharing their information about them with RAND so that they could be contacted later and asked whether they would be willing to participate in an Internet survey.

Members of the ALP tend to have more education and income than the broader U.S. population. There are two main reasons for this sample selection. First, the monthly survey respondents, among whom the members of the ALP are recruited, tend to have more education than the population at large. Second, the majority of ALP members have their own Internet access. Americans with Internet access tend to have more education and income than the broader population.

Detailed Results of Household Survey and Focus Groups

Table G.1
Beliefs About Financial Service Professionals

Respondent Characteristic	Investment Advisers (%)	Brokers (%)	Financial Advisors or Consultants (%)	Financial Planners (%)	None (%)	Observations
What types of financial service providers provide advice about securities (e.g., shares of stocks or mutual funds) as part of their regular business?						
Age						
40 and older	79	63	77	61	3	536
Younger than 40	83	66	82	73	4	116
Education						
College degree or more	82	68	81	68	2	337
No college degree	77	58	75	57	3	315
Household income						
At least $75,000	82	69	80	64	1	290
Less than $75,000	78	59	77	62	4	357
Region						
Northeast	83	65	83	62	2	142
Midwest	80	67	79	64	1	148
West	80	56	76	66	3	119
South	77	63	75	62	5	242
Investment experience						
Experienced	82	68	80	66	2	434
Inexperienced	74	54	74	58	5	217
Uses financial service provider						
Yes	82	70	82	67	1	307

Table G.1—Continued

Respondent Characteristic	Investment Advisers (%)	Brokers (%)	Financial Advisors or Consultants (%)	Financial Planners (%)	None (%)	Observations
No	78	58	74	59	5	341

What types of financial service providers execute stock or mutual fund transactions on the client's behalf?

Age						
40 and older	29	90	28	22	3	536
Younger than 40	27	84	30	26	7	116
Education						
College degree or more	27	91	27	21	3	337
No college degree	31	87	30	25	4	315
Household income						
At least $75,000	24	91	28	22	3	290
Less than $75,000	32	87	29	24	4	357
Region						
Northeast	27	95	25	20	1	142
Midwest	34	85	30	26	3	148
West	24	87	29	19	5	119
South	29	88	29	24	4	242
Investment experience						
Experienced	32	90	32	24	3	434
Inexperienced	24	86	21	21	4	217
Uses financial service provider						
Yes	32	91	35	24	2	307
No	26	88	22	22	5	341

What types of financial service providers recommend specific investments?

Age						
40 and older	83	53	72	50	1	535
Younger than 40	84	40	72	47	4	116
Education						
College degree or more	85	56	74	53	1	337
No college degree	82	45	69	47	3	314

Table G.1—Continued

Respondent Characteristic	Investment Advisers (%)	Brokers (%)	Financial Advisors or Consultants (%)	Financial Planners (%)	None (%)	Observations
Household income						
At least $75,000	84	56	73	54	1	289
Less than $75,000	83	47	71	47	3	357
Region						
Northeast	87	54	72	49	1	142
Midwest	84	50	72	51	2	147
West	82	54	75	50	3	119
South	81	49	70	49	2	242
Investment experience						
Experienced	85	57	76	55	1	434
Inexperienced	79	38	64	39	4	216
Uses financial service provider						
Yes	88	59	77	57	0	307
No	79	43	68	43	4	341
What types of financial service providers provide retirement planning?						
Age						
40 and older	51	13	81	92	2	535
Younger than 40	47	10	78	89	3	116
Education						
College degree or more	51	12	86	93	2	337
No college degree	50	12	74	89	3	314
Household income						
At least $75,000	51	12	83	93	2	289
Less than $75,000	51	12	78	90	3	357
Region						
Northeast	52	15	79	89	3	142
Midwest	52	7	87	93	2	147
West	42	12	78	92	2	119
South	52	13	78	92	2	242

Table G.1—Continued

Respondent Characteristic	Investment Advisers (%)	Brokers (%)	Financial Advisors or Consultants (%)	Financial Planners (%)	None (%)	Observations
Investment experience						
Experienced	55	15	83	93	2	434
Inexperienced	41	6	74	89	3	216
Uses financial service provider						
Yes	55	16	87	93	2	307
No	47	8	74	91	3	341
What types of financial service providers provide general financial planning?						
Age						
40 and older	44	15	82	89	1	535
Younger than 40	31	7	70	86	3	116
Education						
College degree or more	44	13	83	91	1	337
No college degree	40	13	77	86	2	314
Household income						
At least $75,000	39	11	86	90	1	289
Less than $75,000	45	15	75	87	2	357
Region						
Northeast	45	13	85	92	1	142
Midwest	44	16	77	88	1	147
West	38	8	83	86	1	119
South	41	14	77	87	2	242
Investment experience						
Experienced	46	15	86	90	1	434
Inexperienced	34	10	68	84	2	216
Uses financial service provider						
Yes	49	17	86	91	1	307
No	35	10	74	86	2	341

Table G.1—Continued

Respondent Characteristic	Investment Advisers (%)	Brokers (%)	Financial Advisors or Consultants (%)	Financial Planners (%)	None (%)	Observations
What types of financial service providers typically receive commissions on purchases or trades that the client makes?						
Age						
40 and older	43	96	33	22	1	535
Younger than 40	40	94	39	24	3	116
Education						
College degree or more	42	96	36	21	1	337
No college degree	43	95	33	24	2	314
Household income						
At least $75,000	46	98	39	25	1	289
Less than $75,000	40	94	31	20	2	357
Region						
Northeast	38	98	39	20	1	142
Midwest	43	95	32	20	1	147
West	50	96	34	22	1	119
South	41	95	33	25	2	242
Investment experience						
Experienced	45	96	39	24	1	434
Inexperienced	38	95	26	19	2	216
Uses financial service provider						
Yes	49	96	42	26	1	307
No	38	96	28	19	2	341
What types of financial service providers are typically paid based on the amount of assets that the client holds?						
Age						
40 and older	49	38	51	34	12	534
Younger than 40	51	48	47	34	9	116
Education						
College degree or more	54	35	57	37	10	337
No college degree	44	45	43	30	14	313

Table G.1—Continued

Respondent Characteristic	Investment Advisers (%)	Brokers (%)	Financial Advisors or Consultants (%)	Financial Planners (%)	None (%)	Observations
Household income						
At least $75,000	57	35	61	37	9	289
Less than $75,000	43	44	42	31	14	356
Region						
Northeast	57	39	58	37	11	142
Midwest	45	40	41	27	17	147
West	53	39	53	36	8	118
South	46	40	49	35	10	242
Investment experience						
Experienced	56	36	59	39	9	433
Inexperienced	37	48	33	25	16	216
Uses financial service provider						
Yes	58	39	62	36	8	306
No	42	40	40	32	16	341

What types of financial service providers are required by law to act in a client's best interest?

Age						
40 and older	49	44	58	55	19	535
Younger than 40	47	35	61	58	18	116
Education						
College degree or more	48	41	59	60	19	337
No college degree	49	44	58	51	19	314
Household income						
At least $75,000	48	40	59	61	17	289
Less than $75,000	49	44	58	51	21	357
Region						
Northeast	50	43	59	56	15	142
Midwest	45	39	56	54	22	147
West	48	45	55	49	22	119
South	50	42	61	59	18	242

Table G.1—Continued

Respondent Characteristic	Investment Advisers (%)	Brokers (%)	Financial Advisors or Consultants (%)	Financial Planners (%)	None (%)	Observations
Investment experience						
Experienced	50	40	61	59	20	434
Inexperienced	46	47	54	49	18	216
Uses financial service provider						
Yes	55	45	63	60	18	307
No	43	40	55	52	20	341
What types of financial service providers are required by law to disclose any conflicts of interest?						
Age						
40 and older	61	58	56	50	19	535
Younger than 40	66	60	65	53	15	116
Education						
College degree or more	62	60	58	54	18	337
No college degree	61	56	56	47	19	314
Household income						
At least $75,000	64	62	62	57	15	289
Less than $75,000	60	55	54	46	21	357
Region						
Northeast	59	61	57	54	19	142
Midwest	67	63	62	50	15	147
West	60	58	51	45	22	119
South	62	53	58	51	18	242
Investment experience						
Experienced	62	58	60	54	18	434
Inexperienced	62	59	52	44	18	216
Uses financial service provider						
Yes	66	63	62	55	16	307
No	59	55	53	47	20	341

SOURCE: ALP survey.

Table G.2
Commonly Reported Titles for First Individual Reported

Title	All Individual Professionals	Provide Advisory Services Only	Provide Brokerage Services Only	Provide Both Types of Services
Advisor	7	1	1	5
Banker	5	2	0	3
Broker, stockbroker, registered representative	19	0	4	15
CFP	12	1	1	10
Financial adviser or financial advisor	54	7	5	42
Financial consultant	17	2	0	15
Financial planner	34	6	1	27
Investment adviser or investment advisor	18	3	2	13
President or vice president	15	0	1	14

SOURCE: ALP survey.

Figure G.1
Types of Firms That Employ First Individual Professionals Reported

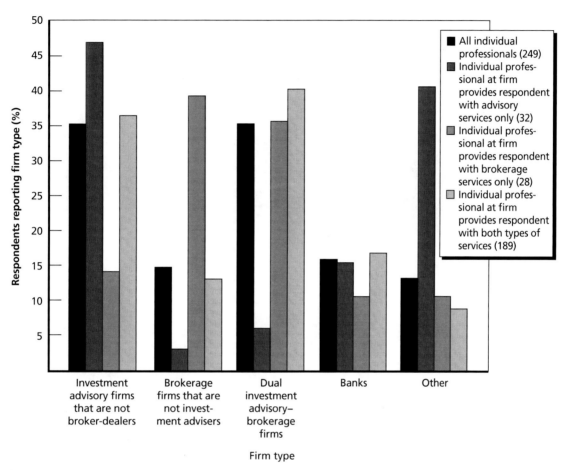

SOURCE: ALP survey.

RAND *TR556-G.1*

**Figure G.2
Types of Firms Used That Are Not Associated with Individual Professionals (First-Reported Firms Only)**

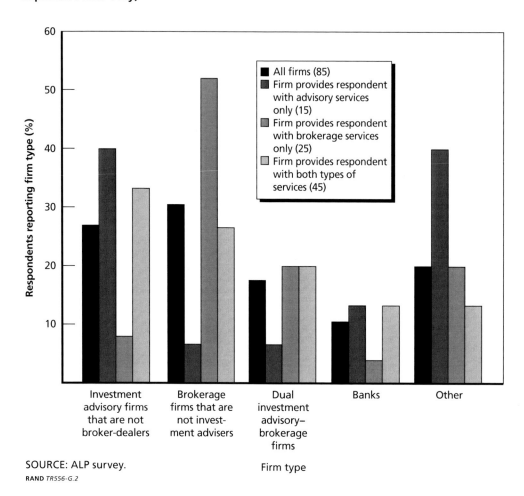

SOURCE: ALP survey.

RAND *TR556-G.2*

Table G.3
Reasons Given for Not Using a Financial Service Provider

Reason	All	Age		Education		Household Income		Region				Investment Experience	
		40 and Older	Under 40	College Degree or More	No College Degree	At Least $75,000	Less Than $75,000	Northeast	Midwest	West	South	Experienced	Inexperienced
No money for investments (%)	47	46	50	33	58	26	60	25	55	47	55	28	67
Too expensive (%)	13	12	17	14	13	16	11	15	11	22	10	17	9
Too hard to choose one (%)	6	5	12	8	5	10	4	7	5	10	5	8	4
I don't need assistance with my financial decisions (%)	21	24	12	29	16	28	18	35	19	15	18	33	10
Had one and didn't like him, her, or firm (%)	8	9	7	9	7	12	6	7	4	15	9	14	2
Other (%)	19	17	29	27	14	27	15	25	19	15	18	23	15
Observations	340	264	76	150	190	130	209	72	84	60	123	175	164

SOURCE: ALP survey.

Table G.4
Desired Assistance with Financial Matters

Service	All	Age		Education		Household Income		Region				Investment Experience		Uses Financial Service Provider	
		40 and Older	Under 40	College Degree or More	No College Degree	At Least $75,000	Less Than $75,000	Northeast	Midwest	West	South	Experienced	Inexperienced	Yes	No
Asset management (%)	30	31	24	38	22	35	26	39	25	27	29	39	12	44	17
College-saving planning (%)	17	12	41	17	17	20	15	12	17	24	17	16	20	14	20
Debt consolidation or management (%)	18	16	30	14	23	14	22	12	18	22	21	10	34	11	24
Developing a budget and saving plan (%)	24	19	46	19	29	19	28	18	27	20	28	16	40	14	33
Estate planning (%)	35	39	19	39	31	41	30	42	33	37	32	42	23	43	28
Executing stock or mutual fund transactions (%)	27	27	25	31	22	29	25	34	22	28	25	34	13	43	13
General financial planning (%)	38	38	41	40	37	38	38	41	39	41	35	41	33	44	33
Investment advising (%)	41	39	47	48	33	41	40	47	46	38	35	48	25	54	28
Retirement planning (%)	62	62	64	66	58	71	55	64	67	63	58	65	56	69	56

Table G.4—Continued

Service	Age			Education			Household Income			Region					Investment Experience			Uses Financial Service Provider	
	All	40 and Older	Under 40	College Degree or More	No College Degree		At Least $75,000	Less Than $75,000		Northeast	Midwest	West	South		Experienced	Inexperienced		Yes	No
Other (%)	3	3	2	2	3		1	3		3	2	2	3		1	5		1	4
Observations	634	521	113	325	309		280	349		137	147	116	233		421	212		296	338

SOURCE: ALP survey.

Table G.5
Focus-Group Participants' Beliefs About Financial Service Providers

Respondent	Investment Advisers (%)	Brokers (%)	Financial Advisors or Consultants (%)	Financial Planners (%)	None (%)	Observations
What types of financial service providers provide advice about securities (e.g., shares of stocks or mutual funds) as part of their regular business?						
Age						
40 and older	80	64	80	66	0	44
Younger than 40	96	57	70	57	0	23
Education						
College degree or more	89	61	76	68	0	38
No college degree	79	62	76	55	0	29
Focus-group location						
Virginia	84	58	84	65	0	31
Indiana	86	64	69	61	0	36
Investment experience						
Experienced	80	62	73	58	0	45
Inexperienced	95	59	82	73	0	22
Uses financial service provider						
Yes	82	74	74	62	0	34
No	88	48	79	64	0	33
What types of financial service providers execute stock or mutual fund transactions on the client's behalf?						
Age						
40 and older	36	77	30	21	0	44
Younger than 40	9	96	9	13	0	23
Education						
College degree or more	18	89	16	14	0	38
No college degree	38	76	31	24	0	29
Focus-group location						
Virginia	23	87	17	13	0	31
Indiana	31	81	28	22	0	36
Investment experience						
Experienced	22	89	18	16	0	45

Table G.5—Continued

Respondent	Investment Advisers (%)	Brokers (%)	Financial Advisers or Consultants (%)	Financial Planners (%)	None (%)	Observations
Inexperienced	36	73	32	23	0	22
Uses financial service provider						
Yes	29	88	21	24	0	34
No	24	79	24	12	0	33
What types of financial service providers recommend specific investments?						
Age						
40 and older	93	41	66	48	0	44
Younger than 40	91	57	70	43	0	23
Education						
College degree or more	97	55	71	47	0	38
No college degree	86	34	62	45	0	29
Focus-group location						
Virginia	90	48	71	55	0	31
Indiana	94	44	64	39	0	36
Investment experience						
Experienced	91	49	64	42	0	45
Inexperienced	95	41	73	55	0	22
Uses financial service provider						
Yes	91	50	68	53	0	34
No	94	42	67	39	0	33
What types of financial service providers provide retirement planning?						
Age						
40 and older	41	11	80	91	0	44
Younger than 40	35	13	83	91	0	23
Education						
College degree or more	42	13	92	95	0	38
No college degree	34	10	66	86	0	29
Focus-group location						
Virginia	35	13	81	97	0	31

Table G.5—Continued

Respondent	Investment Advisers (%)	Brokers (%)	Financial Advisers or Consultants (%)	Financial Planners (%)	None (%)	Observations
Indiana	42	11	81	86	0	36
Investment experience						
Experienced	36	16	80	91	0	45
Inexperienced	45	5	82	91	0	22
Uses financial service provider						
Yes	47	21	79	91	0	34
No	30	3	82	91	0	33

What types of financial service providers provide general financial planning?

Respondent	Investment Advisers (%)	Brokers (%)	Financial Advisers or Consultants (%)	Financial Planners (%)	None (%)	Observations
Age						
40 and older	34	14	75	89	0	44
Younger than 40	30	22	87	96	0	23
Education						
College degree or more	34	21	92	97	0	38
No college degree	31	10	62	83	0	29
Focus-group location						
Virginia	35	19	81	94	0	31
Indiana	31	14	78	89	0	36
Investment experience						
Experienced	36	22	80	91	0	45
Inexperienced	27	5	77	91	0	22
Uses financial service provider						
Yes	35	18	76	91	0	34
No	30	15	82	91	0	33

What types of financial service providers typically receive commissions on purchases or trades that the client makes?

Respondent	Investment Advisers (%)	Brokers (%)	Financial Advisers or Consultants (%)	Financial Planners (%)	None (%)	Observations
Age						
40 and older	49	93	47	33	0	44
Younger than 40	70	100	39	35	0	23
Education						
College degree or more	59	100	49	41	0	38

Table G.5—Continued

Respondent	Investment Advisers (%)	Brokers (%)	Financial Advisers or Consultants (%)	Financial Planners (%)	None (%)	Observations
No college degree	52	90	38	24	0	29
Focus-group location						
Virginia	60	100	43	30	0	31
Indiana	53	92	44	36	0	36
Investment experience						
Experienced	52	100	45	39	0	45
Inexperienced	64	86	41	23	0	22
Uses financial service provider						
Yes	52	100	45	42	0	34
No	61	91	42	24	0	33

What types of financial service providers are typically paid based on the amount of assets that the client holds?

Age						
40 and older	41	48	49	23	9	44
Younger than 40	61	74	39	13	0	23
Education						
College degree or more	59	58	46	24	5	38
No college degree	41	55	45	14	7	29
Focus-group location						
Virginia	60	71	37	20	6	31
Indiana	44	44	53	19	6	36
Investment experience						
Experienced	50	60	41	18	7	45
Inexperienced	55	50	55	23	5	22
Uses financial service provider						
Yes	48	56	48	27	3	34
No	55	58	42	12	9	33

What types of financial service providers are required by law to act in a client's best interest?

Age						
40 and older	66	70	61	55	14	44
Younger than 40	61	48	52	61	26	23

Table G.5—Continued

Respondent	Investment Advisers (%)	Brokers (%)	Financial Advisers or Consultants (%)	Financial Planners (%)	None (%)	Observations
Education						
College degree or more	68	71	58	58	18	38
No college degree	59	52	59	55	17	29
Focus-group location						
Virginia	58	61	48	58	19	31
Indiana	69	64	67	56	17	36
Investment experience						
Experienced	64	67	58	60	20	45
Inexperienced	64	55	59	50	14	22
Uses financial service provider						
Yes	74	74	68	59	15	34
No	55	52	48	55	21	33

What types of financial service providers are required by law to disclose any conflicts of interest?

Respondent	Investment Advisers (%)	Brokers (%)	Financial Advisers or Consultants (%)	Financial Planners (%)	None (%)	Observations
Age						
40 and older	64	75	61	82	16	44
Younger than 40	52	61	61	52	22	23
Education						
College degree or more	61	74	58	82	18	38
No college degree	59	66	66	59	17	29
Focus-group location						
Virginia	65	71	65	97	16	31
Indiana	56	69	58	50	19	36
Investment experience						
Experienced	53	71	53	71	22	45
Inexperienced	73	68	77	73	9	22
Uses financial service provider						
Yes	56	71	53	79	24	34
No	64	70	70	64	12	33

SOURCE: ALP survey.

Supplemental Analysis of Industry Data from 2001 to 2006

In this appendix, we report on an analysis of trends in data derived from regulatory filings made by investment advisers and broker-dealers. This analysis supplements the findings reported in Chapter Four.

Investment Advisers

In Chapter Four, we classify each investment advisory firm as one of five mutually exclusive and exhaustive types:

1. **Dually Registered**: A matching unique firm identifier (hereinafter, CRD number) exists in both the IARD database and a broker-dealer database (either CRD data or FOCUS reports) for the corresponding business quarter.
2. **Reportedly Engaged as Broker-Dealer**: IARD data indicate that the firm has self-reported as being engaged in business as a broker-dealer, but no matching CRD number is found (i.e., not of type 1).
3. **Registered Representative**: IARD data indicate that the firm is a registered representative of a broker-dealer, and the firm is not of type 1 or 2.
4. **Affiliated Activity**: IARD data indicate that a related person is a broker-dealer, municipal securities dealer, or government securities broker or dealer, and the firm is not of type 1, 2, or 3.
5. **Neither Dual nor Affiliated Activity**: The firm is not of type 1, 2, 3, or 4.

As described in Table H.1, the great majority of firms in the IARD data are of the fifth type—neither dual nor affiliated activity—and it is these firms that account for most of the growth in the number of firms in our IARD data from 2001 through 2006. In this appendix, we document the year-to-year changes in the composition of firms and the assets that these firms managed from 2001 through 2006. Here, we include all firms that are listed in the IARD database, rather than restricting attention to those firms that report clients who are individuals. We do so to simplify the analysis. Even with this simplification, we still are left to track ten different categories of firms defined by type of business activity and year of entry into the IARD database.

Table H.1
Number of Advisers of Each Type, by Year

Fourth Quarter of Year	Dually Registered (FOCUS)	Reportedly Engaged as Broker-Dealer	Registered Representative	Affiliated Activity	Neither Dual nor Affiliated Activity
2001	527	124	826	1,803	4,334
2002	538	131	841	1,810	4,455
2003	548	112	858	1,850	4,724
2004	525	105	868	1,872	5,253
2005	518	101	819	1,904	5,742
2006	536	94	855	2,009	6,990

SOURCES: Activities and affiliations reported in IARD database. Dually registered firms determined by match in IARD and FOCUS data.

Changes in Composition of Firms

We report next on the rate of entry into and exit out of each business-type classification and the database as a whole. Note again that database entry or exit reflects a change in registration status of a firm, which may or may not indicate that the firm entered or exited the market.

We begin by reporting on the probability that a firm changes from one type to another across years. Average year-to-year transition probabilities from 2001 through 2006 are reported in Table H.2.[1] The most stable types are dually registered, affiliated activity, and neither dual nor affiliated activity. In each case, about 90 percent of firms stay in the data set *and* stay the same type across years. Most of the firms that exit the type classification actually exit the database. About 7 or 8 percent exit the database each year from these categories.

The group of firms reportedly engaged as a broker-dealer constitutes the least stable type. Only about two-thirds retain this classification from one year to the next. The most likely transition is to exit the database, indicating that perhaps these firms—12 percent of firms in this classification—actually were previously dually registered but simply exited the FOCUS database before exiting the IARD database. An almost equally large share of these firms—10 percent—transitioned to affiliated activity, which is consistent with either the possible reporting problems described in Chapter Four or simply a reporting lag associated with changes in business activities.

About four-fifths of the registered representative firms retained this classification from one year to the next. Most of those that exited this classification either became the neither-dual-nor-affiliated type or exited the database.

The bottom row of Table H.2 describes the initial classification of firms that were not in the IARD database in the fourth quarter of the preceding year. A comparison with the entries in Table H.1 reveals that these firms are more likely than the randomly selected firm to be classified as neither dual nor affiliated activity—70 percent versus 61 percent—and less likely to be either dually registered—4 percent versus 6 percent—or affiliated activity—15 percent versus

---

[1]   The transition probabilities are weighted by the number of observations in each category in each year. These values are nearly identical to those obtained when we drop the data from 2006, when many hedge funds apparently registered for the first time. Only one entry changes by more than 2 percentage points: The probability of transitioning from not being in IARD to being neither dual nor affiliated activity falls from 70 percent to 67 percent.

Table H.2
Distribution of Investment Advisory Firm Types in Year t, Conditional on Type in Prior Year (t–1)

Classification in Year t-1	Dually Registered (FOCUS) (%)	Reportedly Engaged as Broker-Dealer (%)	Registered Representative (%)	Affiliated Activity (%)	Neither Dual nor Affiliated Activity (%)	Not in IARD (%)
Dually registered (FOCUS)	90	1	0	0	0	8
Reportedly engaged as broker-dealer	2	67	4	10	5	12
Registered representative	0	0	81	2	8	8
Affiliated activity	0	0	1	87	4	7
Neither dual nor affiliated activity	0	0	1	2	91	7
Not in IARD	4	1	9	15	70	0

SOURCE: Activities and affiliations reported in IARD database for the fourth quarter of each year from 2001 through 2006. Dually registered firms determined by match in IARD and FOCUS data.

22 percent. That is, the new registrants are less likely to be directly or indirectly engaged in brokerage activities.[2]

To get a better understanding of changes in the market since 2001, we categorized firms according to the classification by type in 2001 or, if the firm was not listed as of 2001, the year of entry into the IARD database. Table H.3 lists the number of firms in each of ten mutually exclusive and exhaustive categories. The entries in the first five rows replicate the entries in the first row of Table H.1. The entries in the last five rows show the number of new entrants each year—that is, the firms that were not in the IARD in the fourth quarter of 2001.[3] Table H.3 indicates that 43 percent of the firms (5,714 out of 13,328) that appear in the IARD database in the fourth quarter of any year from 2001 through 2006 are classified as new entrants.

Table H.4 describes the classification of firms as of the fourth quarter of 2006, conditional on the classification in Table H.3. The first five rows again describe types in the database as of 2001. The entries in these rows may be compared to the year-to-year transition probabilities in Table H.2. The general pattern is the same here, but attrition from the data set (i.e., percentage not in IARD) is much higher, because these entries describe five-year transition probabilities rather than one-year transition probabilities. The five-year probabilities of switching types but staying in the data set are also larger. As a result, the entries on the diagonal (i.e.,

---

[2] This result is less pronounced when we restrict attention to the period 2001 through 2005, thereby excluding the many hedge funds that registered in 2006. As reported previously, the probability of transition from not being in IARD to being neither dual nor affiliated activity falls from 70 percent to 67 percent.

[3] These firms constitute most of the sample on which the entries in the bottom row of Table H.2 are based. Firms are also included in the bottom row of Table H.2 if they were in the database in 2001, transitioned out of it, and then subsequently came back in.

Table H.3
Number of Advisers, by Type in 2001 or Entry Year

Entry Year	Classification	Number of Firms
Fourth quarter of 2001	Dually registered (FOCUS)	527
	Reportedly engaged as broker-dealer	124
	Registered representative	826
	Affiliated activity	1,803
	Neither dual nor affiliated activity	4,334
2002		824
2003		870
2004		1,056
2005		1,026
2006		1,938
Total		13,328

SOURCES: Activities and affiliations reported in IARD database for the fourth quarter of 2001. Dually registered firms determined by match in IARD and FOCUS data. New entrants determined by IARD data.

probability of being of the same type in 2006 as in 2001) are much lower than in the case of one-year transition probabilities.

The entries in the last five rows of Table H.4 supplement the findings on new entrants presented in Table H.2. The 2006 classification of firms does not vary much by entry year but for the higher attrition rates among firms with earlier entry years. Note that the higher attrition rates are pretty much offset by lower shares in the neither-dual-nor-affiliated-activity classification.

Changes in Assets Under Management

The amount and distribution of reported assets under management has changed markedly since 2001. Table H.5 describes total assets under management reported by all firms in the IARD database in the fourth quarter of each year. This table may be compared to Table 4.7 in Chapter Four, which restricts attention to firms with individual clients. The patterns of variation reported in these two tables are similar across years, but the magnitudes are larger here. As in Table 4.7, the growth in assets under management during this period is attributable to assets in discretionary accounts, which grew from $19 trillion in 2001 to $29 trillion in 2006.

Continuing this comparison with Table 4.7, we find that firms with individual clients reported from 53 to 56 percent of all assets under management each year. From 2001 through 2003, firms with individual clients reported about 75 percent of assets in nondiscretionary accounts. This share fell below 60 percent from 2004 through 2006, but this change had little effect on the overall picture, because assets in nondiscretionary accounts constituted only about 10 percent of all assets under management throughout the period.

Next, we consider changes in assets under management by type of firm in 2001 or, for new entrants, by entry year. Figures H.1 and H.2 depict the totals of managed assets in discretionary accounts and nondiscretionary accounts, respectively. The patterns displayed in Figure

Table H.4
Distribution of Investment Advisory Firm Types in 2006, Conditional on 2001 Type or Entry Year

Entry Year	Classification in 2001 or Entry Year	Classification in Fourth Quarter of 2006 (%)					
		Dually Registered (FOCUS)	Reportedly Engaged as Broker-Dealer	Registered Representative	Affiliated Activity	Neither Dual nor Affiliated Activity	Not in IARD
Fourth quarter of 2001	Dually registered (FOCUS)	66	1	0	2	4	28
	Reportedly engaged as broker-dealer	2	25	9	23	10	31
	Registered representative	0	1	42	7	21	29
	Affiliated activity	0	1	2	55	12	30
	Neither dual nor affiliated activity	0	0	1	4	69	26
2002		4	0	6	14	44	31
2003		4	0	6	13	51	25
2004		3	1	8	14	58	17
2005		3	0	9	13	63	12
2006		3	1	6	12	78	0

SOURCES: Activities and affiliations reported in IARD database for the fourth quarters of 2001 and 2006. Dually registered firms determined by match in IARD and FOCUS data. New entrants determined by IARD data.

Table H.5
Assets Under Management, 2001–2006: Investment Advisers That Reported Continuous and Regular Supervisory or Management Services to Securities Portfolios

Fourth Quarter of Year	Number of Investment Advisers	Total Assets ($ trillions)		
		All Accounts	Discretionary Accounts	Nondiscretionary Accounts
2001	6,834	21.00	18.72	2.28
2002	7,102	21.16	18.87	2.29
2003	7,367	20.14	17.89	2.24
2004	7,905	23.95	21.59	2.36
2005	8,428	27.74	25.29	2.45
2006	9,803	32.07	29.13	2.95

SOURCE: Assets under management reported in IARD database.

Figure H.1
Total Assets Under Management in Discretionary Accounts, by Year and 2001 Firm Type or Entry Year

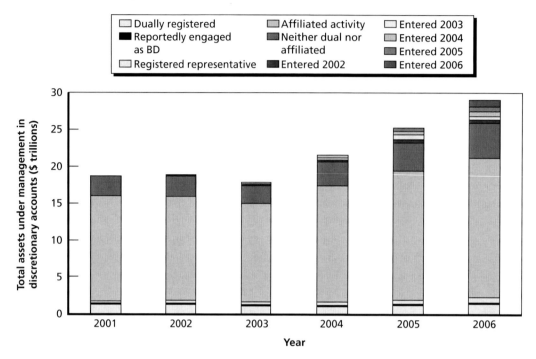

SOURCES: Assets under management reported in IARD database for fourth quarter of each year. Dually registered firms determined based on IARD and FOCUS data. Other firm types and entry years determined by IARD data.
RAND *TR556-H.1*

H.1 may be compared to those in Figure 4.2 in Chapter Four, which depicts assets managed in discretionary accounts by firms with individual clients, with firm type defined contemporaneously. In Figure H.1, we see that about half of the overall growth in discretionary accounts from 2003 through 2006 is attributable to growth in assets managed by firms of the affiliated-activity type in 2001. New entrants account for about one-fourth the overall growth during this interval.

The patterns displayed in Figure H.2 may be compared to those in Figure 4.3 in Chapter Four, which depicts assets managed in nondiscretionary accounts by firms with individual clients, with firm type defined contemporaneously. In Figure H.2, we see a very different pattern of change from 2001 through 2006. In particular, when all investment advisers are included in the analysis, total assets in nondiscretionary accounts are relatively stable during the first four years of the period, which was a period of decline in the sample of firms with individual clients described in Chapter Four. We also find that total assets in nondiscretionary accounts declined for firms of the affiliated activity type in 2001 and increased for dually registered firms, which parallels the findings in Chapter Four. New entrants reported about $480 million in nondiscretionary accounts for the fourth quarter of 2006, accounting for more than 70 percent of the total increase in managed assets from 2001 through 2006.

Figure H.2
Total Assets Under Management in Nondiscretionary Accounts, by Year and 2001 Firm Type or Entry Year

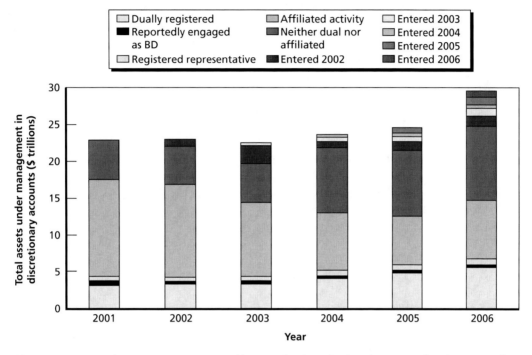

SOURCES: Assets under management reported in IARD database for fourth quarter of each year. Dually registered firms determined based on IARD and FOCUS data. Other firm types and entry years determined by IARD data.
RAND *TR556-H.2*

Broker-Dealers

We continue our supplemental analysis by focusing on broker-dealer firms. In Chapter Four, we classify each broker-dealer firm as one of five mutually exclusive and exhaustive types:

1. **Dually Registered (Database Match)**: A matching CRD number is found in our IARD database on investment advisers for the corresponding business quarter.
2. **Dually Registered (Web-Site Match)**: A matching record was found in the SEC's searchable database of investment advisers—e.g., state-registered (see Appendix A)—but no matching CRD number is found in our IARD database (i.e., not type 1).
3. **Reportedly Engaged in Investment Advisory Services Business**: CRD data indicate that the firm provided investment advisory services, but we found no matching CRD number in our IARD database and no matching record in the SEC's searchable database.
4. **Affiliated Activity**: CRD data indicate that the firm directly or indirectly controls, is controlled by, or is under common control with another entity engaged in the securities or investment advisory business, and the firm is not of type 1, 2, or 3.
5. **Neither Dual nor Affiliated Activity**: The firm is not of type 1, 2, 3, or 4.

In contrast to our data on investment advisers, the broker-dealer data do not allow us to track the number of firms in each classification back over time. Instead, we can track only whether or not a broker-dealer falls into the dually registered (database match) category based on matches between the FOCUS and IARD data. Table H.6 reports the number of dually registered firms and the number of other broker-dealer firms in the FOCUS database in the fourth quarter of each year from 2001 through 2006.

Changes in Composition of Firms

We report next on the rate of entry into and exit out of each category and the database as a whole. Note again that database entry or exit is determined by whether the broker-dealer firm filed a FOCUS report for the fourth quarter of that year, which may or may not indicate that the firm entered or exited the market. The entries in Table H.7 indicate that about 90 percent of firms stay in the data set *and* stay in the same category—either dually registered or other—across years, which is similar to the reported percentage for each of the largest groups of investment advisers (see Table H.2). About half of the broker-dealers that exit the dually registered classification actually exit the database, whereas almost all of the exits from the other category do so. We also note that only 3 percent of new entrants in a given year are dually registered, as described in the bottom row of the table.

To get a better understanding of changes in the market since 2001, we categorize firms according the classification by type in 2001 or, if the firm was not listed as of 2001, the year of

Table H.6
Number of Broker-Dealers of Each Type, by Year

Fourth Quarter of Year	Dually Registered (FOCUS)	All Other Firm Types
2001	527	4,999
2002	538	4,876
2003	548	4,759
2004	525	4,700
2005	518	4,616
2006	536	4,532

SOURCES: FOCUS database for fourth quarter of each year. Dually registered firms determined by match in IARD and FOCUS data.

Table H.7
Classification Distribution of Broker-Dealer Firms in Year t, Conditional on Prior Year (t-1) Classification

Classification	Dually Registered (FOCUS) (%)	All Other Firm Types (%)	Not in FOCUS (%)
Dually registered (FOCUS)	90	5	5
All other firm types	1	91	8
Not in FOCUS	3	97	0

SOURCES: FOCUS database for fourth quarter of each year from 2001 through 2006. Dually registered firms determined by match in IARD and FOCUS data.

entry into the FOCUS database. Table H.8 lists the number of firms in each of seven mutually exclusive and exhaustive categories. The entries in the first two rows replicate entries in the first row of Table H.6. The entries in the last five rows show the number of new entrants each year. Table H.8 indicates that 21 percent of the firms (1,492 out of 7,018) that appear in the FOCUS database in the fourth quarter of any year from 2001 through 2006 are classified as new entrants. Recall that new entrants account for 43 percent of investment advisory firms in the IARD.

Table H.9 describes the classification of firms as of the fourth quarter of 2006, conditional on the classification in Table H.8. The first two rows again describe types in the database as of 2001. The entries in these rows may be compared to the year-to-year transition probabilities in

Table H.8
Number of Broker-Dealers, by Firm Type in 2001 or Entry Year

Entry Year	Classification	Number of Firms
Fourth quarter of 2001	Dually registered (FOCUS)	4,999
	All other firm types	527
2002		349
2003		311
2004		303
2005		290
2006		239
Total		7,018

SOURCES: FOCUS database for fourth quarter of each year. Dually registered firms determined by match in IARD and FOCUS data.

Table H.9
Classification Distribution of Broker-Dealer Firms in 2006, Conditional on Classification in 2001 or Entry Year

Entry Year	Classification in 2001 or Entry Year	Classification in Fourth Quarter of 2006 (%)		
		Dually Registered (FOCUS)	All Other Firm Types	Not in FOCUS
Fourth quarter of 2001	Dually registered (FOCUS)	66	13	21
	All other firm types	3	65	33
2002		4	72	23
2003		4	75	21
2004		1	85	14
2005		4	90	6
2006		2	98	0

SOURCES: FOCUS database for fourth quarter of each year. Dually registered firms determined by match in IARD and FOCUS data.

Table H.7. The general pattern in Table H.9 is the same as in Table H.7, but the attrition rate from the data set (i.e., percentage not in FOCUS) and the probability of switching rates are much higher, because these entries describe five-year transition probabilities rather than one-year transition probabilities. As a result, the entries on the diagonal (i.e., probability of being of the same type in 2006 as in 2001) are much lower than in the case of one-year transition probabilities. As we found with the IARD data, about two-thirds of dually registered firms in 2001 are still dually registered in 2006.

The entries in the last five rows of Table H.9 supplement the findings on new entrants presented in Table H.7. The 2006 classification of firms does not vary much by entry year but for the higher attrition rates among firms with earlier entry years. Note that the higher attrition rates are approximately offset by lower shares in the all—other-firm-types classification.

Balance Sheet and Income Statements

Now we consider the assets and income reported by broker-dealers during the sample period. Figure H.3 depicts the sum of total assets reported in the fourth quarter of each year, by 2001 firm type or, if the firm was not listed as of 2001, the year of entry into the FOCUS database. Recalling that dually registered firms account for only about 10 percent of firms, the figure clearly documents the extent to which dual registrants at the end of 2001 represent far larger operations than their counterparts as measured by assets throughout the period. We also see that new entrants account for a small fraction of total assets by the end of the period.

Figure H.3
Sum of Total Assets, by Year and Firm Type in 2001 or Entry Year

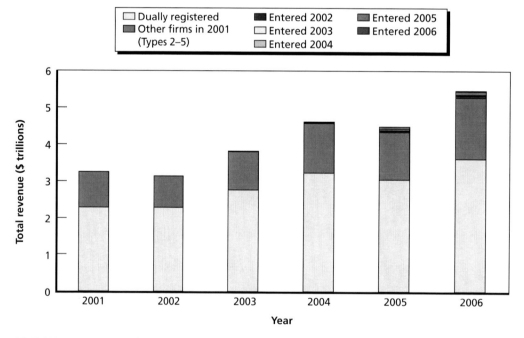

SOURCES: Assets reported in FOCUS database in fourth quarter of each year. Dually registered firms determined based on IARD and FOCUS data in fourth quarter of 2001.
RAND *TR556-H.3*

As we found in Chapter Four, when focusing on mean values and conditioning on contemporaneously defined firm types, the sum of total revenues varied over the period in much the same way as total assets did. These trends are depicted here in Figure H.4. The results for the sum of net income, depicted in Figure H.5, are comparable to results presented in Figure 4.6 in Chapter Four.

We conclude this analysis with supplemental findings on broker-dealer revenues that may be attributed to investment advisory services. Figure H.6 depicts the total of quarterly revenues reported on the FOCUS reports in field 3975, which includes *but is not limited to* investment advisory fees. We report in Chapter Four that these fees constitute less than 7 percent of all reported revenue in the fourth quarter of 2006, which may be verified by comparing the rightmost column in Figure H.6 to the rightmost column of Figure H.4. Comparing the other columns reveals that this share is almost 8 percent in 2001, increases to almost 9 percent in 2003 and then falls each year through 2006.

Figure H.6 also clearly documents the extent to which these fees are generated by firms that were dually registered in 2001, increasing from almost $4 billion in 2001 to almost $6 billion in 2006. Further analysis of the statistics on which Figures H.4 and H.6 are based reveals that the fees reported in field 3975 constitute a larger share of total revenues for dually registered firms during the first half of the period (ranging from 9 to 11 percent) than they do during the second half of the period (declining to 7 percent in 2006). Among other firms in existence in 2001, the share ranges from 4 to 5 percent throughout the period. The declining differential across these two groups may arise from transitions between types over the sample period. Finally, note that new entrants reported a small fraction of these fees.

Figure H.4
Sum of Total Revenue, by Year and Firm Type in 2001 or Entry Year

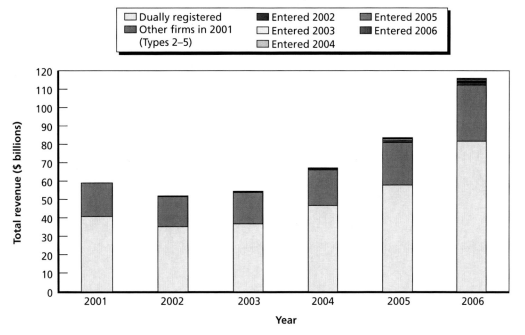

SOURCES: Revenue reported in FOCUS database in fourth quarter of each year. Dually registered firms determined based on IARD and FOCUS data in fourth quarter of 2001.
RAND *TR556-H.4*

Figure H.5
Sum of Net Income Before Federal Taxes, by Year and Firm Type in 2001 or Entry Year

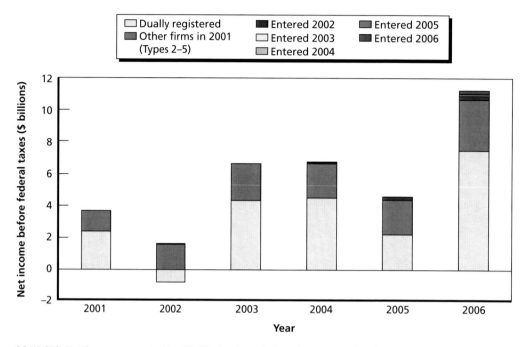

SOURCES: Net income reported in FOCUS database in fourth quarter of each year. Dually registered firms determined based on IARD and FOCUS data in fourth quarter of 2001.
RAND *TR556-H.5*

Figure H.6
Sum of Reported Fees for Account Supervision, Investment Advisory, and Administrative Services, by Year and Firm Type in 2001 or Entry Year

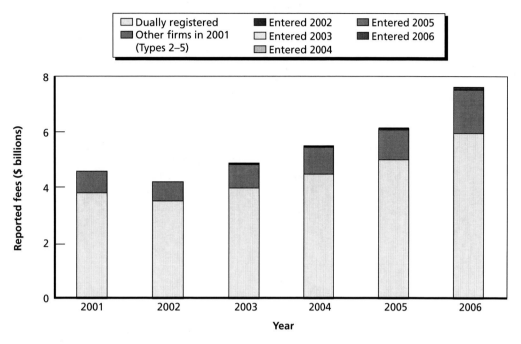

SOURCES: Fees reported in field 3975 in FOCUS database in fourth quarter of each year. Dually registered firms determined based on IARD and FOCUS data in fourth quarter of 2001.
RAND *TR556-H.6*

References

ACA Compliance Group, Investment Adviser Association, *IM Insight*, and Old Mutual Asset Management, *2007 Investment Management Compliance Testing Survey: Summary Report*, September 4, 2007. As of December 28, 2007:
http://www.investmentadviser.org/public/2007%20IM%20Testing%20Report.pdf

Al Mamun, Abdullah, M. Kabir Hassan, and Van Son Lai, "The Impact of the Gramm-Leach-Bliley Act on the Financial Services Industry," *Journal of Economics and Finance*, Vol. 28, No. 3, 2004, pp. 333–347.

Alexander, Gordon J., Jonathan D. Jones, and Peter J. Nigro, "Does Mutual Fund Disclosure at Banks Matter? Evidence from a Survey of Investors," *Quarterly Review of Economics and Finance*, Vol. 41, No. 3, Autumn 2001, pp. 387–403.

Armstrong, David, and John Hechinger, "Fidelity Alters Fees It Charges Buyers of Bonds; Move Aims to Court Individuals by Providing More Disclosure of Pricing and Commissions," *Wall Street Journal*, September 21, 2004, p. D1.

B/D Solutions Consulting, "Frequently Asked Questions," undated Web page. As of December 29, 2007:
http://www.bdsolutions.com/bdfinop/acct_faq.php

Bergstresser, Daniel, John M. R. Chalmers, and Peter Tufano, *Assessing the Costs and Benefits of Brokers in the Mutual Fund Industry*, working paper, Harvard Business School, 2006.

Black, Barbara, "Brokers and Advisers—What's in a Name?" *Fordham Journal of Corporate and Financial Law*, Vol. 11, No. 1, 2005, pp. 7–30.

Bowen, John J., Jr., "The CPA Alliance: When Investment Advisers Partner with CPAs, the Whole Is Greater Than the Sum of the Parts," *Financial Planning*, September 1, 2002, p. 1.

Carlson, Stephen L., and Frank A. Fernandez, "The Costs of Compliance in the U.S. Securities Industry," *Research Reports*, Vol. 7, No. 2, February 22, 2006, pp. 1–31.

C.F.R.—*see* Code of Federal Regulations.

Chakravarty, Sugato, and Asani Sarkar, "A Model of Broker's Trading, with Applications to Order Flow Internalization," *Review of Financial Economics*, Vol. 11, No. 1, 2002, pp. 19–36.

Chao, Chiang-Nan, Robert J. Mockler, and Dorothy Dologite, "Online Trading: The Competitive Landscape," *Review of Business*, Vol. 23, No. 3, September 2002, pp. 44–48.

Chevron, USA, Inc. v NRDC, Inc., 467 U.S. 837, 104 S. Ct. 2778, June 25, 1984.

Clark v Lamula, 583 F.2d 594, 2nd Cir., August 24, 1978.

Clark, Bob, "Squeeze Play: How Will the Broker-Dealer Industry React This Time Around to Shrinking Profits," *Financial Planning*, March 1, 2003, p. 1.

Code of Federal Regulations, Title 17, Section 240.17a-3, "Records to Be Made by Certain Exchange Members, Brokers and Dealers," 1948.

———, Title 17, Section 240.17a-5, "Reports to Be Made by Certain Brokers and Dealers," last amended June 21, 2004. As of December 29, 2007:
http://ecfr.gpoaccess.gov/cgi/t/text/text-idx?c=ecfr&sid=0df425c18f27fb197f850b9747ee6b72&rgn=div8&view=text&node=17:3.0.1.1.1.2.94.372&idno=17

Coles, Jeffrey L., Jose Suay, and Denise Woodbury, "Fund Advisor Compensation in Closed-End Funds," *Journal of Finance*, Vol. 55, No. 3, June 2000, pp. 1,385–1,414.

Colonial Realty Corp. v Bache and Co., 358 F.2d 178, 2nd Cir., March 10, 1966.

Cowan, Lynn, "Merrill Brokers Staff Its Call Centers," *Wall Street Journal*, November 20, 2002, p. B.5.G.

Damato, Karen, "An Out-of-the Box Plan for Mutual Fund Prospectuses," *Wall Street Journal*, April 15, 2005, p. C1.

Das, Sanjiv Ranjan, and Rangarajan K. Sundaram, "Fee Speech: Signaling, Risk-Sharing, and the Impact of Fee Structures on Investor Welfare," *Review of Financial Studies*, Vol. 15, No. 5, Winter 2002, pp. 1,465–1,497.

Eckblad, Marshall, and Pamela Black, "Behind the Numbers: Broker-Dealers Are Reporting Healthy Growth—Especially in Fee Revenue," *Financial Planning*, June 1, 2006, p. 1.

Elton, Edwin J., Martin J. Gruber, and Christopher R. Blake, "Incentive Fees and Mutual Funds," *Journal of Finance*, Vol. 58, No. 2, April 2003, pp. 779–804.

Ferrell, Allen, "A Proposal for Solving the Payment for Order Flow Problem," *Southern California Law Review*, Vol. 74, No. 4, May 2001, pp. 1,027–1,088.

———, "Much Ado About Order Flow," *Regulation*, Vol. 25, No. 1, Spring 2002, pp. 58–63. As of December 28, 2007:
http://www.cato.org/pubs/regulation/regv25n1/v25n1-8.pdf

Financial Industry Regulatory Authority, "Recommendations to Customers (Suitability)," National Association of Securities Dealers rule 2310, last amendment effective August 20, 1996.

———, "Rule 15c3-1: Net Capital Requirements for Brokers or Dealers," National Association of Securities Dealers manual, last amendment effective June 21, 2004.

———, "Fair Dealing with Customers," National Association of Securities Dealers rule IM-2310-2, last amendment effective August 1, 2006.

———, "Mark-Up Policy," National Association of Securities Dealers rule IM-2440-1, last amendment effective July 5, 2007a.

———, "Application for Membership," National Association of Securities Dealers by-laws, Article III, Section 1, last amendment effective July 30, 2007b.

———, "Best Execution and Interpositioning," National Association of Securities Dealers rule 2320, last amendment effective September 28, 2007c.

———, "Supervision," National Association of Securities Dealers rule 3010, last amendment effective December 19, 2007d.

———, "Members' Responsibilities Regarding Deferred Variable Annuities" National Association of Securities Dealers rule 2821, effective May 5, 2008.

Fin. Planning Ass'n v SEC, 375 U.S. App. D.C. 389, 482 F.3d 481, March 30, 2007.

FINRA—*see* Financial Industry Regulatory Authority.

Fishman, Michael J., and Francis A. Longstaff, "Dual Trading in Futures Markets," *Journal of Finance*, Vol. 47, No. 2, June 1992, pp. 643–671.

Fusilier, Marcelline, and Mark Schaub, "Broker-Client Contact and Client Satisfaction: Are Client Attitudes Towards Brokers Bullish and Bearish with the Stock Market?" *Journal of Financial Services Marketing*, Vol. 8, No. 1, August 2003, p. 63.

Garbade, Kenneth D., and William L. Silber, "Best Execution in Securities Markets: An Application of Signaling and Agency Theory," *Journal of Finance*, Vol. 37, No. 2, May 1982, pp. 493–504.

Goforth, Carol R., "Stockbrokers' Duties to Their Customers," *Saint Louis University Law Journal*, Vol. 33, No. 2, Winter 1989, pp. 407–445.

Goldstein v SEC, 371 U.S. App. D.C. 358, 451 F.3d 873, June 23, 2006.

Hanly v Securities and Exchange Com., 415 F.2d 589, 2nd Cir., July 24, 1969.

Hecht v Harris, Upham and Co., 430 F.2d 1202, 9th Cir., June 8, 1970.

Horowitz, Jed, "Wachovia Offers 50% Payout Plan to Lure Brokers," *Wall Street Journal*, December 15, 2004, p. 1.

Huhmann, Bruce A., and Nalinaksha Bhattacharyya, "Does Mutual Fund Advertising Provide Necessary Investment Information?" *International Journal of Bank Marketing*, Vol. 23, No. 4, 2005, pp. 296–319.

Independent Order of Foresters v Donald, Lufkin and Jenrette, 157 F.3d 933, 2nd Cir., October 7, 1998.

Investment Adviser Association, and National Regulatory Services, *Evolution Revolution: A Profile of the Investment Advisory Profession*," June 2005. As of December 27, 2007:
http://www.investmentadviser.org/public/evolution_revolution-2005.pdf

———, *Evolution Revolution: A Profile of the Investment Adviser Profession*, July 2006. As of December 27, 2007:
http://www.investmentadviser.org/public/evolution_revolution-2006.pdf

Investment Company Institute, "Ownership of Mutual Funds Through Professional Financial Advisers," *Fundamentals*, Vol. 14, No. 3, 2005, pp. 1–4.

Investment Counsel Association of America, and National Regulatory Services, *Evolution Revolution: A Profile of the U.S. Investment Advisory Profession*, September 2002. As of December 27, 2007:
http://www.investmentadviser.org/public/evolution-revolution_2002.pdf

———, *Evolution Revolution: A Profile of the Investment Advisory Profession*, May 2003. As of December 27, 2007:
http://www.investmentadviser.org/public/evolution_revolution-2003.pdf

———, *Evolution Revolution: A Profile of the Investment Advisory Profession*, May 2004. As of December 27, 2007:
http://www.investmentadviser.org/public/evolution_revolution-2004.pdf

Jablon v Dean Witter and Co., 614 F.2d 677, 9th Cir., February 29, 1980.

Jamieson, Dan, "Managed Account Industry Braces for Scrutiny," *On Wall Street Journal*, June 1, 2004, p. 1.

Kehrer, Kenneth, "Broker Integration: What Some Banks Are Doing," *ABA Banking Journal*, Vol. 93, No. 5, May 2001, pp. 28–31.

Kehrer, Kenneth, and John Houston, "Thud! Why Your Stock Sales Strategy's Flopping," *ABA Banking Journal*, Vol. 95, No. 11, November 2003, pp. 24–25.

Kim, Jane J., "Banks Push Customized Accounts; Latest 'Separately Managed Account' Offerings Have Lower Fees, Minimums; Brokers Fight Back," *Wall Street Journal*, June 20, 2006, p. D1.

———, "Picking an Account That Fits; Brokers Introduce UMAs as Full-Service Choice for the Just Wealthy," *Wall Street Journal*, June 9, 2007, p. B1.

Kristof, Kathy M., "Schwab Clients Complain of Obscure Fee," *Los Angeles Times*, May 3, 2004, p. C4.

Lauricella, Tom, "Brokerage Firms Begin to Reveal Details of Sales Pacts," *Wall Street Journal*, October 1, 2004, p. C1.

Lawson, Diana, Richard Borgman, and Timothy Brotherton, "A Content Analysis of Financial Services Magazine Print Ads: Are They Reaching Women?" *Journal of Financial Services Marketing*, Vol. 12, No. 1, August 2007, pp. 17–29.

Leib v Merrill Lynch, Pierce, Fenner and Smith, Inc., 461 F. Supp. 951, E.D. Mich., October 30, 1978.

Liu, Wei-Lin, "Motivating and Compensating Investment Advisors," *Journal of Business*, Vol. 78, No. 6, November 2005, pp. 2317–2349.

Lowe v SEC, 472 U.S. 181, 105 S. Ct. 2557, June 10, 1985.

Markham, Jerry W., "Mutual Funds Scandals—Comparative Analysis of the Role of Corporate Governance in the Regulation of Collective Investments," *Hastings Business Law Journal*, Vol. 3, No. 1, Fall 2006, pp. 67–156.

Markham, Jerry W., and Thomas Lee Hazen, *Broker Dealer Operations Under Securities and Commodities Law: Financial Responsibilities, Credit Regulation, and Customer Protection*, Vol. 23, St. Paul, Minn.: West Group, 2006.

Meinhard v Salmon, 249 N.Y. 458, 164 N.E. 545, N.Y., December 31, 1928.

Mills, Rob, "Regional Firms: Increasingly Retail-Oriented, but Holding Their Own," *Research Reports*, Vol. 6, No. 6, 2005, pp. 11–17.

National Regulatory Services, and Investment Adviser Association, *Evolution Revolution: A Profile of the Investment Adviser Profession*, July 2007. As of December 27, 2007:
http://www.investmentadviser.org/public/evolution_revolution-2007.pdf

National Regulatory Services, and Investment Counsel Association of America, *Evolution Revolution: A Profile of the U.S. Investment Advisory Profession*," July 2001. As of December 27, 2007:
http://www.investmentadviser.org/public/icaanrsbooklet.pdf

Oberlin, Cliff, and Jill R. Powers, "Making the Switch: Looking for a New Broker-Dealer? Here's a Road Map to Guide You as You Search for the Right Partner," *Financial Planning*, June 1, 2003, p. 1.

"On the Cutting Edge: These Four Broker-Dealers Have Found Success by Creating Their Own Unique Business Models," *Financial Planning*, June 1, 2006, p. 1.

Opdyke, Jeff D., "UBS to Unmask Fees and Accounts; Big Brokerage House Is Among the First to Disclose How Wall Street Operates," *Wall Street Journal*, May 5, 2005, p. D2.

Opinion Research Corporation, "Regulation of Stockbrokers and Financial Advisors: What American Investors Understand, Think Is Right: Summary of Survey Findings," briefing for Zero Alpha Group and Consumer Federation of America, October 27, 2004. As of December 28, 2007:
http://www.zeroalphagroup.com/news/RIvestmentZAG_CFAFINAL_102704.ppt

Palomino, Frédéric, and Andrea Prat, "Risk Taking and Optimal Contracts for Money Managers," *RAND Journal of Economics*, Vol. 34, No. 1, Spring 2003, pp. 113–137.

Pekarek, Edward, "Pruning the Hedge: Who Is a 'Client' and Whom Does an Adviser Advise?" *Fordham Journal of Corporate and Financial Law*, Vol. 12, No. 5, 2007, pp. 913–976.

Pessin, Jaime Levy, "Compliance Work Alters Finance Firms," *Wall Street Journal*, November 2, 2005, p. 1.

———, "Concern Over Brokers at Banks; NASD Worries That Risks Aren't Adequately Disclosed at Branches," *Wall Street Journal*, October 28, 2006a, p. B4.

———, "Wall Street Aims to Simplify Disclosures for Clients," *Wall Street Journal*, October 31, 2006b, p. D2.

Plaze, Robert E., "The Regulation of Investment Advisers by the Securities and Exchange Commission," working paper, Division of Investment Management, U.S. Securities and Exchange Commission, October 1, 2006.

PLI—*see* Practising Law Institute.

Practising Law Institute, *Corporate Law and Practice: Course Handbook Series*, New York, August 8, 2007.

Public Law 106-102, Financial Modernization Act of 1999, November 12, 1999.

Schaeffer, John R., "Considerations for Choosing Between a Regional or National Broker-Dealer," *National Underwriter*, Vol. 105, No. 14, April 2, 2001, pp. 27–28.

SEC—*see* U.S. Securities and Exchange Commission

Securities Industry and Financial Markets Association, *Expanded Securities Industry DataBank*, undated(a) Web page. As of December 29, 2007:
http://www.sifma.org/research/statistics/expanded_databank.html

————, *User Guide to Securities Industry DataBank*, undated(b). As of December 28, 2007:
http://www.sifma.org/research/statistics/other/Databank-user-guide.pdf

Segal, Julie, "Fund Firms, Broker-Dealers Formalize Distribution Pacts," *Fund Action*, August 23, 2004, p. 1.

Siegel and Gale, LLC, and Gelb Consulting Group, Inc., *Results of Investor Focus Group Interviews About Proposed Brokerage Account Disclosures: Report to the Securities and Exchange Commission*, March 10, 2005. As of December 28, 2007:
http://www.sec.gov/rules/proposed/s72599/focusgrp031005.pdf

SIFMA—*see* Securities Industry and Financial Markets Association.

Smith, Elizabeth Reed, "Investment; An Assortment of Advice, but at What Price?" *New York Times*, July 20, 2003, p. 3.

Smith, Tom, and Robert E. Whaley, "Assessing the Costs of Regulation: The Case of Dual Trading," *Journal of Law and Economics*, Vol. 37, No. 1, April 1994, pp. 215–246.

TD AMERITRADE Holding Corporation, "TD AMERITRADE Survey Reveals Need for Clarity," press release, Omaha, Neb., May 10, 2006. As of December 28, 2007:
http://www.tdainstitutional.com/pdf/Announcement%2005.06.06.pdf

Tibergien, Mark C., and Bob Clark, "The Broker-Dealer Disconnect: The Success of a Broker-Dealer Is Tied to the Success of Its Reps, but Most Firms Don't Really Know How to Help Their Reps Become More Successful," *Financial Planning*, June 1, 2002, p. 1.

Tiburon Strategic Advisors, *A Comprehensive Overview of the Fee-Accounts, Turnkey Asset Management Programs (TAMPs), and Separately Managed Accounts Markets*, October 2005. As of December 27, 2007:
http://www.tiburonadvisors.com/05.10.28%20-%20Tiburon%20Research%20Release%20-%20Fee-Accounts%20Public%20Release.html

Tully, Daniel P., and Arthur Levitt, *Report of the Committee on Compensation Practices*, Washington, D.C.: U.S. Securities and Exchange Commission, April 10, 1995.

U.S. Census Bureau, *Current Population Survey*, Washington, D.C., March 2007.

U.S. Securities and Exchange Commission, "Investment Adviser Public Disclosure," undated Web page. As of December 29, 2007:
http://www.adviserinfo.sec.gov/IAPD/Content/Search/iapd_OrgSearch.aspx

————, "Staff Study, Financial Planners," *Federal Securities Law Reporter*, paras. 84,220–, March 16, 1988.

————, "(Financial and Operational Combined Uniform Single) FOCUS Report: Information Required of All Brokers and Dealers Pursuant to Rule 17a-5," form X-17A-5 Schedule I, SEC1675, last updated June 2002. As of December 29, 2007:
http://www.sec.gov/about/forms/formx-17a-5_schedi.pdf

————, "Certain Broker-Dealers Deemed Not to Be Investment Advisers," releases 34-51523 and IA-2376, file S7-25-99, Code of Federal Regulations, Vol. 17, Part 275, April 15, 2005. As of December 27, 2007:
http://www.sec.gov/rules/final/34-51523.pdf

————, "Uniform Application for Investment Adviser Registration," form ADV, SEC1707, updated April 2006. As of December 29, 2007:
http://www.sec.gov/about/forms/formadv.pdf

————, "Uniform Application for Broker-Dealer Registration," form BD, SEC1490, updated April 2007a. As of December 29, 2007:
http://www.sec.gov/about/forms/formbd.pdf

————, "Interpretive Rule Under the Advisers Act Affecting Broker-Dealers," *Federal Register*, Vol. 72, No. 188, September 28, 2007b, pp. 55,126–55,132.

U.S. Statutes, Title 48, Section 881, Securities Exchange Act, June 6, 1934.

U.S. Statutes, Title 54, Section 847, Investment Advisers Act, November 1, 1940.

Weiss, Harry J., "SEC and SRO Enforcement Developments," in Carmen J. Lawrence and Neal Sullivan, *Coping with Broker/Dealer Regulation and Enforcement, 2007*, New York: Practising Law Institute, October 24, 2007, pp. 75–96.

Yang, Zhilin, and Xiang Fang, "Online Service Quality Dimensions and Their Relationships with Satisfaction: A Content Analysis of Customer Reviews of Securities Brokerage Services," *International Journal of Service Industry Management*, Vol. 15, No. 3, 2004, pp. 302–326.

ZAG—*see* Zero Alpha Group.

Zero Alpha Group, "Survey: In Blow to SEC Rule Proposal, 9 Out of 10 U.S. Investors Back Equally Tough Broker, Investment Adviser Regulation," press release, Washington, D.C., October 27, 2004. As of November 27, 2007:
http://www.zeroalphagroup.com/news/cfazagsurvey102704.cfm